# Touring *the* Universe

## A Practical Guide to Exploring the Cosmos thru 2017

### Ken Graun

ken

# A Ken Press Book

*"Bringing Astronomy to Everyone"*

Published by Ken Press, Tucson, Arizona USA
(520) 743-3200 or office@kenpress.com

**Publisher's Cataloging-in-Publication Data**

Graun, Ken.
    Touring the universe:  a practical guide to exploring the cosmos until 2017 / by Ken Graun.
    p. cm.
    Includes index.
    LCCN 2002091872
    ISBN 1-928771-15-7

    1. Astronomy — Observers' manuals. 2. Astronomy — Amateurs' manuals.

QB64.G73  2003          520
                 QB102-701645

**Other Ken Press Books by Ken Graun**

What's Out Tonight? 50 Year Astronomy Field Guide, 2000 to 2050
Our Earth and the Solar System
Our Galaxy and the Universe
The Next Step:  Finding and Viewing Messier's Objects
David H. Levy's Guide to the Stars (planispheres, co-author)

Visit us at:
**www.whatsouttonight.com**

Printed in Canada

# Table of Contents

# Acknowledgements

Scott Tucker (left) and Dean Koenig

Larry Moore

Ken Don

You can't go through life without the support of others, and writing a book is no different. This book was inspired by the proddings of Kris Koenig and his older brother Dean Koenig. Within a span of six months, both mentioned that I should write a full-color, beginning astronomy book for adults. I know this wasn't a coordinated effort because their twists were different, but maybe this is a case for genetically like minds thinking similarly. Anyway, I thought about what they said and agreed, so I pursued this book wholeheartedly, ahead of others in the queue.

The support needed to complete a book does not have to be direct. My astronomy buddies, Ken Don, Larry Moore, Scott Tucker, Joe Jakoby, as well as David and Wendee Levy, have provided uplifting friendship that keeps me pushing forward. I thank them for being who they are and the kinship they provide.

I lied a little about Larry Moore and Scott Tucker not providing any direct support. Scott and Dean Koenig spend most of their recreational time with astrophotography. I thank them immensely for letting me use their beautiful photos which rival those from professional observatories. Larry Moore also kindly let me use several of his photos that he has taken over the years.

My parents have supported my interest in astronomy since childhood. Without their love and encouragement, I would not be who or where I am today. I thank them from my heart and I am glad that both have seen the fruits of their labor.

Shortly after I came to Tucson in 1988, I met the talented art director Debbie Niwa, who has been instrumental in creating many of my wonderful covers. Not only do I appreciate her artistic ability, but I have also enjoyed our philosophical and political chats.

Isabelle Houthakker did the final editing and has assisted me in other projects. Her attention to detail is very much appreciated, because mine runs dry at the end of a project like this.

Finally, I want to acknowledge the patience and understanding of my wife, Suzanne and daughter, Adrea. Without their tolerance and giving of "space," this book could not have been written.

Thank you all.

Kris Koenig next to a 30-inch diameter reflector telescope.

# Introduction

Why 2017? That was the question that came up time and again when I told people the planned title of this book. Why stop at 2017 when 2020 is such a nice round number and only three more years?

Well, there is a good reason. I want everyone in the United States to keep 2017 on their minds. I want North Americans to plan on traveling to a 60-mile-wide strip stretching from Lincoln City, Oregon to Charleston, South Carolina, for the August 21, 2017 total solar eclipse of the Sun. This is going to be one spectacular event that everyone in the United States will have an opportunity to experience, and see something that they will remember for the rest of their lives. I guarantee it. Send this book back to me in September 2017 if you don't agree.

As you can probably guess, the intent of this book is to get as many people to step out and experience the beauty of the Universe. I am not steering you to become a fanatic, just a participator. All of nature is beautiful, but please experience its grandest displays. Hopefully, this will lead to a greater appreciation of what has been given to us, as well as a desire to preserve it.

In August 2017, you will be able to witness an event like this that lasts just two minutes but will provide a life-long memory.

I wrote this book to accommodate a wide range of astronomy enthusiasts. It details a plethora of observing activities for those just beginning or others who are more knowledgeable. Those who are just beginning won't need binoculars or a telescope to enjoy the heavens, only a small commitment of time. For the most part, nature does the work for you, so all you have to do is look up and enjoy the show.

Now, if you have a basic knowledge of astronomy or get the "bug," I have noted over 100 objects on the star charts that you can observe with binoculars or a small telescope. This should keep you busy while you decide where you want to go next with this wonderful science.

Astronomy is dynamic. Meteors streak across the sky, the Moon waxes and wanes, eclipses occur, comets come and go and stars occasionally flare up. There is always something exciting, interesting or different happening. For this reason, I am providing 16 years of celestial information to keep you abreast of the most predictable events so that you can pick up wherever you may have left off.

Now go out and enjoy the splendors of the heavens. You won't regret it!

**Ken Graun**
Tucson, Arizona
July, 2002

The author at home in Tucson.

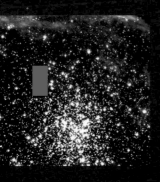

**14.5 billion years ago.** The Universe began from a "Big Bang."

**14.4 billion years ago.** First batch of largest stars had died from supernovae explosions.

**4.5 billion years ago.** Sun and solar system formed.

**4.4 billion years ago.** Moon forms from object that collided with Earth.

**540 million years ago.** Life suddenly proliferates during the Cambrian period.

**65 million years ago.** Dinosaurs wiped out by cosmic impact.

**100,000 years ago.** Homo sapiens begins to spread across the globe.

**4240 BC.** Egyptians institute the first 365-day calendar.

**3000 BC.** Babylonians predict eclipses.

**2296 BC.** Chinese make the first known record of a comet.

**763 BC.** Babylonians make the earliest known record of a solar eclipse.

**500 BC.** Pythagoreans teach that Earth is a sphere.

**270 BC.** Aristarchus of Samos (Greek island near Turkey) challenges Aristotle's teachings by asserting that the Sun is the center of the solar system and that the planets revolve around the Sun.

**240 BC.** Chinese records indicate first known visit of Halley's Comet.

**165 BC.** Chinese astronomers record sunspots.

**635 AD.** Chinese record that a comet's tail always points away from the Sun.

**1300.** Eyeglasses become common.

**1504.** Christopher Columbus of Spain uses knowledge of a total lunar eclipse to frighten a group of Native Americans.

**1543.** On his deathbed, Nicolas Copernicus of Poland, publishes his works stating that the Sun is the center of our solar system.

**1604.** Johannes Kepler of Germany observes a supernova in the constellation Ophiuchus — the last supernova observed in our galaxy. In 1609, he publishes fundamental laws of planetary orbits.

**1609.** Galileo Galilei of Italy builds one of the earliest refractor telescopes and observes four of Jupiter's moons.

**1668.** Isaac Newton of England makes the first reflecting telescope and in 1687, publishes theory of gravity.

**1682.** Edmond Halley of England observes "The Great Comet." He predicts its return in 1758. In his honor it is named after him.

**1781.** Charles Messier of France, a comet hunter, publishes his famous catalog listing a hundred star clusters and nebulae. William Herschel of England discovers Uranus.

**1801.** Piazzi of Italy discovers the first asteroid, Ceres.

**1821.** Catholic church lifts ban on teaching the Sun-centered Copernican system.

**1839.** Harvard College Observatory, the first official observatory in the United States, is founded. A 15-inch refractor is installed in 1847.

**1846.** Johann Galle of Germany discovers Neptune using the predictions of its position by Urbain Le Verrier of France and John Couch Adams of England.

**1863.** William Huggins of England uses the spectra of stars to show that the same elements that exist in stars also exist on Earth.

**1864.** John Herschel, son of William Herschel, publishes a catalog of nebulae and star clusters that contains more than 5,000 entries.

**1877.** Giovanni Schiaparelli of Italy thinks he has discovered channels on Mars.

**1882.** David Gill photographs Halley's comet and notices the multitude of stars surrounding the comet — the idea of stellar cataloging by photography is born.

**1884.** International meeting in Washington, DC, sets the Prime Meridian through Greenwich, England.

**1897.** George Hale sets up the Yerkes Observatory in Williams Bay, WI. The Yerkes telescope, at 40 inches, is still the largest refracting telescope ever built.

**1912.** Studies of short-period variable stars in the Small Magellanic Cloud by Henrietta Leavitt lead to the period-luminosity law of Cepheid variables — a key that is used to unlock the distances to the stars.

# A History of Astronomy

**1913.** Russel and Hertzsprung propose theory of stellar evolution.

**1917.** Hale builds 100-inch reflecting telescope at Mount Wilson, CA.

**1924.** Hubble demonstrates that galaxies are true independent systems rather than parts of our Milky Way system. In 1929, he establishes that the more distant a galaxy is, the faster it is receding.

**1930.** Clyde Tombaugh discovers Pluto from Flagstaff, Arizona.

**1931.** Jansky founds radio astronomy.

**1938.** Bethe and Weizsäcker of Germany propose that the energy produced by stars is the nuclear fusion of hydrogen into helium.

**1946.** V-2 rocket carries a spectrograph to record a spectrogram of the Sun.

**1947.** Spitzer speculates that astronomers might put telescopes of various kinds in orbit around Earth.

**1948.** The 200-inch Hale reflecting telescope is completed at Palomar, California.

**1949.** Whipple suggests that comets are "dirty snowballs." A rocket testing ground is established at Cape Canaveral, Florida.

**1955.** US Vanguard project for launching artificial satellites is announced.

**1957.** First artificial satellite, *Sputnik I,* is launched by the Soviet Union on October 4.

**1958.** Wernher von Braun's team launches the first American satellite to reach a successful orbit around Earth.

**1961.** Soviet cosmonaut Yuri Gagarin becomes the first human being to orbit Earth. Alan Shepard, Jr., becomes the first US astronaut in space.

**1962.** John Glenn, Jr. is the first American to orbit Earth. US *Mariner 2* becomes the first spacecraft to voyage to another planet — Venus.

**1965.** US *Mariner IV* reaches the vicinity of Mars.

**1966.** Soviet *Luna 9* becomes the first spacecraft to soft land on the Moon.

**1969.** On July 20, US astronaut Neil Armstrong becomes the first human to stand on the Moon.

**1970.** Soviet *Venera 7* becomes the first spacecraft to soft land on a planet — Venus.

**1976.** US *Viking 1* & *2* land on Mars. Space probes *Voyager 1* & *2* are launched on journey to outer planets.

**1981.** First space shuttle, *Columbia,* launched.

**1987.** Astronomers discover first planet orbiting a star.

**1990.** *Hubble Space Telescope* (HST) placed in orbit around Earth.

**1994.** Comet Shoemaker-Levy 9 slams into Jupiter.

**1997.** *Pathfinder* becomes the first roving vehicle on another planet — Mars.

**1998.** *Lunar Prospector* detects frozen water at poles on Moon.

**1998/99.** Construction on the *International Space Station* begins.

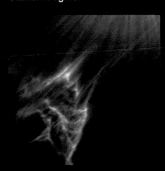

**Picture Captions:**
**First column.** Double star cluster in the Large Magellanic Cloud.
**Second column.** Birthing area of a young, massive, ultra-bright star.
**Fourth column.** Heart of the Whirlpool Galaxy (designated M51).
**Fifth column.** Gas in the Pleiades or Seven Sisters star cluster.

# PART I

# Armchair Tour of the Universe

Hubble Deep Field.
Almost every fuzzy object
and speck in this picture is
a galaxy. Galaxies are all
that astronomers see when
they look deep into space,
past the stars of our own
Milky Way Galaxy.

# Our Solar System

*I begin this armchair tour with our own solar system because of its familiarity. It is our cosmic back-yard and serves as a good stepping-stone to the stars. Like everything in the Universe, our solar system had a beginning. For us, it started 4.5 billion years ago, when the Sun and planets condensed out of a giant hydrogen cloud. We're middle-aged now and have matured a bit since those earlier years.*

A solar system is a star that has planets, asteroids and comets revolving around it. Stars are at the center of every solar system because they are so large and massive that their gravity keeps all the other objects bound to them.

Solar systems form inside huge hydrogen clouds called nebulae. They start as protoplanetary disks, which are concentrations of hydrogen gas and other elements that eventually come together to form the gases, rocks, metals and various ices which make up the planets and stars. These disks take a million or so years to produce newborn solar systems.

Our Earth is part of a solar system that has nine planets and billions of asteroids and comets. We call the star that we orbit the "Sun" or "Sol." The diameter of our solar system out to Pluto is over seven billion miles. If you got in a car and drove this distance at 75 miles per hour, it would take you 11,000 years. Light, which travels at 186,282 miles per second, could go this far in 11 hours!

Astronomers have and are discovering planets around other stars, but they do not yet have the instrumentation to detect planets as small as Earth.

Solar systems form within giant hydrogen clouds called nebulae, like the Eagle Nebula pictured here. This nebula is so large that many solar systems are forming inside. See page 28 for more about this cloud.

A star is a huge ball of mostly hydrogen gas that creates energy by a special process called nuclear fusion. Since stars are very massive, they produce tremendous pressure and heat at their centers, which forces hydrogen atoms together to become helium atoms. During this "fusing" process, a very small amount of excess matter gets converted into an enormous amount of energy. This is the same energy that is produced from nuclear hydrogen bombs. We see some of this energy as the light of stars or the brilliance of our Sun.

Although our Sun is huge, approaching a million miles in diameter, it is only an average-sized star. Its mass, that is, the amount of matter it contains is equivalent to 330,000 Earths. Its surface temperature averages 10,000°F, but its core temperature is estimated to reach 27 million degrees.

Our Sun is composed of 92.1% hydrogen, 7.8% helium, 0.061% oxygen and even smaller amounts of other elements. It is yellowish in color because of its surface temperature. Cooler stars look reddish, and hotter ones look blue or white.

A star like our Sun will shine for 10 to 12 billion years. At the end of its life it will puff up and become a red giant, then shrink down to a white dwarf, a star about the size of Earth.

When you glance at the Sun, the bright part that you see is the photosphere. Photo means light, so you are seeing the part of the Sun that gives off visible light. If you attach a solar filter to a telescope, you can often see sunspots. These dark spots are cooler than their surroundings and indicate areas of intense magnetic fields. Because the Sun rotates, sunspots "move" across its surface, forming, growing and finally dissolving away. Many are larger than Earth.

**Our Sun is a star just like all the others in the night sky. It only appears bigger and brighter because we are orbiting close to it.**

### Sun

Our Sun is a star just like the other stars in the night sky; however, it is special to us because it is the star that our planet, Earth, orbits. And because of its majestic brilliance, metaphorically it is the center of our Universe.

**Top.** The appearance of our Sun through a regular white-light solar filter, which is the most common type of solar filter used by amateurs. Numerous sunspots are frequently visible during the height of 11-year cycles.

**Middle.** It takes a special hydrogen-alpha filter to see prominences that jet off from the Sun's surface. The chromosphere outlines this surface.

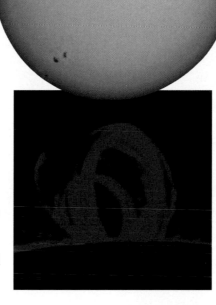

Immediately above the photosphere is a thin red layer of gas, about 1,000 miles thick, called the chromosphere. This layer separates the lower photosphere from the outer corona. The corona is a magnificent veil of hydrogen gas that reaches temperatures of millions of degrees and extends millions of miles from the surface. The corona is visible as an irregular halo surrounding the Sun during a total solar eclipse.

Our Sun becomes active about every 11 years. During these times, the number of sunspots, prominences and flares increases. Over 100 sunspots per day can often be counted. Huge prominences jet off from the surface and some loop back. And flares also shoot out charged particles into the solar system creating the wonderful displays of the northern Aurora Borealis and the southern Aurora Australis.

Mercury resembles our Moon. Like our Moon, it is small in size, pitted with craters, and has no atmosphere. Its craters were formed from a heavy bombardment of asteroids and comets during the first billion years of the solar system's existence. The interior of Mercury, once molten, has cooled and is now solid. It is composed mostly of iron ore.

Mercury is difficult to study with a telescope because it is so close to the Sun. All of the close-up pictures of it were obtained by the one spacecraft, *Mariner 10,* that visited it in 1975.

Since Mercury orbits inside Earth's orbit, it cycles through phases like our Moon. When we see phases, we are seeing nothing more than the day and night sides of the planet at the same time.

***Mercury in the sky.*** Mercury is visible as a fairly bright star several times a year; however, most people never see it, because it can only be seen for a short time after sunset or before sunrise.

## The Terrestrial Planets

*The first four planets, in their order from the Sun, are Mercury, Venus, Earth and Mars. These planets are known as the "terrestrial planets" because they are similar to Earth in size and composition. Composed of hard, rock-type materials, these planets have solid surfaces that you can stand and walk on. All four terrestrial planets orbit inside the asteroid belt; the remaining planets orbit outside.*

## Venus
Venus was named after the Roman goddess of love. It is the planet closest and most similar in size to Earth. Like Earth, Venus is a terrestrial planet that is composed of rock-type material, so it has a surface that you can stand and walk on.

If you are at least middle-aged, you may remember Venus referred to as Earth's sister planet. This connotation ended once we learned more about conditions on the planet's surface.

Venus' atmosphere consists mostly of the colorless gas carbon dioxide. However, within this colorless atmosphere are opaque white clouds so thick that it is impossible to see through them to the surface. No one knew what lay beneath these clouds until exploratory spacecraft started visiting the planet in the late 1970s.

(Continued on page 12)

## Mercury
The planets were named after ancient Roman and Greek mythological gods. Mercury, the closest planet to the Sun, was identified with the Roman god who had wings attached to his feet and a helmet on his head. He swiftly delivered messages to the other gods. As the name so well implies, the planet Mercury revolves rapidly around the Sun, more swiftly than any of the others.

Mercury has no atmosphere and is pitted with craters just like our Moon. *Mariner 10* has been the only spacecraft to visit this planet (in 1975). Less than half of its surface was photographed.

# Our Solar System at a Glance

Our solar system consists of the Sun and orbiting planets, asteroids and comets. Our Sun is a star just like all the other stars in the night sky. It appears brighter and larger because we orbit close to it. In 1987, astronomers discovered the first planets orbiting other stars, and many more since. One estimate is that half of the stars may have solar systems. At this time, astronomers do not have the instrumentation to detect planets as small as Earth.

## How did our solar system form?
Inside a huge gas cloud called a nebula, like the one pictured on page 8 — the Sun and planets condensed out of a dense disk of hydrogen gas and other elements.

## How old is our solar system?
The Sun, Earth and all the other planets formed about 4.5 billion years ago.

## How big is our solar system?
Its diameter out to Pluto's orbit is over 7 billion miles or 11 light hours. The outer reaches of our solar system, where the most distant comets reside, stretch halfway to our nearest solar neighbor, the star Proxima Centauri, which is 4.2 light years away.

## What type of star is our Sun?
Our Sun is a very average star, in size, temperature and its color.

## How long will our Sun last?
A star like our Sun will shine for 10 to 12 billion years. Near the end of its life, it will shed its outer atmosphere in one final heave. Outwardly, this will produce a planetary nebula like those pictured on page 34. The remaining core will shrink to become a white dwarf, a star about the size of Earth.

## What are the major differences between the planets?
Mercury, Venus, Earth and Mars are known as the Terrestrial Planets because they are Earth-like and have surfaces that you can stand on. Jupiter, Saturn, Uranus and Neptune are known as the Gas Giants, because they are large and composed mostly of hydrogen gas. They do not have surfaces that you can stand on. Pluto is a third type of planet that is composed of ices and rocks.

## Where and what is the asteroid belt?
It lies between Mars and Jupiter and consists of about a billion giant rocks, some rich in metal ores. These represent leftover material from the formation of the solar system.

## Where are all the comets?
There are three belts of comets. The innermost has orbits inside Jupiter's. The next group has orbits that extend past Pluto, while the majority reside in a giant cloud surrounding the solar system.

## Solar System Basics

| | Diameter in Miles | Rotation on Axis | # of Moons | Distance from Sun — Miles | Distance from Sun — Light Time | Revolution about Sun | Mass Earth = 1 | Gravity Earth = 1 | Atmosphere |
|---|---|---|---|---|---|---|---|---|---|
| SUN | 865,000 | 30 days | – | – | – | – | 333,000 | 28 | 92% hydrogen, 7.8% helium |
| MERCURY | 3,032 | 59 days | 0 | 36 million | 3.2 minutes | 88 days | 0.06 | 0.38 | None. High 800°F, low −300°F |
| VENUS | 7,521 | 243 days | 0 | 67 million | 6 minutes | 225 days | 0.82 | 0.90 | 96% carbon dioxide, high 900°F |
| EARTH | 7,926 | 24 hours | 1 | 93 million | 8.3 minutes | 365 days | 1 | 1 | 77% nitrogen, 21% oxygen |
| MARS | 4,222 | 24.6 hours | 2 | 142 million | 13 minutes | 687 days | 0.12 | 0.38 | 95% carbon dioxide, 2.7% nitrogen |
| JUPITER | 88,844 | 9.8 hours | 39 | 484 million | 43 minutes | 11.8 years | 318 | 2.53 | 90% hydrogen, 9% helium |
| SATURN | 74,900 | 10.2 hours | 30 | 887 million | 80 minutes | 29 years | 95 | 1.11 | 97% hydrogen, 3% helium |
| URANUS | 31,764 | 17.9 hours | 21 | 1.8 billion | 2.7 hours | 84 years | 15 | 0.90 | 83% hydrogen, 15% helium |
| NEPTUNE | 30,777 | 19.2 hours | 8 | 2.8 billion | 4.2 hours | 164 years | 17 | 1.14 | 74% hydrogen, 25% helium |
| PLUTO | 1,429 | 6.4 days | 1 | 3.7 billion | 5.5 hours | 248 years | 0.0025 | 0.08 | 100% methane, low −419°F |

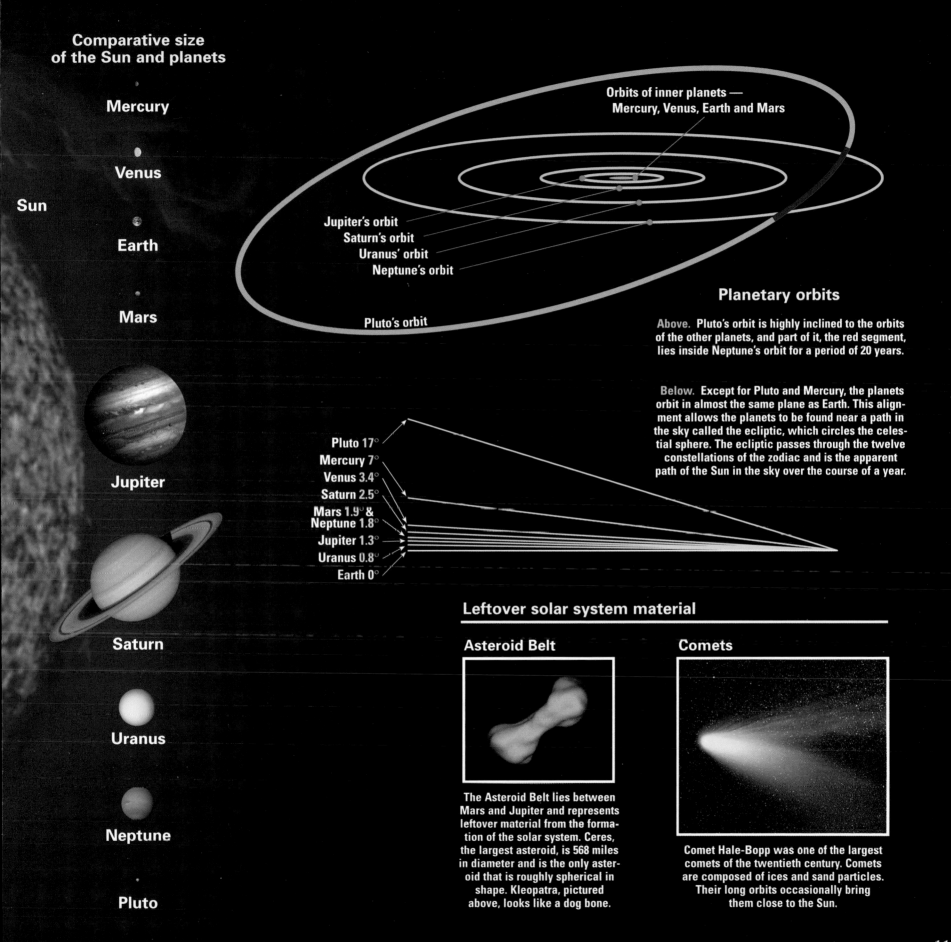

## Comparative size of the Sun and planets

Sun

Mercury

Venus

Earth

Mars

Jupiter

Saturn

Uranus

Neptune

Pluto

Orbits of inner planets —
Mercury, Venus, Earth and Mars

Jupiter's orbit
Saturn's orbit
Uranus' orbit
Neptune's orbit

Pluto's orbit

### Planetary orbits

**Above.** Pluto's orbit is highly inclined to the orbits of the other planets, and part of it, the red segment, lies inside Neptune's orbit for a period of 20 years.

**Below.** Except for Pluto and Mercury, the planets orbit in almost the same plane as Earth. This alignment allows the planets to be found near a path in the sky called the ecliptic, which circles the celestial sphere. The ecliptic passes through the twelve constellations of the zodiac and is the apparent path of the Sun in the sky over the course of a year.

Pluto 17°
Mercury 7°
Venus 3.4°
Saturn 2.5°
Mars 1.9° &
Neptune 1.8°
Jupiter 1.3°
Uranus 0.8°
Earth 0°

## Leftover solar system material

### Asteroid Belt

The Asteroid Belt lies between Mars and Jupiter and represents leftover material from the formation of the solar system. Ceres, the largest asteroid, is 568 miles in diameter and is the only asteroid that is roughly spherical in shape. Kleopatra, pictured above, looks like a dog bone.

### Comets

Comet Hale-Bopp was one of the largest comets of the twentieth century. Comets are composed of ices and sand particles. Their long orbits occasionally bring them close to the Sun.

# Our Solar System

The white clouds in Venus' atmosphere are made of sulfuric acid. Venus has numerous volcanos that continually release sulfur dioxide which combines with a small amount of water vapor to form the widespread sulfuric acid clouds.

Venus is also hot! What happens inside a car that is out in the Sun with its windows rolled up? The interior temperature rises because the windows trap the sunlight's heat. The same thing happens to Venus. Its atmosphere of carbon dioxide acts like the windows of a car, trapping the heat energy of sunlight. This type of heating is called the greenhouse effect. On Venus, the greenhouse effects pushed the temperature near the surface to 900°F, the hottest of any planet and hot enough to melt the metal lead.

Overall, Venus' atmosphere contains about 100 times more gas than Earth's. This "heavy" atmosphere creates tremendous pressure at Venus' surface — more than 90 times greater than ours, and equal to the pressure found at an ocean depth of 3,000 feet.

Venus' barren surface is riddled with rocks and volcanos. Scientists believe that its surface may circulate with its upper level interior and thus renew itself every 100 million years or so.

Surprisingly, the former USSR landed the *Venera 13* and *14* probes on Venus in 1982. These landers were able to transmit pictures of the surface and other data for one to two hours before succumbing to the hostile environment.

Venus rotates nearly upside down compared to the other planets. As a result, if you viewed Venus from the top of the solar system (from the direction of Earth's north pole), it would appear to rotate backward. Also, Venus rotates very slowly on its axis. It takes longer to rotate once on its axis than to revolve around the Sun.

**Above**. A colorized image (produced from radar) of the surface of Venus. It is riddled with active volcanos. **Right**. The *Pioneer Venus Orbiter* circled Venus from 1978 to 1992 and gathered general information about the planet. In 1992, it ran out of positioning fuel and burned up in Venus' atmosphere.

*Venus in the sky.* Often, Venus is the brightest "star" in the sky. Its white clouds make it highly reflective and its closeness to Earth makes it even brighter. Because Venus orbits inside Earth's orbit, it displays phases.

## Earth

The Earth is our home, and as far as we know, the only planet with life. No one understands exactly how life developed on Earth, but scientists feel certain that two major factors are necessary for life to start and then to flourish. First, a planet must have liquid water. Our Earth's surface is 71% water. Second, the temperature must stay in a narrow range. If the Earth were just a little closer or a little farther away from the Sun than it is now, it would be either too hot or cold for life to *flourish*. There are many other factors necessary for life to flourish, but if these two conditions were not met, humans, animals and plants would not exist in the abundance that they do now.

A false-color mapping of Venus produced from radar imagery by the spacecraft *Magellan* in the early 1990s. Blue indicates low altitude areas and red the higher terrain. Areas of the same color are at the same altitude. Venus' surface can only be mapped with radar because its opaque-white, sulfuric acid clouds are too thick to see through.

The original seven American Mercury astronauts. **Top, from left**: Alan Shepard (first American in space), Virgil "Gus" Grissom and L. Gordon Cooper. **Bottom, from left** are Walter Schirra, Donald "Deke" Slayton, John Glenn (first American to orbit the Earth) and Scott Carpenter. The Mercury program was America's first attempt to send a man into space. The Gemini program followed, with the goal of gaining experience in manned orbits and reentry. This led to the Apollo program that landed 12 men on the Moon from July 1969 to December 1972.

### Moon

The Moon is visible at night as well as during the day. It forever cycles through phases, from crescent to full and back. The phases occur as the Moon circles the Earth and are nothing more than our seeing its day and night sides at the same time.

On July 20, 1969, Neil Armstrong became the first person to walk on the Moon. The last astronauts to visit were Eugene Cernan and Harrison Schmitt, in December 1972. Schmitt, a geologist, was the first scientist in space and the only scientist to walk on the Moon.

The Moon is full of craters. They vary in size from just inches to over 100 miles in diameter. Most of these bowl-shaped depressions were formed over four billion years ago when meteoroids, asteroids and comets bombarded its surface. In contrast to the cratered areas, there are darker, smoother areas called maria or plains. These plains were formed when very large asteroids or comets struck deep into the Moon, releasing interior lava that flowed to the surface. Scientists believe that the interior of the Moon has now completely cooled and is no longer molten.

The Moon was most likely formed when an object as large as Mars slammed into the Earth over four billion years ago. This impact produced a ring of rocky material that orbited the Earth and eventually coalesced to become the Moon. How do we know this? The astronauts who went to the Moon brought back rocks that contain the same materials as those found in the Earth's crust.

***Observing the Moon.*** If you can observe the area around the terminator, which is the "line" that separates the lighted side from the dark side, with high power (200x to 400x magnification), you will feel as though you were flying over its surface.

### Mars

Mars is named after the Roman god of war because of its "red" color. However, when we think of Mars, we often think of Martians. This idea started in the late 1800s when Giovanni Schiaparelli of Italy and Percival Lowell of America made drawings of what they thought to be channels or canals. Lowell believed that the channels were canals built by Martians to transport

**Top**. A picture of Earth taken by the Apollo 17 crew on their way to the Moon in 1972. This was the last manned mission to the Moon. **Below Earth**. The Command and Service Modules circled the Moon with one astronaut aboard while the other two landed in the Lunar Module which Edwin "Buz" Aldrin is climbing down in the **above** picture. Buz became the second person to walk on the Moon. **Left**. A closeup of the crater Tycho, near the terminator and with the Earth hovering above. Tycho is a prominent crater that has magnificent emanating rays. This photograph was taken by the orbiting spacecraft *Clementine* in 1994.

water from the poles to the lower latitudes. Mars does not have canals or Martians, but these ideas ignited imaginations throughout the world that have lasted to this day.

Mars shares many similarities with Earth. These include mountains, volcanos (extinct on Mars), hills, plains, grand canyons, sand dunes, craters, polar caps, weather and clouds. As you can see from the pictures on the next page, the surface of Mars resembles a rocky desert.

Since Mars' diameter is a half of Earth's, its total surface area is about the same as the total land area on our planet. The difference in altitude between the highest and lowest points on Mars is 19 miles. Valles Marineris (Val-Les Mar-A-Nair-Us), its deepest canyon, is four times deeper than the Grand Canyon and stretches over 2,500 miles. Olympus Mons is not only the largest inactive volcano in the solar system, but also Mars' highest point. Its cauldron alone is 55 miles across and the area of its lava flow is the size of the state of Arizona. Mars is riddled with craters, but the largest one is Hellas, a whitish oval in the southern hemisphere with a diameter of 1,200 miles. Hellas boasts the lowest point on Mars.

The surface rocks are reddish due to a form of oxidation or rust. There are large areas of coloration caused by regional differences in the hues of the rocks and sand. The boundaries of these regions shift because of wind storms.

Overall, Mars appears to be geologically stable and volcanically inactive. Early in its history, it most likely had active volcanos and a thicker, warmer atmosphere supporting liquid surface water that flowed, and carved some of its terrain. Today's surface appears to have changed little in the past few billion years.

Mars' north polar cap is mostly made of frozen water; its southern cap is made of frozen carbon dioxide, commonly known as "dry ice."

Other than Earth, Mars is the most hospitable planet in our solar system. However, we could only live there in a protected environment. Its atmosphere is thin, unbreathable and cold.

# Our Solar System

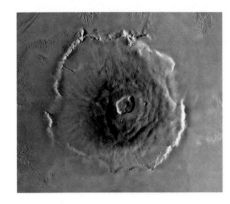

The atmospheric pressure at Mars' surface is 1/100 that of Earth's and would be the same as what we experienced 20 miles above our surface. High performance jets can fly to a height of just over 20 miles. Commercial jetliners top out at 7 miles where the air pressure is 1/6 of sea level pressure. Oxygen is usually required to get to the top of Mount Everest, which is 5.5 miles high with half the air pressure of sea level. Even though Mars' atmosphere is thin, evidence of dust devils have been observed and the winds can "kick up" to produce huge, planet-wide dust storms.

Mars' atmosphere is 95% carbon dioxide, 2.7% nitrogen, 1.6% argon and less than 1% oxygen. Compare this to Earth's 77% nitrogen, 21% oxygen and less than 1/10 of 1% carbon dioxide. Although Mars' atmosphere is not poisonous, you could not breathe it to stay alive.

The average temperature is cold, around −81°F, but varies from −274°F to 72°F. The 72°F would last for just brief periods, close to the surface, around noon. Frost forms on surface rocks but evaporates as the day warms.

Because of Mars' low atmospheric pressure, any liquid water on its surface would boil away into vapor. Likewise, if we stood on the surface

without a space suit, the low atmospheric pressure coupled with the heat from our bodies would cause our blood to slowly boil. To walk around on Mars, you would need a light space suit providing adequate air pressure, warmth and oxygen.

Water is absolutely necessary for humans to survive an extended stay on another planet. Its usefulness extends beyond drinking and watering plants, because it can also be used to make oxygen for breathing as well as hydrogen for fuel. Mars has frozen water at its north pole and underground, which will make it easier for people to stay and live there.

The two moons of Mars, Phobos and Deimos, are believed to be captured asteroids because their irregular shapes and composition resemble these. Phobos is 17 x 13 miles in size and orbits Mars in 7.7 hours, at a distance of 5,800 miles. Deimos is 10 x 8 miles in size, orbiting in 1.3 days, at a distance of 14,600 miles.

Is there life on Mars? Many suspect that there may be microbial life in its soil; however, the answer to this question is years away and will most likely come only after extensive soil samples are taken and analyzed.

***Mars in the sky.*** About every two years, the orbits of Mars and Earth bring them close to one another, allowing the surface colorations of Mars to be observed even with small telescopes. During this same time, Mars is at its brightest and even outshines Jupiter.

**Top**. Olympus Mons' area of lava flow covers an area equal to the state of Arizona. The center cauldron spans 55 miles. **Upper right**. Mars' south pole boasts a permanent cap of frozen carbon dioxide or dry ice. **Right**. A *Hubble Space Telescope* picture of Mars showing the surface coloration and clouds around the poles. **Below**. A 360° vista taken by the *Mars Pathfinder* in 1997. Mars is a rocky desert. *Sojourner*, the first rover vehicle on another planet, is parked next to the rock.

took t
the sk
these
micro
This i
switch
tograp
erly, tl
as the
betwe
that m
would
Tombɑ
dot ju
two pl

public
People
Pluto,
submi:
Oxforc

I
Its diɑ
6.4 daɣ
facing
the sɑr

P
spacec
Pluto h
dozen

P
cult to

through
have th
during
those w

Af
second
formatic
years ag
"dirty sr
ture of
include
cals suc
ammon

## Mars Recap

### Physical characteristics

**Diameter** of 4,222 miles, which is about half of Earth's.
**Total land or surface area** is about the same as all the land area on Earth.
**Rotates** on its axis in 24 hours, 37 minutes (its day).
**Revolves** around the Sun in 1.9 years or 687 days (its year).
**Tilt on axis** is 25.2°, so it has "seasons."
**Gravity** is 1/3 of Earth's.

### Weather & atmosphere

**Atmosphere** is 95% carbon dioxide, 2.7% nitrogen, 1.6% argon and 0.2% oxygen.
**Atmospheric pressure** is 1/100 of Earth's.
**Temperature** varies from −274° F to 72° F.
The **north pole** has a permanent cap of frozen water ice, while the **south pole** has a permanent cap of frozen carbon dioxide, otherwise known as "dry ice."
**Other weather elements** include clouds, surface frost, huge dust storms, and dust devils. There is no rain or lightening.

### Geology

Mars has the **largest inactive volcano** in the solar system, named Olympus Mons, which is more than 15 miles high with a 55-mile-wide cauldron. It also has its own grand canyon called **Valles Marineris** which is 2,500 miles long. The terrain suggests that its surface was once carved by massive quantities of water. Overall, the planet appears **geologically stable** since it does not have active volcanos or moving tectonic plates like Earth. Also, there is **no magnetic field**, suggesting a core that has cooled.

## The Asteroid Belt

The asteroid belt lies between Mars and Jupiter. It is composed of about a billion chunks of rock that vary in size from a dozen feet to more than 500 miles across. Their total mass is about 1/5 the mass of our Moon. Distances from the Sun vary from around 175 to 375 million miles, so orbits range from 3.5 to 6.5 years.

None of the asteroids have atmospheres. Most have odd shapes and resemble potatoes. They are pitted with craters, formed when the asteroids struck one another. Their colors range from reddish and light brown to dark gray. Asteroids vary in composition, from silicates, that is, sand, quartz and other rock-type materials, to metals such as nickel and iron. They represent remnants left over from the formation of the solar system and are not material from a planet that exploded.

Not every asteroid lies in the asteroid belt. Today, public interest in asteroids focuses on those that could possibly collide with Earth. There may be up to 700 "Apollo-Amor" asteroids that present collision hazards. This category has lengths of over 1/2 a mile and crosses the orbits of either Mars or Earth. Astronomers are hoping to find all of these by 2010. It is estimated that one large "Apollo-Amor" asteroid strikes the Earth every 250,000 years, but none are expected to do so in the foreseeable future. The orbits of these asteroids change because of the gravitational influence of Jupiter.

The asteroid Ida, as imaged by *Galileo*, a spacecraft passing by on its way to Jupiter. Ida is 32 miles in length and has a small moon about a mile in diameter named Dactyl (visible as the spot to the right).

Verrie

The twin planets
Uranus, **above**, i
the Sun than Ne
its atmosphere i
more distant bro
atmosphere gen
spots, which are
Great Red Spot.
Neptune's spots
dissipate, like hu

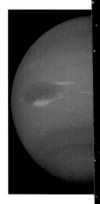

comple
ever im
*N*
with th
like wit
look be
Neptun
200x m

# The Universe at a Glance

## The Universe is full of galaxies:

**1** If you held the Universe in your hands, and looked close, you would see fuzzy specks everywhere. Each of these fuzzy spots would be a galaxy. There may be about 125 billion galaxies in the Universe. A galaxy is a grouping of stars — anywhere from a billion to a trillion that are held together by their collective gravity. This *Hubble Space Telescope* photo is a snapshot of deep space. All of these specks are galaxies billions of light years away. Galaxies are all that astronomers see when they look deep into space.

*A galaxy is a grouping of stars — anywhere from a billion to a trillion that is held together by their collective gravity.*

**2** Galaxies cluster together. Our Milky Way Galaxy is a member of what astronomers call the Local Group which totals about three dozen galaxies, including the famous Andromeda Galaxy.
Clusters of galaxies are further organized into superclusters that stretch across huge expanses of the Universe.

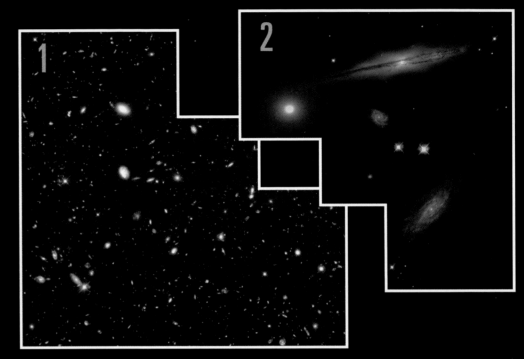

**NOTE:** *Many of the objects on these pages can be seen with a small telescope.*

## There are three basic types of galaxies:

**3a** Over 80% of all the galaxies in the Universe are of the elliptical type. These are shaped like balls or elongated balls and represent the largest and smallest galaxies. This galaxy is in Virgo[1].

**3b** Spiral galaxies, like this one in Pisces[1] represent at most 10% of the galaxies. They are fairly large and strikingly visible. Shaped like dishes, they have a bulged center out of which curved arms radiate. Spirals have active star formation occurring in their arms.

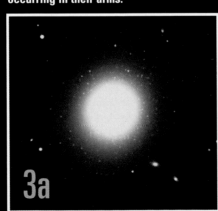

**3c** Finally, there are irregular galaxies that have irregular shapes or scrambled insides. Some are the result of galaxies colliding and merging. Others get deformed by the gravity of larger galaxies pulling on them. Here is a close-up of an irregular galaxy with mixed-up insides, in Ursa Major, designated **M82** .

[1] Galaxies are much farther outside our galaxy and are not actually in these constellations, but lie in their direction.

# Stars are born within gas clouds called nebulae that reside in galaxies:

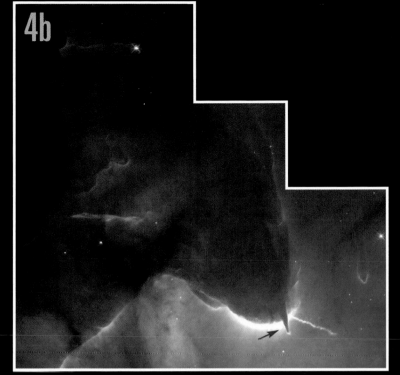

**4a** The Omega Nebula in the constellation Sagittarius. Nebulae are gas clouds composed mostly of hydrogen and helium. Within, pockets of gas sometimes condense to become stars.

**4b** A closeup of the Trifid Nebula in Sagittarius. The arrow points to a column of hydrogen gas and dust: within it a star is forming. This nebula spreads across 30 light years and is 5,000 light years away. Planets sometimes form along with birthing stars to create new solar systems.

# Stars are born together in clusters:

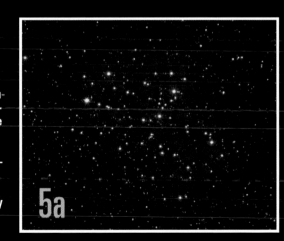

**5a** Anywhere from a dozen to a hundred or more stars can be born from a nebula. Here is a beautiful cluster, designated M6, located in the constellation Scorpius. The Pleiades, visible in winter, are the best known example of a naked-eye cluster.

**5b** Special clusters, called globular clusters, contain thousands to hundreds of thousands stars. Older stars comprise these objects which resemble cotton balls. They often surround galaxies. Our Milky Way Galaxy has about 200 in a spherical halo.

# Even in death, stars bring beauty

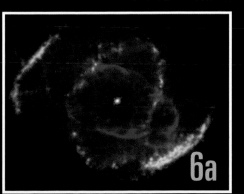

All stars die. In their death throes, many form either a planetary nebula or supernova remnant.

**6a** Planetary nebulae have nothing to do with planets. That's just an old name that stuck. They are the shedded atmospheres of average-sized stars like our Sun before these shrink down to become white dwarfs.

**6b** Stars with masses much greater than our Sun die with violent supernova explosions. Although they leave behind a remnant, the star shrinks down to become a neutron star or black hole. As the remnants expand into space, they are recycled back into new stars and planets.

# Galaxies

The beauty of the Universe. This spiral galaxy is in the direction of the southern hemisphere constellation Horologium. It is 30 million light years away and spans 70,000 light years. The outer blue ring is an area of active star formation (births). The red areas in the ring indicates stars fluorescing the clouds around them.

What the heck? Look closely at this photograph. What you see are two spiral galaxies, but one is in front of the other at a highly inclined angle. These galaxies are 140 million light years away and lie in the direction of the constellation Hydra.

If our Milky Way Galaxy were one inch across, which is the size of a quarter, the Andromeda Galaxy would be a mere 23 inches away, and the Universe would stretch for only 2 miles in every direction.

## Galaxies

*When we look up into the night sky, we see stars. Stars are the most common object in the Universe and represent the building blocks of galaxies.*

The debate over the true nature of galaxies was concluded at the end of 1924, after Edwin Hubble had photographed many with the new 100-inch diameter Hooker telescope located at Mount Wilson, California. He had conclusive proof that they *were* islands of stars. This ushered in a new age of astronomy.

There are about 125 billion galaxies and they contain all the stars in the Universe. Practically speaking, there are no stars between galaxies. Galaxies are held together by the collective gravity of their stars which revolve around a concentration at their centers or nuclei. Most galaxies are circular in shape, resembling either dishes or balls, however; some are irregular looking.

### Elliptical Galaxies

The most common shape is the elliptical, accounting for at least 80 percent of all galaxies. These resemble balls or elongated balls. The smallest and largest galaxies are elliptical. Overall, the stars in ellipticals are smaller and older than the stars in our sky.

## Universe Facts

**Age:** Between 12 & 16 billion years old.

**Beginning:** The Universe began from an "explosion" called the *Big Bang.*

**Type:** Expanding Universe? At this time, astronomers' best guess is that the Universe may exist and expand forever.

**Chemical elements in the Universe:** 75% hydrogen, 25% helium and just traces of all the other elements.

**Number of galaxies in the Universe:** Around 125 billion (125,000,000,000).

**Types of galaxies in the Universe:** Elliptical (>80%), spiral (<10%), irregular (<10%).

**Objects inside galaxies:** Mostly stars, nebulae, star clusters, globular clusters, neutron stars, black holes, white & brown dwarfs, planets & all other solar system objects.

Inside these galaxies, there is little gas and dust to form new stars. Unlike the orderly orbits of the planets around our Sun, the stars in ellipticals orbit their galaxy nuclei "every which way."

### Spiral galaxies

The second most common galaxy shape is the spiral, which accounts for at most 10 percent of all galaxies. Our Milky Way Galaxy, which is the galaxy that we live in, is a spiral. Spirals look flatter, like dishes. They have a round bulged center out of which curved arms radiate. Spirals often have lots of gas and dust in their arms, from which new stars are born. Although these only account for a small percentage of galaxies, their arms and nuclei are often bright, so they stand out more than the others. Astronomers classify spirals by how tightly wound their arms and how elongated their nuclei are.

### Irregular galaxies

Finally, there are two kinds of irregular galaxies. One kind appears to be the result of the collision of galaxies. The other is usually a smaller galaxy being distorted or pulled on by the gravity of a nearby larger galaxy. In either case, these galaxies have mixed up insides, often with no cores or nuclei and often containing large amounts of gas and dust (out of which new stars can form). The Large and Small Magellanic Clouds, visible from the southern hemisphere, are two irregular galaxies that are being distorted by the gravity of our galaxy.

### Red shift

After Hubble settled the debate over the true nature of galaxies in 1924, he wanted to know their distances from us. In 1929, he made another important discovery. He found that the farther away a galaxy was, the faster it was also moving away. With this information, he and other astronomers discovered that *all* distant galaxies were moving *away* as if from an explosion. Eventually, this information helped to scientifically establish the idea of the Big Bang.

Something happens to the light from distant receding galaxies. The lines in the spectrums of their light (see caption at top right) shift or move towards the red part. The amount of the shift indicates how fast the galaxy is moving away and even provides a clue as to the distance. The lines in spectrum can also shift towards the blue part, indicating movement towards us. Both of these phenomena are the same effect as the change in pitch heard when a train approaches and moves away. This shifting of the spectrum has proved immensely helpful in determining the movement or speed of most celestial objects.

### Galaxies bump but stars don't

For their size, galaxies are millions of times closer to one another than the stars they house. For example, our Milky Way Galaxy and the Andromeda Galaxy are only 20 diameters apart from one another. On the other hand, for their diameters, our Sun and the closest star, Proxima Centauri, which is in the constellation Centaurus, are 29 million times farther away from one another.

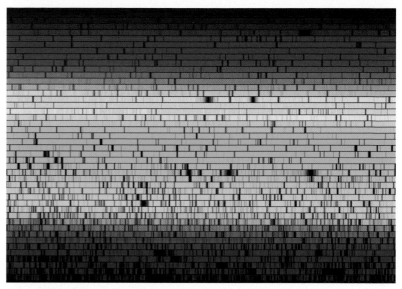

**The visible spectrum of the star Arcturus** (a very bright star in the constellation Bootes — see star charts E and F). Astronomers use a special instrument called a spectrograph to spread out the light from stars or other celestial objects. In doing so, they find many dark lines on the spectrum indicating different chemical elements. If a star or galaxy is physically moving away from us, all of the lines move slightly to the left or towards the red part of the spectrum. This is called a red shift. The opposite happens if the object is moving towards us. How do astronomers know if the lines shift? There is a second, comparison spectrum made at the same time as the original but from a stationary, built-in light source in the instrument. This picture is a series of 50 long strips stacked on top of each other.

Proportionately, there are truly enormous amounts of space between stars, but not between galaxies. For this reason, it is often said that two galaxies could pass through one another without any of the stars colliding.

Galaxies cluster in groups. These groups are gravitationally bound and the galaxies within them revolve together around one another, but not in any orderly fashion. The closeness of galaxies combined with their disorderly revolutions make galactic collisions happen "often." There is evidence to show that our Milky Way and the Andromeda galaxies may collide some day.

### Which came first, the chicken or the egg?

It appears that most elliptical and spiral galaxies have supermassive black holes at their very centers (see more on page 36). Astronomers are not sure if galaxies formed around black holes created at the beginning of the Universe, or if the central black holes were later formed by the galaxies. In either case, this leads us to the evolution of galaxies.

Some astronomers think that elliptical galaxies may be the result of spiral galaxies colliding with one another. When they look deep into space, which is the same as looking back into time, they find that spiral galaxies were smaller and more numerous previously than they are today. Since galaxies do collide, it is reasonable to conclude that the collision of two or three spirals produce an elliptical. Like anything that is not known for certain in science, this idea will be studied further.

## Our Milky Way Galaxy & Band

We are more aware of our Sun than of any other celestial body. None of the nighttime stars come close to matching its brilliancy because they are so much farther away. Hence, from our vantage point, it is not obvious that the Sun is just one star out of more than 100 billion that comprise our galaxy. And it is far less obvious that there are more galaxies in the Universe than stars in our Milky Way.

The name of our galaxy came from the irregular pale path that stretches across the night sky — the Milky Way Band. One of the first references to this path being called "milky" appeared in a hymn by Homer from 800 BC. Like the ancients, we appreciate the beauty of the band, but unlike them, we understand that it represents the faint glow of billions of stars too far away to be seen individually. When astronomers discovered that the stars in the band represented the bulk of those in our galaxy, our galaxy retained the name it had been called for ages, the Milky Way.

Our galaxy is a spiral and it is bigger than most galaxies. As a spiral, it is flattish, but has a bulged center out of which curved arms radiate. One distinguishing aspect of our galaxy is that its core or nucleus is somewhat elongated and is what astronomers call a slightly barred center. The core contains the highest concentration of stars, which on average are older than the stars in the arms. The core or bulged center is about 30,000 light years away in the direction of the constellation Sagittarius. Astronomers have discovered that at the very center of the core lies a supermassive black hole, with a mass of about 2.5 million Suns.

If we could view our entire galaxy like we can view the Andromeda Galaxy, we would see several distinct arms curving outward from the core. In fact, there are four primary arms as well as many shorter branches and spurs. Our Sun is in a shorter outer arm called the Orion-Cygnus arm. The arm closer in is called the Sagittarius, and the one farther out the Perseus (see drawing on the next page).

### Why we can't see our galaxy

It's hard to see the outside of something when you are on the inside! When you are inside your home, you can't see it from the outside, but you have clues as to its shape from the layout of the interior. The same idea applies to us, positioned inside our Milky Way Galaxy. Often, I get asked why we can't send a spacecraft out to take a picture. Well, with our present technology, the spacecraft would have to travel for billions of years to get far enough away to take a picture of our whole galaxy. So far, the farthest a spacecraft has gotten from our Sun is a little past Pluto, nowhere close to even the nearest star!

So, the best view we can get of our galaxy is from where we are — the inside. Since our galaxy is a spiral, most of its stars are spread across a flat dish. Therefore, when looking around at night, what you see is a circular band of mostly faint, faraway stars — the Milky Way Band. To get a similar effect, place your head inside a hula hoop and look around.

### Ancient beliefs

Everything about the sky was a mystery to ancient civilizations. Their knowledge of nature was not as developed as ours. And some of their religions, which we now look upon as myths and legends, often included "elements" taken from nature. For many of these civilizations, the Milky Way Band was considered to be the River of Heaven and was thought of as the road that departed souls took to reach their final resting place. Some Native Americans also believed that the bright stars in the Milky Way Band were campfires where departed souls camped and rested.

**Shaped like a flat dish.** This edge-on, false-colored picture of our galaxy was obtained by taking infrared images of the Milky Way Band that stretches across the entire celestial sphere. "Nearby" gas and dust visually obscure much of our inside view, but infrared heat-type radiation passes through and provides us with a good cross-sectional view of our galaxy. The black and white picture to the right shows some of the nebulae and dust surrounding our bulged center, or nucleus. This bulge is about 10,000 light years wide and 6,500 light years thick. The white line indicates the plane of our galaxy..

This galaxy, designated NGC 1232, probably resembles our Milky Way Galaxy more than any other. It is 100,000 light years in diameter, about 50 million light years away and is located in the direction of the constellation Eridanus, known as "The River."

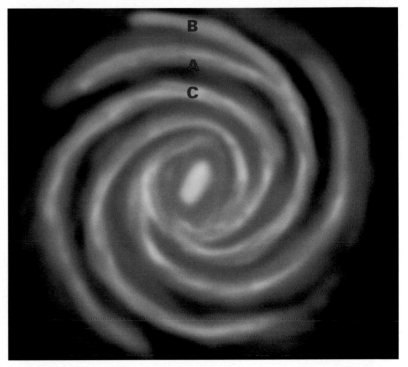

A drawing of the major arms of our galaxy, based on surveys using radio telescopes that mapped the lanes of hydrogen gas clouds. The brightness and prominence of the arms is greatly exaggerated. **A** indicates the Sun's position in the Orion-Cygnus arm, **B** is the outer Perseus arm, and **C** the inner Sagittarius arm.

## Our Milky Way Galaxy

**Type of galaxy:** Spiral galaxy with a slightly straight or "barred" center.

**Diameter:** 75,000 to 100,000 light years.

**Center:** Our Sun is about 30,000 light years from the center, which is in the direction of the constellation Sagittarius (visible during the summer in the southern sky).

**Total mass:** About 1 trillion times the mass of the Sun.

**Number of stars:** About 100 billion (100,000,000,000).

**Revolution of the Sun around galaxy's center:** About 220 million years.

**Closest companion galaxies:** The Large and Small Magellanic Clouds which are respectively 160,000 and 195,000 light years away. They are visible from the southern hemisphere.

**Local group:** Our galaxy is one of about three dozen in a small cluster of galaxies called the "Local Group."

The heart of the Milky Way, that is, the direction to the center of our Milky Way Galaxy, is between the constellations Sagittarius and Scorpius. This area of the Milky Way Band is also the widest and brightest. Although it is visible just above the southern horizon from July to September, city lights and pollution can easily wash it out. The reddish area near the center is the Lagoon Nebula. See Chart G on page 84. Picture by amateur astronomer Larry Moore.

# Pillars of Creation
## Where stars come to be

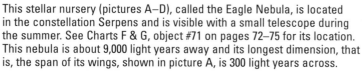

This stellar nursery (pictures A–D), called the Eagle Nebula, is located in the constellation Serpens and is visible with a small telescope during the summer. See Charts F & G, object #71 on pages 72–75 for its location. This nebula is about 9,000 light years away and its longest dimension, that is, the span of its wings, shown in picture A, is 300 light years across.

**A.** The entire Eagle Nebula as photographed by an Earth-based telescope from Kitt Peak, near Tucson, Arizona. Some nebulae, like this one, are given names for their shape.

**B.** This famous picture was taken by the *Hubble Space Telescope*, which orbits 375 miles above the Earth. It is often referred to as the "Pillars of Creation," because stars are being born inside the pillars or columns. The *Hubble Space Telescope* can capture greater detail than Earth-based telescopes because it is above our turbulent atmosphere. The pillar on the left is about 50 light years tall. Can you identify where the pillars are in the bottom picture?

**C & D.** Enlargements of the top left pillar. Astronomers have identified protostars, which are cocoon-type concentrations of hydrogen gas within many smaller columns or fingers. The arrows point to three fingers. The cocoon concentrations are hidden by the gas and dust, but are visible in infrared "light." The width of the smallest fingers is about one quarter of a light year or nearly 200 times the diameter of our solar system.

For comparison, our Sun has a diameter of 4.6 light *seconds*, and our solar system has a diameter of just 11 light *hours*. The closest star to the Sun is just over 4 light *years* away.

## INSIDE GALAXIES
# Birth of Stars

Stars are born inside giant clouds called nebulae (the singular is nebula) that are composed mostly of hydrogen and some helium molecules. In our galaxy, there is an abundance of nebulae in the arms, which is where most new stars are born.

### Out of the cloud

Nebulae can easily span 150 or so light years. These clouds are large and "thin," and for the most part, would be considered vacuums on Earth because they contain as few as 1,600 atoms per cubic inch. However, much higher gas concentrations can occur and astronomers have identified several ways in which this happens. The simplest is from clouds colliding. For example, gas thrown from a supernova explosion can ram other clouds. Also, nearby starlight can play a role by pushing on clouds, causing accumulations (yes, sunlight or starlight can push and move molecules in space). When concentrations occur, they may have diameters of 300 times that of our solar system. The concentrations are large and massive, thus they have gravity. When a concentration has enough mass (matter), gravity slowly takes over and further condenses the cloud. By this time, the cloud is rotating (most objects in the Universe have some spin) and heating up as it further contracts. Because the cloud rotates, its shape starts to flatten out and can resemble a donut with a bulged center.

### Ignition

This whole concentration of gas and dust is often referred to as a cocoon. Inside, around the center, there is a protostar. The cocoon is opaque because its dust blocks light. The protostar becomes a star when the temperature and pressure at its core become so great that sustained nuclear fusion takes place. Nuclear fusion is the process of forcing or "fusing" four hydrogen atoms together to become one helium atom. Fusing takes lots of energy, but it also releases tremendous amounts by converting matter into energy according to Einstein's famous equation $E=mc^2$. What is the matter that gets converted? Four hydrogen atoms weigh 1% more than one helium atom. It is this 1% that gets converted into pure energy.

When the new star gets hot enough, it will reveal itself by pushing away leftover gas and dust from the cocoon. Astronomers can see newborn stars within their opaque cocoons by using telescopes with instrumentation that can detect heat or infrared radiation. Similar technology is used in some night goggles.

The Horsehead Nebula in the constellation Orion. It lies about one Moon's diameter due south of the left belt star, Alnitak. Here is an example of an unlit or dark nebula (the "head") silhouetted against a bright nebula farther behind. This photograph was taken by seasoned amateur astronomer Dean Koenig using a 4-inch diameter refractor and a special digital camera designed specifically for astrophotography (see Astrophotography, starting on page 112). To visually see this nebula, you need at least a 20-inch diameter telescope and very dark skies. The Horsehead is 1,500 light years away and about 2.5 light years in height.

### Double and multiple

About half of all stars are part of a multiple star system where two or more stars born together end up revolving around one another. Our Sun is a single star and has no orbiting sibling. Many binary stars can be viewed with a small telescope. *Castor*, in the constellation Gemini, is a favorite and is easily seen with a small 4-inch telescope.

### Solar systems

Since 1987 and up until the time this book was written, astronomers have found almost 100 planets orbiting stars. How are planets formed? They condense out of the protostar disk along with the new star. Planets, like the Earth, aggregate from dust. The dust molecules of metals and silicates (materials of rock) collide to form larger particles of matter. Initial clumps are as fine as the soot of cigarette smoke.

## INSIDE GALAXIES
### Nebulae

Nebulae are often referred to as molecular clouds because they contain molecules of hydrogen, helium, other elements and compounds. Nebulae vary in size and shape but can span several to hundreds of light years. Today, most nebulae are found in the arms of spiral galaxies. Some represent recycled material from stars that have died and some may represent original material left over from the Big Bang.

Nebulae are all basically the same, but they are lit differently. Nebulae that are not near any stars appear black. We see these as silhouettes when they are in front of stars or other bright nebulae.

The Horsehead Nebula, pictured on page 29, is a good example of this type. Other nebulae glow in a fashion similar to neon signs. The hydrogen in these emission nebulae are excited to fluoresce a pinkish color by the highly energetic ultraviolet light of some nearby stars. A third type of nebula is just dimly lit by reflecting light from nearby stars. These reflection nebulae appear bluish in color from scattering light, in an effect similar to what makes our daytime sky blue.

## INSIDE GALAXIES
### Star Clusters

Stars are born in groups or clusters. It would be rare for just one star to be born from a nebula. Hundreds of clusters can easily be observed with a small telescope.

### Open clusters

An open cluster is a group of stars born together from the same nebula. The number of stars varies from a dozen to a thousand or so. The best-known open cluster is the Pleiades or Seven Sisters, pictured on the next page and indicated on Chart B. Often, open clusters break apart because their stars slowly move away from one another and because they can get spread about as they revolve around the galaxy. Our Sun was most likely born in a group that has broken up.

### Globular clusters

Globular clusters are distinct from open cluster. They resemble cotton balls and contain anywhere from 10,000 to a million stars. Overall, the stars in globulars are older than most

---

**Left page.** The Rosette Nebula in the constellation Monoceros. In our sky, this is a huge nebula because it spans more than two Moon diameters; however, it is very faint. Although several of my friends say they can see it in their telescopes (about 8-inch diameters), I cannot see it. This picture looks as though it was taken with a professional-sized scope, but it was actually imaged by amateur astronomer Dean Koenig using a 4-inch refractor and a digital camera designed specifically for astrophotography. The exposure was 2.25 hours. The detail is equivalent to a picture taken at the Kitt Peak observatory complex, near Tucson, Arizona, with a 36-inch diameter telescope. The area in the sky that this nebula spans is greater than can be captured with the 4-inch telescope in one exposure, so two exposures were taken and joined together. The Rosette is 5,000 light years away and stretches 116 light years across at its greatest length.

**Above center.** The Great Nebula in Orion (bottom, bright pinkish one). This is one of the few nebulae just visible to the naked eye. It is part of Orion's sword, below his belt. Amateur astronomer Scott Tucker took this photograph using a 6-inch refractor and film camera with an exposure time of one hour (see Astrophotography starting on page 112). In the sky, this nebula covers an area greater than the Moon, but in reality, it is 39 light years across and 1,500 light years away. Details in this nebula can be seen with small telescopes. Orion's nebula is lit by four young energetic stars that excite its hydrogen atoms to fluoresce. These stars are known as the Trapezium and are easily visible at 75x in any telescope (see Chart C on page 66). Astronomers have found evidence of other stars forming in this cloud. Just hints of the top blue reflection nebula can be seen in a small telescope, appearing as faint mist.

# Inside Galaxies

The pictures of most nebulae and star clusters are of those located in our galaxy. However, this star cluster, designated NGC 1850, is 166,000 light years away and is located in the Large Magellanic Cloud, a smaller companion galaxy to our own (see Chart J, page 80). Astronomers believe that this unique cluster may represent a young globular cluster because it is only 50 million years old and contains about 10,000 stars.

The Pleiades or Seven Sisters (designated M45), located in the constellation Taurus are visible during the winter (Chart B) with the naked eye. However, the nebulosity around them is more difficult to see. This cluster, which looks beautiful in binoculars, contains about 100 stars that are 407 light years away and span 14 light years. These stars are about 70 million years old. Although it might seem reasonable to conclude that the nebulosity around these stars is left over from when the stars formed, it is actually just another cloud that the stars are passing through.

other stars. Our Milky Way Galaxy has about 200 globular clusters that surround the nucleus in a ball-like halo. They are not restricted to the plane of the galaxy where our Sun resides. Globular clusters are easy to see in small telescopes, but they are spectacular in 12-inch or larger telescopes!

## INSIDE GALAXIES

### Stars Galore
When you think of a galaxy, think of stars. A galaxy is a collection of billions of stars bound by their collective gravity. In the Universe, there are more stars than anything else and since the beginning of time, their births have represented a natural process that is repeated over and over.

### Shining brightly
Stars shine from light created as a by-product of nuclear fusion that occurs at their centers when hydrogen atoms are converted into helium atoms. For a star the size of our Sun, this process takes place in an area equal to 1.6% of the total volume of the star, but containing half of its total mass. The density in this region is so great that a photon (a packet of light) ricochets for about 170,000 years before reaching the surface.

Star shine brightly and give off tremendous amounts of energy because they convert massive quantities of hydrogen into helium. In our Sun, 700 million tons of hydrogen are converted to helium *every* second, but even at this rate our Sun can produce light for billions of years.

### Normal size, mass, brightness, temperature and life
Stars come in all sizes, but even the smallest are large and massive. Our Sun is an average-size star. It has a diameter of 865,000 miles and a mass 330,000 times that of Earth. The diameter of normal-size stars varies from about 1/3 to 10 times the diameter of our Sun. Star mass, or the amount of matter that a star contains, varies from 1/10 to 40 times that of our Sun. Their brightness varies from 1/100 to over 1,000,000 times that of our Sun and the smallest stars have surface temperatures of just 5,000°F while the largest reach 70,000°F. Our Sun will last about 10 billion years, while the smallest stars may last a trillion and the largest only a million.

These ranges apply to normal stars. There are stars that are much smaller or much larger than mentioned above, but they represent special cases of stars that are at the ends of their lives. This includes stars known as white dwarfs, neutron stars, black holes, giants and supergiants.

### Yardstick stars
Cepheid variables are a famous category of stars. Historically, these stars gave astronomers the "yardstick" tool for measuring the distances to many objects within our galaxy and even nearby galaxies (but not to the distant ones).

# Stars
are like atoms to the Universe for they are the building blocks of galaxies.

The star *Betelgeuse* in the constellation Orion. This is one of the few images of a star other than our Sun and was taken by the orbiting *Hubble Space Telescope*. This red supergiant star is 58 light years away and has a diameter of almost a billion miles.

## Red Supergiant

This very small yellow dot is the size of our Sun compared to this red supergiant which has a diameter 1,000 times larger. This makes it slightly smaller than Antares, the brightest star in the constellation Scorpius (visible during the summer). Red supergiants are "puffed up" stars in a final stage of their lives before they explode as supernovae.

The length of this white line represents the distance from the Earth to the Sun, which is 93 million miles.

## Star Facts

**Our Sun:** Our yellowish colored Sun is a typical or average star. It has a diameter of 865,000 miles, a mass 333,000 times that of Earth and an age of about 4.5 billion years. Its technical designation is G2 V, which means that it has an average surface temperature and is typical in its class.

**Mass of stars:** The mass or amount of matter stars contain varies from just 1/10 to over 40 times the mass of our Sun.

***Normal* sizes:** Diameters vary from about 1/3 to more than 10 times the diameter of our Sun.

**Composition:** The composition of normal stars is 75 percent hydrogen and 25 percent helium gas, including traces of other elements.

**Life span:** The smallest stars may last a trillion years or more, while the largest may last only a million years. Our Sun will have a total life of about 10 billion years.

### Element Forging
The fusion process inside stars initially fuses hydrogen to helium. Helium is then fused to make carbon and oxygen. Stars like our Sun cannot create or fuse elements "heavier" than oxygen which is the eighth element in the periodic table. More massive stars can fuse about 30 elements of the periodic table. Supernovae explosions account for the heaviest elements.

### Interior Circulation
The energy created at the center of stars circulates inside. Depending on their mass, stars' interiors circulate differently. This is one factor that causes different outcomes at their deaths.

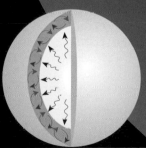

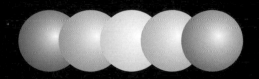

The color of a star depends on its surface temperature. Hotter stars appear blue or white, while cooler stars are red. There are no green stars because green is in the middle of the spectrum and gets washed out.

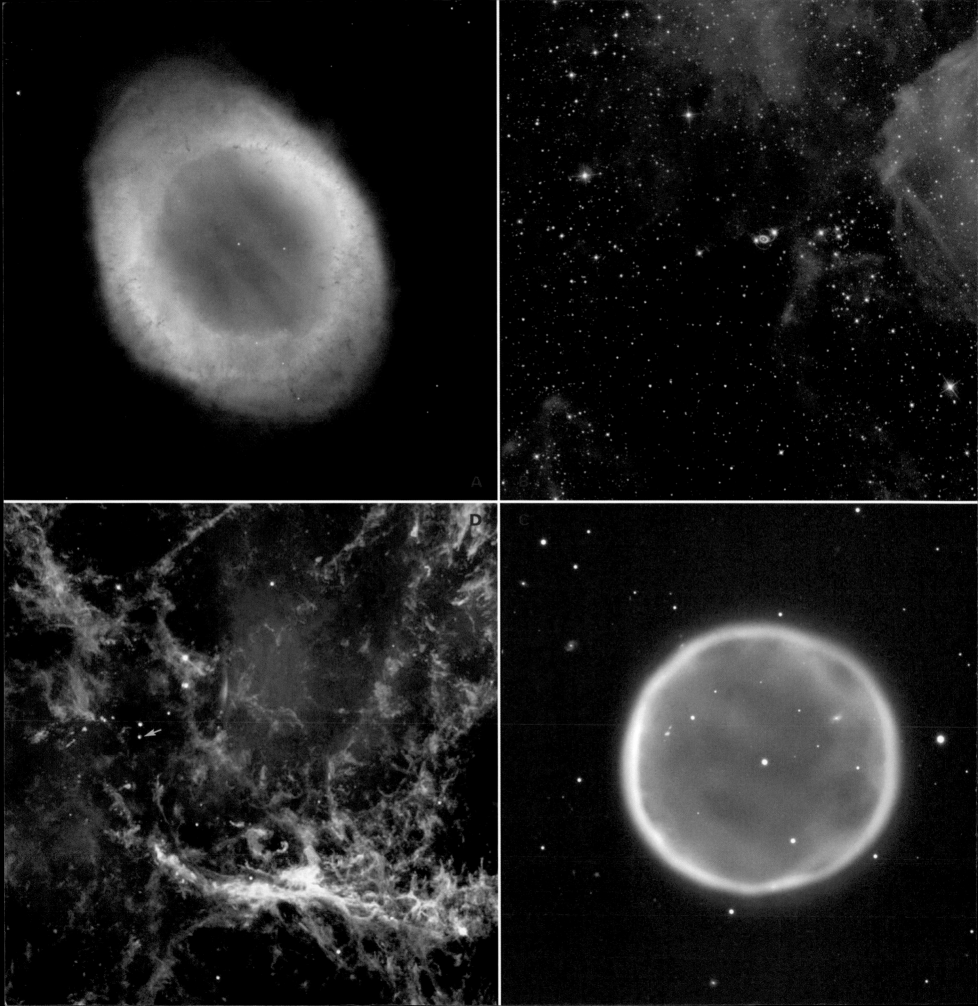

Variable stars change in brightness, which can take from a few days to a year or more. Cepheid variables are named after the first-known of it kind, observed in the constellation Cepheus, the King, visible in the northern sky. These types of variables can be either giant or supergiant stars near the ends of their lives. They slowly change in brightness over a period of a few days to months by expanding and contracting in size — their diameters changing anywhere from 5 to 10 percent. *Polaris*, the North Star, is a Cepheid variable, but its brightness changes very little. In 1912, Henrietta Leavitt discovered that the true brightness (compared to our Sun) of a Cepheid variable solely depends on its pulsation period. If the true brightness of a star is known, then it is easy (for astronomers) to calculate its distance. For a down-to-Earth example, if we took a 60 watt light bulb (a known brightness) and moved it to any distance, that distance could be found simply by measuring its new apparent brightness (the brightness of light falls off by a factor of exactly four when its distance is doubled). So, astronomers have used this discovery to measure the distances of Cepheid variables in star clusters, nebulae and even *nearby* galaxies.

### Galactic alchemy
When the Universe was formed, it created just two elements — hydrogen and helium. The other elements of the periodic table were produced by stars. These include metals and the various silicates or materials that make up rocks. Our Sun is a "second generation" star, and like the planets it contains elements created from stars that have lived and died. Some of the heavy elements, like gold, could only have been formed by supernova explosions.

### Giants and supergiants
Really large stars are "puffed up" stars near the ends of their lives. Towards the end of our Sun's life, it will expand to about the size of Mercury's orbit and will be considered a red giant. Stars that are much more massive than our Sun become super-

giants. Their outer atmospheres can expand to at least 1,500 times the diameter of our Sun (the diameter of Earth's orbit is equal to 200 Suns). The outer atmosphere of the supergiant Betelgeuse in the constellation Orion would almost reach the orbit of Jupiter.

## INSIDE GALAXIES
### Dying Stars
*Stars live long lives, but eventually they will all "die" by running out of fuel for nuclear fusion.*

### The smallest live the longest
The smallest "normal" stars, which have masses about 1/10 that of our Sun, live long lives. These stars are called red dwarfs because they are small in diameter and red in color. They slowly and efficiently fuse hydrogen into helium for possibly a trillion or more years. Red dwarfs die quietly, becoming cold dark cinders. Our Universe is not old enough for a red dwarf to have died yet.

### Stars the size of our Sun
Medium-sized stars like our Sun die in a different way. These stars burn hotter and faster than the smallest stars, so their lifespans are shortened to around 10 billion years. They end up with a core of helium and an outer shell of hydrogen that never got used for fusion. There is an incredible balancing act in the interiors of all stars. Stars are relatively stable because they balance the outward forces produced at their cores by the weight or mass of all the gas above them. However, with medium-sized stars, there comes a point when the helium core must contract to maintain balance. But in doing so, it heats up tremendously (the energy of the collapse produces the extra heat), so much so that it ignites the outer shell of hydrogen, causing it to fuse into helium and expand enormously — to diameters as large as Earth's orbit. These medium-size stars become giant stars.

### From planetary nebulae to white dwarfs
The thin outer atmospheres of giant stars eventually expand to form what are called planetary nebulae. The remains of the stars shrink to what are known as white dwarfs, very dense stars, about the size of Earth, with very energetic hot surfaces exceeding 45,000°F. This is hot enough to produce highly energetic ultraviolet light that not only pushes the gas around it outward, but also excites the gas to fluoresce, that is, to give off its own light.

Planetary nebulae have nothing to do with planets! It is an old name that stuck, used before anyone understood the true nature of these celestial objects. The word "planet" was originally coined because many of these nebulae are roundish, resembling planets to a degree. See pictures on the opposite page.

Planetary nebulae expand to 3 or more light years in size and eventually dissipate, perhaps lasting for 10,000 years. They are not always round because their shape can be affected by magnetic fields generated by the dying stars.

**A.** The Ring Nebula (designated M57), located in the constellation Lyra, is visible during the summer months. This is a favorite object and can be seen with a small telescope. It is 1,140 light years away, and less than one-half a light year in length, which makes it 335 times larger than the diameter of our solar system.

**B.** A supernova explosion (designated 1987A) that occurred in the Large Magellanic Cloud (visible from the southern hemisphere) in 1987. This is the most notable and nearest supernova explosion to happen in our lifetime.

**C.** This pretty blue planetary is in the constellation Hercules. It is 7,000 light years away and has a diameter of 5 light years. A special blue-green filter was used to isolate its light, emitted by excited oxygen atoms.

**D.** A closeup of the heart of the Crab Nebula in Taurus, remnant of a supernova explosion that happened on July 4, 1054 AD. It is 6,500 light years away and stretches over 11 light years. The original star had a mass of about 10 times our Sun. What remained after the explosion became a pulsar, which is a rapidly rotating neutron star. Neutron stars are about 10 miles in diameter. This one has a mass 1.4 times that of our Sun and spins on it axis 30 times a second. It is indicated by the arrow.

## INSIDE GALAXIES
### Dying Stars:  Supernova Explosions

*The last supernova in our galaxy occurred in 1604. They are rare events. The light they produce is anywhere from 600 million to 4 billion times the brightness of our Sun. They can remain bright for several months, but then fade over the course of a year. Since they actually shine brighter than an entire galaxy, astronomers and amateur astronomers look for them by scanning galaxies for very visible bright spots.*

### Two types

There are two types of supernova explosions. The fainter is produced when a massive star uses up its nuclear fuel. When this happens, the huge core collapses suddenly, sending out a shock wave that blasts the remaining outer atmosphere outward.

The brightest supernovae occur in a binary star system where two stars orbit extremely close to one another. This close proximity enables one of the stars, a white dwarf, to gravitationally pull in incredible amounts of atmospheric material from its companion. This eventually increases the mass of the white dwarf tremendously, forcing it to collapse, causing the element carbon (leftover material created by fusion in the original star before it "died" and became a white dwarf) to ignite in a furious nuclear fusion that consumes the whole star and produces the most violent explosion known in the Universe.

### Neutron stars, black holes and pulsars

The fainter supernovae can create neutron stars or black holes depending on how much material or mass was left after their explosion. A neutron star is an object about 10 miles in diameter, with a sugar cube size piece of its material weighing in at 100 million tons. Pulsars are rapidly rotating neutron stars (rotating as fast as 1,000 times per second).

### Nova flashes

At one time, astronomers thought that a nova might be a moderated supernova. Well, after collecting and analyzing data on novae, they discovered that novae are quite different. A nova is like a repeating camera "flash." Nova flashes occur in binary systems, where two stars are orbiting near one another. One of the stars, a white dwarf, gravitationally pulls off some of the outer atmosphere of its companion. When a substantial amount of the hydrogen atmosphere has accumulated on the white dwarf's surface, it ignites like a nuclear fusion bomb. Both stars remain intact after the explosion, to begin the process anew. A nova flash can cause a 100,000 fold brightening. Like many situations in nature, a nova and the brightest supernova have similar setups (binary systems with white dwarfs), but small differences produce dramatically different outcomes.

## INSIDE GALAXIES
### Black Holes

*The most mysterious objects in the Universe may conjure up thoughts of devouring monsters, but black holes are nothing more than fairly tame dead stars.*

### What exactly is a black hole?

The idea of a black hole was proposed shortly after Isaac Newton developed his famous equation about gravity in 1687. A black hole is a celestial object so dense, the gravity it produces will not even allow light to escape from its surface.

### Small to large

Black holes come in a variety of masses, from low or "small" mass to supermassive. A low mass black hole is one that has a mass of at least three times that of our Sun. Supermassive black holes are believed to reside at the center of most, if not all, galaxies. These are estimated to have masses millions of times greater than that of our Sun.

### Becoming a black hole — no application necessary

Low mass black holes can form from the remains of supernova explosions. If the mass of a star that remains after one of these explosions is three or more times that of our Sun, the object will automatically collapse to become a black hole. Anything less massive than three solar masses will become a neutron star or white dwarf. Our Sun does not have enough mass to become a black hole — it will become a white dwarf. A low mass black hole can only be created from stars much more massive than our Sun.

Supermassive black holes, located at the center of galaxies, may become very massive by pulling in extra matter, such as nebulae clouds, when galaxies collide.

### Zero in size?

According to the mathematics, all black holes, no matter how massive, have zero diameters. This seems difficult to believe, so scientists are studying this idea further to see if black holes might have small diameters. But scientists are fairly sure of one thing, that the "smallest" black holes, those with just three times the mass of our Sun, would have a diameter smaller than the periods printed on these pages.

### Event horizon

Although black holes may only be the size of periods at the end of sentences, they create around themselves a larger area of no return called an "event horizon." If you enter the event horizon, you cannot escape from the black hole. The diameter of the event horizon increases with mass. A black hole with a mass of three of our Suns has an event horizon 11 miles in diameter, whereas a black hole with a mass of a million Suns has a diameter of 5,600,000 miles, which is 14 times smaller than Mercury's orbit around the Sun.

## Black holes are not vacuum cleaners

If our Sun suddenly became a black hole, the planets would continue to orbit the black hole just like they did the Sun. A black hole does not act like a vacuum cleaner and suck things into it! A spacecraft could visit a black hole safely by orbiting around it. If something gets close to a black hole, it will get pulled in, but this is no different than a spacecraft crashing into a planet if it comes too close without entering an orbit.

# The End of the Universe

*The Universe came into existence about 14 billion years ago from a Big Bang, but what will be its fate? Will it last forever? Most everything in nature has a beginning and end, so, why shouldn't the Universe?*

## The expanding Universe

The Big Bang was an explosive type of event that popped our Universe into existence. Astronomers are not certain why the Universe began this way, it just did. They know that the Universe is expanding because in every direction they look, galaxies are fleeing away, just like from an explosion.

## Density does it

Density is the weight of a substance per unit of volume. For example, a block of balsa wood weighs less than a block of aluminum, which weighs less than a block of gold. If the blocks are the same size, these substances take up the same amount of volume but have different weights because they have different densities. In this example, gold has the highest density. The density of the Universe may be the key to determining its final fate.

If the density of the Universe determines its fate, what could happen to it? The Universe will either continue to expand and exist forever, or will one day stop expanding and collapse back on itself. But which will happen?

If the density of the Universe is high enough, then the Universe's gravity will eventually slow its expansion to a stop, reverse its direction and finally make it collapse. This will result in all the matter and energy in the Universe coming together in what astronomers call the "Big Crunch." If the density of the Universe is too low, the Universe will continue to expand forever. In this case, the Universe will not have enough gravity to stop the expansion. The expansion will continue forever with matter getting spread out over time. Eventually, all the stars will die and all the black holes will evaporate away. This Universe will end up cold and barren.

## The end

What will eventually happen to the Universe? At this time, we do not know for sure. Astronomers and scientists have to take many more measurements before they can try to answer this question. Along the way to finally answering it, they will make more discoveries and there will be surprises, that is, they will discover things about the Universe that they had never thought of. Now, don't get too worried about the end of the Universe, because whatever occurs, it is not going to happen for a very long time.

# A Really Big Mystery

*Our knowledge of the Universe has come a long way since recorded history, but the Universe is still mostly mysterious to us. We know its basic content, but we are having a harder time finding and understanding what holds it all together.*

At this time, the biggest mystery about the Universe is "missing matter." This is not a trivial concern, because astronomers and physicists can account for at most 10% of all the matter in the Universe. It is Newton's law of gravity, a law that has enabled us to send spacecrafts to our planets, that tells us something is "wrong." According to the math, there should be a lot more matter in galaxies than we have been able to measure. As we currently understand it, galaxies should fly apart because there is not enough matter to create the gravity necessary to hold them together.

Astronomers and physicists are busy looking for explanations. In the race to understand this, they have proposed everything from new forms of "exotic" matter to tinkering with Newton's law of gravity. The solution eludes us, but solving this problem will lead to a better understanding of how the Universe works. I also believe that this will open doors to a future that we can only experience in today's science fiction.

**Right.** A "jet" created by a supermassive black hole at the center of an elliptical galaxy (designated M87) that can be found in the direction of the constellation Virgo. This large galaxy is 55 million light years away. Black holes can shoot off jets of electrons from matter circling inward. **Smaller picture above** shows a ring created from matter circling in on the black hole.

*Friendship 7*

**ED**
**S**

# Highlights of Space Exploration

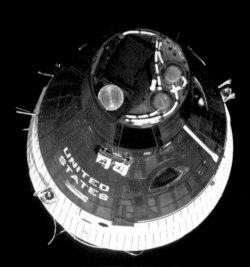

n all, there are about 2,500 satellites orbiting Earth and another 3,500 pieces of debris made up of such things as nose-cone shrouds, hatch covers and objects like wrenches that have escaped from manned missions.

**1957.** *Sputnik 1* of USSR becomes the first satellite to orbit the Earth.

**1958.** *Explorer 1* becomes the first US satellite. NASA is founded.

**1959.** *Luna 2* of USSR impacts Moon. *Luna 3* orbits and photographs Moon.

**1960.** *Tiros 1* of US becomes first weather satellite.

**1961.** Yuri Gargarin of USSR becomes first human in space and first person to orbit Earth. One month later, Alan Shepard becomes first American in space.

**1962.** John Glenn becomes first American to orbit Earth. *Telstar 1* broadcasts first live transatlantic television.

**1963.** Valentia Tereshkova of USSR becomes first woman in space.

**1964.** *Ranger 7* of US orbits Moon and relays photographs.

**1965.** First *Gemini* launch, a precursor to the *Apollo* mis-

sions. US *Mariner 4* launched to Mars, later returns photos. USSR launches *Venera 3* to Venus, later impacts surface.

**1966.** USSR *Luna 9* followed by US *Surveyor 1* become first spacecrafts to soft-land on the Moon. US & USSR place spacecrafts in orbit around Moon.

**1967.** USSR *Soyez 1* crashes, killing Vladimir Komaroc.

**1968.** First two *Apollo* missions — second orbits Moon.

**1969.** Neil Armstrong and Edwin Aldrin become first individuals to set foot on the Moon. US *Mariner 6 & 7* return closeup pictures of Mars.

**1970.** *Apollo 13* experiences an explosion on the way to the Moon, but successfully returns. USSR *Venera 7* becomes first spacecraft to soft-land on Venus and return data.

**1971.** USSR *Salyut 1* becomes first space station. *Apollo 15* astronauts drive first

Moon rover. US *Mariner 9* becomes first spacecraft to orbit Mars.

**1972.** US *Pioneer 10* launched to Jupiter. *Apollo 17* becomes last manned mission to Moon.

**1973.** *Skylab* and *Skylab 2* become first US space stations. US *Mariner 10* launched to flyby Venus and Mercury.

**1974.** USSR places two more space stations into orbit, *Salyut 3 & 4*.

**1975.** US *Apollo 18* and USSR *Soyuz 19* dock.

**1976.** US *Viking 1 & 2* soft-land on Mars and return pictures.

**1977.** US *Voyager 2* followed by *Voyager 1* launched to explore the four gas giants.

**1978.** Two US *Pioneer* missions reach Venus and map its surface.

**1979.** The European Space Agency (ESA), established in 1973, launched its first rocket and goes on to launch 100 more by 2000.

**1981.** First US space shuttle *Columbia* launched.

**1982.** USSR *Venera 13* soft-lands on Venus.

**1983.** Sally Ride becomes first US woman in space aboard shuttle *Challenger*.

**1984.** First untethered space walk, conducted during shuttle *Challenger* mission. USSR cosmonauts spend record 237 days in space aboard *Salyut 7*.

**1985.** Japan launches *Sakigake* to rendezvous with Halley's Comet.

**1986.** Shuttle *Challenger* explodes upon liftoff. Core unit of the USSR space station *Mir* is placed into orbit. Three spacecrafts rendezvous with Halley's Comet.

**1989.** Shuttle missions deploy spacecrafts *Magellan* and *Galileo* that go on to explore Venus and Jupiter. *Voyager 2* flies by Neptune. US *Cosmic Background Explorer* (COBE) launched.

**1990.** Shuttle *Discovery* deploys *Hubble Space Telescope* in orbit around Earth.

**1993.** Contact lost with US Mars *Observer* just prior to placing in orbit.

**1995.** US *Solar and Helispheric Observatory* (SOHO) placed at a distant point in Earth's orbit to study Sun. US *Galileo* arrives and placed in orbit around Jupiter.

**1997.** *Pathfinder* becomes the first roving vehicle on another planet — Mars.

**1998.** *Lunar Prospector* detects frozen water at poles on Moon. Construction on the *International Space Station* begins.

**1999.** *Chandra X-ray observatory* deployed from shuttle to orbit Earth 1/3 of way to Moon. Contact with US *Mars Polar Lander* lost on entry. US *Mars Climate Orbiter* lost thru navigational error.

**2001.** After 15 years in orbit, Russia's *Mir* space station burns up in Earth's atmosphere. US Mars *Odyssey* placed in orbit around the red planet to conduct mineralogical analysis of surface. US *NEAR Shoemaker* becomes first spacecraft to orbit and then land on an asteroid.

**2003.** US is scheduled to launch two rovers for exploring Mars' surface. Japan's *Nozomi* scheduled to arrive and be placed in orbit around Mars.

**2004.** US *Cassini* expected to arrive and be placed in orbit around Saturn.

**Picture Captions:**
**Upper left.** John Glenn entering his Mercury *Friendship* 7 spacecraft on February 20, 1961.
**Middle.** Gemini 6 rendezvous with Gemini 6, December 15, 1965.
**Far right.** July 16, 1969 lift-off of Apollo 11 to the Moon atop the 363-foot tall Saturn rocket.

# Self-guided Tour of the Universe

# Guide to the Heavens

*As you explore the night sky, whether occasionally or regularly, you will experience powerful moments which will become cherished memories. How you explore the night sky is up to you. Whether by just looking up or investing in a telescope for a closer view, you will open doors to nature's grandest handiwork, her awesome and beautiful Universe. May your journey lead you to joy and appreciation, understanding and awareness of what truly is heavenly.*

Observing the heavens and all that they contain is much like going on vacation and visiting another locale. For both, you need transportation, maps, guides and a calendar of events. What we choose to see is based on our interests, time and energy. And there are always those one-time special exhibits or events, but remember, if you don't catch these, then you'll miss them.

Your experiences are your own and you make what you want of them. It doesn't matter if you travel first class or coach, or are on a limited budget, because you can have a downright sensational experience either way. Tipping included.

## Part II overview

This part of the book is your guide to exploring the heavens. There is something for everyone because it covers a range of activities. Some require telescopes, but many don't.

If you want to explore without a telescope, you will find that there is plenty to do, as listed on page 43.

If you have a hunger to explore with a telescope, start with the Moon, work your way over to the planets (if they are out) and then seek the brightest deep sky objects.

## General Observing Considerations

A major factor in determining the amount of time spent observing is comfort. Sitting comfortably and staying warm are at the top of the list. There are also night vision concerns. Here are some of my thoughts on these considerations.

**Outdoor furniture.** Lawn chairs or similar folding/reclining furniture eliminate the strain of standing for long periods of time and provide comfortable horizontal positioning for viewing the sky overhead. Shop outdoor stores or catalogs for the latest in outdoor portable chairs or loungers, because they seem to get better and more innovative every year. For most of my observing, I use cloth or nylon-covered chairs because they are warmer against the body. In a pinch, leaning against the car is an alternative, but that can be cold and dirty.

**Dress for warmth.** In general, be prepared by dressing warmly and/or having extra garments handy for when the temperature drops. *I can't overemphasis this point, no matter what time of year it is.* Sky watching is a sedentary activity, so your body can get cold quickly, especially if it is windy. If you plan on observing for just an hour, bring a jacket, hat and gloves, even during the summer. If you are traveling to a location away from home, go prepared for conditions worse than you anticipate. You can take off what you have, but you can't put on what you don't. Do we ever learn? Not too long ago, I went observing with friends and failed to bring a jacket. Lucky for me, one of my wiser-minded companions let me borrow his extra one. I would have had to come home early had it not been for his consideration.

I would say that "cold feet" is the complaint I hear most often. Wear double socks with heavy shoes or hiking boots. Disposable hand warmers placed in your shoes can help keep your feet warm. Speaking of disposable warmers, I have found them very effective at keeping me warm on cold nights. Some manufacturers produce various sizes to fit shoes, gloves, etc. I have experienced five or more hours of glorious heat from these warmers. According to friends, reusable warmers don't get as hot or last as long as disposable ones. I would be interested in your experience. Personally, I like reusable products, but I'd rather stick with guaranteed warmth when I am outside and away from home.

**Night vision & red-light flashlights.** Bright outdoor lights hardly affect observing the Moon and planets, because these objects are bright themselves. However, if you want to see fainter stars or observe nebulae and galaxies through a telescope, you must get away from bright lights so your eyes can "dark adapt," which makes them much more sensitive to low light levels ("night vision" is another term for "dark-adapted" eyes). As long as you are away from bright lights, your eyes will automatically adapt to the dark, taking just a few minutes to initially adapt and about 15 to 30 minutes to achieve a deeper adaptation. All of us have experienced different degrees of night vision when walking around our living places at night. The difference between dark-adapted and non-dark-adapted eyes in seeing low levels of light is dramatic! If your eyes are not dark-adapted, you will simply not be able to see faint objects like nebulae and galaxies.

Using a red-light flashlight during observing activities will immensely help to preserve your night vision. Red-light flashlights can be purchased at your local telescope store or from advertisers in the popular monthly astronomy magazines.

In the northern hemisphere, all the stars appear to revolve daily around *Polaris*, the North Star, because the Earth's axis points in its direction. This picture was taken by pointing a camera at *Polaris* and keeping the shutter open for about 20 minutes. Because the Earth spins, it acts like a gyroscope and one property of a gyroscope is that it keeps its axis pointing in the same direction, even if the whole gyroscope is moved above, just like when the Earth revolves yearly around the Sun.

As a general word of warning, using white-light flashlights at astronomical events really irritates staff members and others who are often quite curt about turning them off. This is an overreaction, but nonetheless, it happens.

## Movement in the Heavens

The motions of Earth are what cause the majority of the movements we see in the sky.

Most heavenly movement is a result of the Earth's daily rotation on its axis, which produces the appearance that all celestial objects revolve around the Earth. The most obvious examples are the Sun's movement across the sky during the day and the stars moving through it at night.

The daily rotation of the Earth is perpetual, so every celestial object appears to move across the sky over the course of a day. Although we only see the Sun during daylight, the stars are there. Because celestial objects are constantly "moving" across the sky, telescopes have to be nudged every few minutes (unless they are motorized) to keep objects centered in their eyepieces.

All rotating or spinning objects share a common property. Left alone, without any outside influence, their axes keep their orientations. In Earth's case, this means that our axis of rotation, which passes through the poles, always points in the same direction, towards the star *Polaris*, the North Star. Therefore, all the stars will appear to revolve around Polaris (see picture above).

A second heavenly movement is caused by Earth's yearly revolution around the Sun. This produces two major effects: first, this is the why we see a slightly different set of constellations each month (see illustration on the next page). But, maybe more

Red-light flashlights are helpful for preserving your night vision while you are observing. Various models are available and most rely on red LEDs, so their batteries have a long life. Most telescope stores stock them. Personally, I like the type that allows the brightness to be varied. Styles change yearly.

# Naked-eye Observing

importantly, our annual revolution gives rise to the ecliptic and the constellations that make up the zodiac.

If we could see the stars during the day, we would quickly notice that the Sun moves amongst them. And, over the course of a year, the Sun would complete a great circle which passes through twelve* constellations that we have dubbed the "zodiac." This great circle or path of the Sun is called the ecliptic. Unfortunately, we don't get a good feel for the Sun's movement through

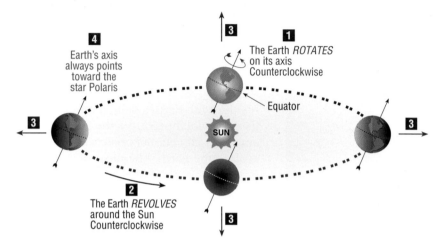

**Heavenly Movements**

**1** Our days and nights, as well as the daily rising and setting of the Sun, Moon and stars, happen because the Earth rotates on an axis.

**2** The Earth's revolution around the Sun creates our year and is the reason that the stars change from month to month.

**3** The night side of the Earth points in a slightly different direction every night of the year; however, it takes about a month for us to notice any change in the evening stars.

**4** The Earth acts like a gyroscope as it spins daily on its axis. One property of a gyroscope is that, as it spins, its axis will always point in the same direction even if the gyroscope is moved about. So, even though the Earth revolves around the Sun, its axis always points in the same direction, and the star Polaris just happens to be near to where it points.

the constellations because we can't see the stars around the Sun during the day. The ecliptic is tilted 23.5° to the celestial equator (a projection of our equator onto the sky) because it corresponds to the tilt of the Earth on its axis. The ecliptic's northern-most point is in the constellation Taurus (Summer Solstice) while its southernmost point is in Sagittarius (Winter Solstice). It crosses the celestial equator in Pisces (Vernal Equinox — beginning of spring) and Virgo (Autumnal Equinox). The ecliptic is noted on the star charts starting on page 64.

A third type of heavenly movement is caused by the revolutions of the Moon and planets. The Moon's revolution around Earth produces its monthly phases, whereas the revolution of the planets, which is counterclockwise around the Sun, moves them eastward through the constellations of the zodiac. The

*In our modern era, there are actually 13 constellations that the Sun passes through, the 13th being Ophiuchus, which lies between Sagittarius and Scorpius.

Moon and planets also move through the constellations of the zodiac because their orbits are close to the same plane as Earth's orbit. This makes them appear to follow the same path through the constellations as the Sun. This idea is useful because if you know where the ecliptic is, or the constellations of the zodiac, then you can find any visible planet somewhere near this path.

Why don't we see the stars moving individually? All the stars (and the Sun) *are* moving in different directions through space. However, constellation patterns appear "fixed" and do not seem to change because the stars are so far away (the very closest is over 25 trillion miles away) that it takes thousands of years for any of them to move far enough to be noticed. This is why we call the stars "fixed," and use them as reference points for movements within our solar system.

## Observing with the Naked Eyes

One can easily spend a lifetime exploring and enjoying the wonders of the sky without any optical instruments. The ancients did just that until Galileo and others turned the first telescopes upwards in 1609.

In general, most of us are anxious to use a telescope for celestial exploration, but I will tell you firsthand that at least half of my most memorable moments have been when viewing the sky with just my naked eyes. There is nothing grander than staring at the heart of the Milky Way Band during the summer or witnessing the splash of a meteor across the sky. Identifying the constellations gives you a warm feeling that brings them home, and experiencing a total solar eclipse is beyond description. All of these activities or events are to be enjoyed to their fullest without optical aid. I believe much of your enjoyment will come from this.

Since there are many ways to enjoy and participate in astronomy without using instruments, I have listed some of the most popular on the next page.

### Thoughts on identifying and learning the constellations

Every time I am with people who do not know the constellations, they always enjoy having them pointed out. The stars, their patterns and ancient lore are fascinating to most of us. Fortunately, it is fun and relatively easy to learn the brightest constellations. The ability to go out and identify them will bring you closer to the night sky and nature. The stars will become your lifelong friends, always there and supporting you by providing a framework for celestial events and memories.

On pages 62–81, I have provided constellation charts that cover the entire sky, both the northern and southern hemispheres. At the bottom of these charts, I have indicated the early evening hours when the charts match the stars in the sky. But what about other hours of the night? These charts can be used to navigate the entire sky for any hour of the night, but if it gets confusing, I recommend purchasing a planisphere (see top of next page), which is a special type of star chart that allows you to "dial-in" the stars for any time and date, instead of having to turn and match pages.

If you have *never* found a constellation, and you want to learn them by yourself, you may need a little practice to orient yourself to the night sky. Your first times out may prove frustrating, but like with any new skill, you *will* become proficient through practice.

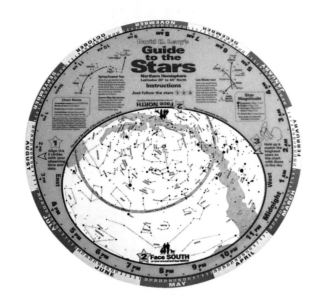

A planisphere is a circular star chart that allows you to dial-in the stars for *your* observing time and date. As you can see, the hours of the day and days of the year are printed around the circumference. This type of star chart consists of two pieces of plastic riveted together at their centers. The stars present in the oval are those that will be visible in your sky.

The David H. Levy planisphere is one of the best current-day planispheres. It comes in two sizes, a jumbo 16-inch diameter and a traditional 11-inch diameter. There is also a Spanish version (16-inch diameter) as well as one for the southern hemisphere (11-inch).

## Suggestions for those wanting to find and learn the constellations

**1** Get a jump start by enlisting the help of someone who can identify the constellations. In several minutes, he or she can provide you with a framework that will last a lifetime.

**2** Find a dark area and steer clear of cars and other bright or glaring lights.

**3** Avoid nights when the Moon is shining brightly because this will make the stars more difficult to see.

**4** Stay outside at least 15 minutes for your eyes to adapt to the dark. You will then be able to see many more stars. Also, to keep your night vision, use a red-light flashlight to read star charts.

**5** Initially, when using star charts, face either due north or due south.

**6** Try to match the brightest stars in the sky with the brightest stars on the star charts, or vice versa. NOTE: Don't confuse the planets with the brightest stars. Venus, Mars, Jupiter and Saturn normally outshine the brightest stars. If you practice facing north (in the northern hemisphere), you can avoid the planets.

**7** The constellations are big. If you extended your arm, Orion spans one hand length and the Big Dipper over one hand length.

**8** If you are having difficulty finding the constellations, practice in many short sessions over several days, weeks or months, instead of long, drawn-out sessions.

**9** If you want to learn and observe the constellations at times other than those indicated on star charts, get a special type of star chart called a "planisphere" which allows you to "dial-in" the stars for any hour of the day and any day of the year (see picture above). These are also great for traveling.

**10** Make sure you have fun!

## Top 10 Naked-eye Observing Activities

1. **Learn the <u>constellations</u> and <u>bright stars</u> while following their parade throughout the year (pages 60–81)**

2. **Learn to identify the <u>brightest planets</u> and watch them wander through the constellations (pages 92–102)**

3. **Watch <u>Moon</u> phases (page 86)**

4. **Observe <u>meteor showers</u> (page 109)**

5. **Observe the <u>Milky Way Band</u> (page 74)**

6. **Observe total <u>solar eclipses</u> and <u>lunar eclipses</u> (page 91)**

7. **Observe <u>aurorae</u> (page 110)**

8. **Observe Moon and Sun <u>halos</u> (page 111)**

9. **Observe bright <u>comets</u> (page 108)**

10. **Visit <u>planetariums</u> or <u>observatories</u> (page 119)**

# Binoculars

Although most of us want a telescope for observing the heavens, I rate binoculars excellent as an instrument for celestial exploration. They offer the comfort of two-eye viewing and capture greater vistas than is possible with telescopes. And, since many of us already own a pair of binoculars, we can use them to go out and start observing right away. Today, almost all middle-of-the-line binoculars, ranging in price from $200 to $350, offer good optical performance.

Binoculars add a dimension to observing that cannot be achieved with telescopes. In my opinion, the most beautiful sights of the Pleiades (M45, see page 64) and the Praesepe (M44, see page 69) come through binoculars. These clusters fill the binoculars' field of view and give the impression that the stars are floating in front of you.

### Classification of binoculars ★ 7x50, etc.

The magnification and lens diameter of binoculars are designated by a pair of numbers with an "x" between them. A few examples are 8x20, 10x40 and 7x50 (7x50 is pronounced seven-by-fifty). Generally you will find this description somewhere on the binoculars. The "x" actually belongs to the first number and signifies power, while the second, larger number is the diameter of either front lens in millimeters.

Binoculars are classified by their magnification and front-lens diameter. This pair is a 10x50, which is indicated on the focusing knob. 10x is the magnification and 50 the diameter of either front lens in millimeters.

### Comparing binoculars for *astronomical* use — Using that little "x"

The Royal Astronomical Society of Canada has come up with a useful "measure" for comparing the *astronomical* performance of binoculars. This measure involves simply multiplying the magnification by the lens diameter to obtain a comparison number called the "Visibility Factor" (e.g. 8x20 = 160). Higher numbers indicate better performing binoculars for astronomical use. According to this formula, and verified by field use, some smaller lens diameters can perform as well as those with larger diameters (10x40 = 400 compared to 7x50 = 350). This Visibility Factor can be most helpful when you are choosing from a plethora of *similar* binoculars — the one with the highest value will be best for astronomy.

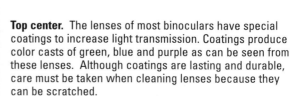

### Other considerations when purchasing binoculars

**Roof prisms vs. Porro prism binoculars.** Both (types) of these binoculars perform well. The roof prism binoculars look like two straight tubes next to one another. The porro prism binoculars look more "traditional," having eyepieces offset from the front lenses. Roof prisms are usually more expensive because the tolerances for their internal prisms must be higher in order to achieve good imagery. (BAK-4 prisms are the standard quality for these units.) They are also more compact, which may be an advantage for traveling.

**Magnification limitations.** Binoculars usually provide just one magnification, generally ranging from 7x to 10x because they are designed for hand-held use. Some binoculars have zoom capability, but most amateur astronomers avoid these because their optical quality is sometimes not as good as units with single magnifications.

**Viewing comfort and eyeglasses.** Binoculars should be comfortable to look through. The "eye relief," of eyepieces, controls viewing comfort (more on page 54) because it determines the distance you must place your eyes from the eyepieces in order to take advantage of the full view provided by the optics. Generally, but not always, higher magnifications mean less eye relief. It is always a good idea to try binoculars before you buy to make sure they are comfortable to look through. If you must wear glasses, binoculars with short eye reliefs may be difficult to use. Many binoculars have rubber guards that either fold back, push or twist in/out to accommodate eyeglass wearers.

**Top center.** The lenses of most binoculars have special coatings to increase light transmission. Coatings produce color casts of green, blue and purple as can be seen from these lenses. Although coatings are lasting and durable, care must be taken when cleaning lenses because they can be scratched.

**Left.** Parallelogram-type mounts are great for groups. The binoculars stay on target even if moved up or down to accommodate different height individuals. Note the reflex-sight finder on top of the binoculars to aid in pointing.

**Comfortable ergonomics.** Some binoculars are more comfortable to hold than others. Although this may not be an immediate concern when using binoculars in conjunction with a tripod, it will become one for daytime and casual use.

**Multi-coated optics.** Binoculars incorporate a number of lenses and prisms. Special coatings on their surfaces help to increase light transmission tremendously. Although it is difficult to tell if the interior surfaces are coated, the exterior front lenses and eyepieces should show a distinct green or bluish-purple cast, indicating that these surfaces are coated. Binoculars with multi-coated optics tend to look dark when you peer into the front lenses. Many binoculars are inscribed with the words "Multi-Coated" on their exterior, but there is no industry standard definition of this term.

**Field of view.** One of the greatest advantages of binoculars over telescopes is that they let you see a large area of the sky at once. Some binoculars even feature extra-wide fields of view; however, I would avoid these for astronomical use because the stars around the edges of their fields of view often appear out of focus.

**Large, high-powered binoculars.** If you really like binoculars for astronomical use, but want more power, there are large binoculars like 15x60, 17x70, 20x100 and others that might interest you! Obviously, these large instruments require sturdy mounts and tripods.

## Tripods

Attaching your binoculars to a camera tripod is very helpful when exploring the heavens because it steadies your view and eliminates arm fatigue. You can also lean on the tripod, which makes it easier to stand in one spot for a long period of time.

There are also specialized parallelogram-type binocular mounts that are particularly useful with groups because they keep an object in view even when the binoculars are moved up or down to accommodate individuals of different heights. Parallelogram-type mounts can be used when standing or adapted for sitting and reclining positions (see picture on page 44).

Today, most binoculars come with a tripod socket that allows attachment to a tripod head; however, you need to purchase an adapter. Many older binoculars don't have sockets, so you may have to get creative to latch these down.

## Porro-Prism Binoculars

**Above.** You may already have a pair of these binoculars lying around, so observing the sky is just a matter of finding them and stepping outside. Porros are a proven design identified by the offset of the eyepieces from the front lenses. Although this design is bigger and thus bulkier than roof-prism binoculars, it can edge out the performance of roof-prism binoculars at a lower cost.

## Roof-Prism Binoculars

**Below.** Nature lovers and hikers often prefer this type of binoculars because they are compact in comparison to porro-prism binoculars; however, they are usually more expensive. Although these binoculars look like two small, side-by-side refractor telescopes, they incorporate several internal prisms to provide upright imagery. Quality roof-prism binoculars perform just as well as porro-prism binoculars.

## Aiming towards the sky

Binoculars are easy to aim during the day, but they are much harder to aim at objects in the night sky. The bright stars are not a problem, but areas where there are fainter stars can pose difficulties. For this reason, many amateurs attach small reflex-sight finders (see picture on page 44 and more on page 53) to their binoculars to facilitate aiming. These finders project red dots. Most reflex-sights can be removed so the binoculars can be stored in their case.

Tripod adapters are used to attach binoculars to tripods. Note: Some adapters won't fit the tighter barrel constraints of roof-prism binoculars.

## Binocular Recommendations

**Use:** For many amateurs, binoculars are an adjunct, used in conjunction with a telescope; however, some people use them as their sole means of exploration.

**Diameter of objective and magnification:** I recommend purchasing a pair that can be used for both astronomical and daytime adventures: 7x40, 10x40, 7x50 or 10x50 are good choices. Those with magnifications above 10x are difficult to hold steadily.

**Optical design:** Both roof- and porro-prisms are good designs. Roof-prisms are more compact but usually more expensive.

**Tripod consideration:** For exploring the heavens, I highly recommend using a camera tripod to steady your view and eliminate arm fatigue.

**Cost:** Expect to spend $250 or more for a pair with good optics. These should last a lifetime.

**Warranty:** Some companies offer a lifetime alignment warranty.

**Return policy:** Inquire about the return policy if you purchase by mail.

# The Three Basic Telescopes

## Refractor

When most people think of a planet, they think of Saturn. When they think of a telescope, they think of a refractor.

A refractor is a telescope with a front lens that brings light to a focus at the rear of the instrument. Refractors were the first telescopes. It all started around 1608 when Galileo and other scientists heard about the invention and made their own instruments for astronomical use. Refractors were used extensively by astronomers until the early 1900s, when they were replaced by reflectors that were larger and less costly to build. The largest refractor in the world, completed in 1897, is the 40-inch diameter Yerkes refractor at Williams Bay, Wisconsin. Among amateurs, refractors have enjoyed a resurgence because their optical quality has improved dramatically over the past years.

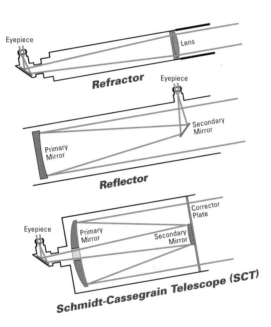

The three most common telescopes use different means to bring light to a focus.

### The refractor attraction

Refractors are easy to use and practically maintenance free. Unless severely jarred, the optics may never need alignment. The only maintenance is an occasional cleaning of the outside front objective. Today, the tubes are physically shorter than they used to be, which makes these telescopes easier than ever to set up, use and store. Refractors are often the telescope of choice for astrophotography. Some of the best celestial photos have been taken with this type of telescope.

### The down side

Refractors are great instruments to explore the heavens, but unfortunately, inexpensive refractors have done more to taint first impressions of observational astronomy than almost any other factor. I have heard, firsthand, numerous reports of disappointment from people who purchased refractors from department stores, or purchased a lower line name brand model. The irony and "up side" to all this is that middle-of-the-line refractors perform better than ever and the top-of-the-line perform the best of any telescope.

### Cost, APOs and size limitations

Per aperture inch, a quality refractor costs more than any other type of telescope. For example, for $3,000, you could purchase either a 4-inch quality refractor (without mount), a 15-inch Newtonian reflector (with mount) or an 11-inch GO TO SCT (with mount and described on page 48).

Although $3,000 dollars is a lot of money for a quality 4-inch refractor, a middle-of-the-line, good-quality, 3-inch refractor can be purchased for $400 to $1,000. The $3,000 refractor represents the highest quality type and is known as an APO (pronounced A-P-O, an abbreviation for apochromatic, which means "free of any optical aberrations"). These telescopes provide incredibly sharp images and for this reason, I enjoy looking through an APO telescope more than any other type of telescope.

The largest readily available diameter for refractors is 4 inches (100mm). Diameters of just 5 to 6 inches must often be special ordered, sometimes with waiting periods of several years.

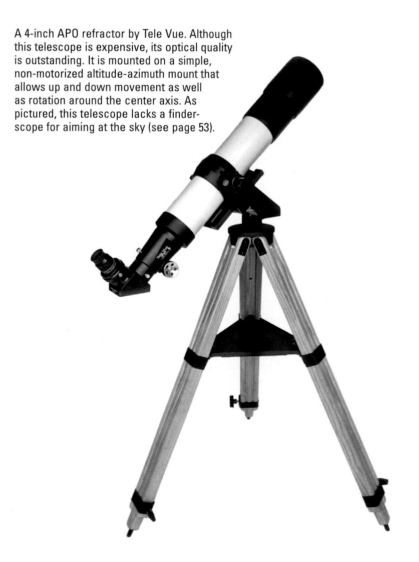

A 4-inch APO refractor by Tele Vue. Although this telescope is expensive, its optical quality is outstanding. It is mounted on a simple, non-motorized altitude-azimuth mount that allows up and down movement as well as rotation around the center axis. As pictured, this telescope lacks a finder-scope for aiming at the sky (see page 53).

## Newtonian Reflector

The Newtonian reflector has been a workhorse for both professionals and amateurs since its invention in 1668 by Isaac Newton. This type of telescope has a concave parabolic mirror at the rear of its tube that focuses light to an eyepiece near the front end. Amateurs enjoy using reflectors more than ever, in diameters ranging from 4 to more than 36 inches.

### Least expensive per inch

The Newtonian reflector is the least expensive telescope per aperture inch. Generally, this telescope is set on a simple, non-motorized mount, called an alt-az mount (short for altitude-azimuth), which moves up and down and rotates to any compass point, similar to binocular mounts at tourist attractions. The optics for reflectors with diameters of 10 inches or less are usually housed in tubes, while those with diameters of 12 inches or more are often placed in an open-frame, truss-tube assembly that can be disassembled and stored compactly (see pictures below). An 8-inch Newtonian sells for about $500, a 10-inch for around $650.

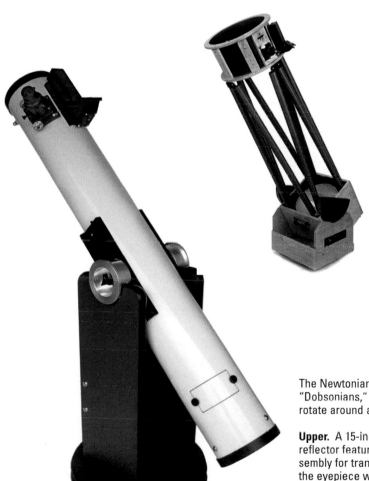

### A little more maintenance

The Newtonian reflector requires occasional to frequent optical alignments, and occasional cleaning of its mirrors. Aligning or collimating the mirrors is easy to perform after you have done it a few times (the basic collimation procedure is outlined on page 57) and there are specialty "tools" to aid in the process. Collimation *must* be performed after each assembly of truss-tube reflectors.

The mirrors of reflectors need occasional cleaning because they are exposed to the elements. Depending on use and environmental conditions, yearly cleanings (or longer intervals) may be all that's needed. Don't worry about some dust on the mirrors, which is normal and does not affect viewing. About every 10 to 20 years, the reflective coating may need to be replaced.

### "Light buckets"

The largest refractors are about 6 inches in diameter, compared to 14 to 16 inches for SCTs (see next page), but the largest reflectors zoom to 36 inches. Large-diameter Newtonian reflectors provide the brightest images of galaxies and nebulae because they collect more light (hence the term "light bucket") than their smaller counterparts. Image brightness depends on the surface area of the lens or mirror. A 20-inch-diameter Newtonian gathers over 11 times more light than a 6-inch lens or mirror.

### Manual labor

Today, more than ever before, Newtonian reflectors are set on simple, non-motorized mounts. This can be a boon or, a bane depending on your orientation and intentions. These simple mounts have allowed manufacturers to hold down costs, enabling amateurs to afford the largest diameter telescopes ever. However, these telescopes are limited to visual use only and cannot effectively be used for astrophotography. Although it is possible to buy a mechanism that will allow these telescopes to follow celestial objects for short periods of time, for the most part they are manual and must be continually nudged to keep an object in view.

### A little help from a friend

Newtonians mounted on simple alt-az mounts can be equipped with "encoders" and a hand controller to help find celestial objects. This allows the telescope to work similarly to the GO TO telescopes described on page 51. The only difference is that you move the telescope by hand, watching directional arrows on the hand-controller's display. Visit your local telescope store for more information. Once installed, these systems do work well.

The Newtonian reflectors pictured here, that is, telescopes set on simple mounts, are often referred to as "Dobsonians," after John Dobson, who popularized simplicity in the 1970s. These non-motorized mounts rotate around a base and move up and down to point in any direction.

**Upper.** A 15-inch-diameter Newtonian reflector manufactured by Discovery Telescopes. This Newtonian reflector features an open truss-tube design that reduces overall weight and facilitates assembly/disassembly for transportation or storage. With larger Newtonians like this, ladders are often needed to reach the eyepiece which is located near the top, next to the Telrad finder. Discovery Telescopes is a US manufacturer of Dobsonians with 6-inch to 24-inch diameter mirrors. Visit www.discovery-telescopes.com.

**Left.** A homemade 6-inch Dobsonian reflector outfitted with a Telrad finder. The panel near the bottom end of the tube can be removed to clean the mirror.

# The Three Basic Telescopes

## Schmidt-Cassegrain Telescopes (SCT) & Other Hybrids

The Schmidt-Cassegrain Telescope (often called S-C-T) is the telescope of choice amongst amateurs, but what is it? Schmidt-Cassegrain is the name of an optical design inspired by Barnard Schmidt (1879–1935) and Guillaume Cassegrain (1625–1712). This type of telescope is often referred to as a hybrid because it contains elements of both reflecting and refracting telescopes. Like a Newtonian reflector, it has a rear primary mirror that focuses light, but it also incorporates a front lens or corrector plate that not only seals the tube from the environment but also helps to fold the optics, making this telescope very compact. The eyepiece holder is at the end of the tube, similarly to a refractor, but for the focused light to get there, it must pass through a hole in the middle of the mirror. This design has been so successful that a 5.5-inch diameter version made by Celestron has been used on Space Shuttle missions.

### Computer automated GO TO technology

Today, a major attraction of SCTs is that most come with a mount incorporating computerized GO TO technology (see more on page 51). This simply means that after you set up the telescope and align it to two bright stars (a five-minute process guided by prompts from a hand controller, detailed on page 52), the telescope will automatically move to and follow objects chosen from its huge database. These telescopes can even take you on a tour of the night sky, providing sights of the best objects visible from your location.

**Above.** Celestron's 11-inch diameter Nexstar GPS Schmidt-Cassegrain Telescope. Like most SCTs, this telescope comes complete with an integral mount and stand. The finderscope on this telescope has been replaced with a Telrad.

**Below.** The internal optics and tube of an SCT are sealed from the environment by the front correcting plate.

### Other hybrids

There are several hybrid designs. The most common after the SCT is the Maksutov (sometimes referred to as the Maksutov-Cassegrain or just Mak), designed by the Russian optician Dmitri Maksutov (1896–1964). The SCTs and Maks look similar but the Maks have an actual lens in front, call a meniscus, that is thick and highly concave. Some people prefer this design because it performs optically a little better than SCTs. Maks are readily available in diameters of 3 to 4 inches, with larger diameters now becoming more available.

### Best value, cost

Why are SCTs the telescopes of choice amongst amateurs? Simply because they offer the most features for your money. Manufacturers generally sell SCTs as turnkey systems, meaning that they include everything — the telescope on a computerized mount, the tripod, a finder and an eyepiece (you will have to purchase more eyepieces). And SCTs breakdown and store well. An 8-inch can easily be packed and hidden in a closet. The 8-inch is the most popular size and sells for about $2,400. I highly recommend this telescope if you can afford it.

### Maintenance

For the most part, maintenance on SCTs and Maksutovs is minimal. Occasionally, the outside front element should be cleaned — at most yearly, but depending on use. The optics of the Maksutov are like refractors and are permanently aligned, whereas those of the SCTs may need occasional collimation depending on use and jarring by transportation. Collimating SCTs requires some skill and not all telescope stores can provide this service. Sometimes there are members of local astronomy clubs who can perform this adjustment.

# Using Your Telescope

## Basic Practices for Simple-Mounted Telescopes

Telescopes are not difficult to use, but like any "new" piece of equipment or tool, they require familiarity and practice for effortless use. So I highly recommend that you become acquainted with your telescope during the day to avoid groping aimlessly and becoming frustrated with it at night. Even the simplest telescope requires some orientation to ensure an evening of smooth sailing.

Whenever you observe, set up your telescope and accessories while it is still light. This will not only make it easier to see what you are doing, but also allow time for the optics to reach the outside temperature, which helps to provide better image quality. Obviously, you want to position your telescope away from bright lights and where a generous portion of the sky is visible. When I observe at home, I also like easy access to the house for additional accessories and star charts.

All professional and amateur telescopes have idiosyncrasies. Smooth operation depends on discovering these surprises and learning to deal with them. Clyde Tombaugh, the discoverer of Pluto, had to work around a glitch he found in the mount holding the telescope he used to find the ninth planet. Today, telescopes are better than ever, but be prepared for minor idiosyncrasies.

### General Suggestions for More Enjoyable Observing

★ Use an adjustable chair to comfortably reach the eyepiece when using a refractor or reflector telescope.

★ Use a red-light flashlight to read charts and take notes.

★ Use a small table for placing notes and other items.

★ Beforehand, check nuts and bolts on tripod, mount and telescope for proper tightness, etc.

★ Have extra batteries available for the telescope or other accessories that require them.

★ Keep tools handy for any adjustments.

★ Keep eyepieces readily available but housed or secured so that they cannot roll or fall if bumped.

★ Keep star charts handy and possibly housed in plastic pouches/bags to keep dew off.

★ You may need a dew removing system (by Kendrick) to keep dew off the optics of your refractors and SCTs.

★ Wear proper clothing and don't forget about bug spray, drinks, etc.

## Eyepieces and focusing

Eyepieces are inserted into the focuser for refractors and reflectors. The focusing knob is turned until stars appear pinpoint. Generally the telescope must be refocused for a different observer or if the eyepiece is changed. Usually, you start with lower magnifications (higher mm numbers on eyepieces, see page 54) to find objects, and switch to higher magnifications when the object is centered in the eyepiece.

## Sitting comfort

It is much more comfortable to observe from a sitting position, but the chair must be adjustable to accommodate the different heights reached by the eyepiece. I use a pneumatic-type "drummer's" stool; however, adjustable seats made specifically for observing are available.

## Moving and aiming the telescope

Non-motorized telescopes are moved by hand. In the case of Newtonian reflectors, you grab the front end of the tube and move it in the required direction.

**Top.** Being comfortable while observing is important for your enjoyment. Adjustable chairs are great for positioning your eye wherever the eyepiece lands. This popular observer's chair by StarBound has a good height range.

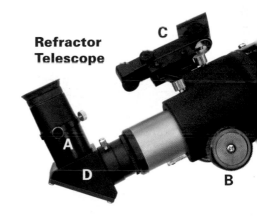

**Refractor Telescope**

**Middle and Bottom.** Eyepieces are inserted in the focuser at **A** and focusing is accomplished by turning the knobs, **B**. The focuser is at the rear for refractors (middle) and front for Newtonian reflectors (bottom). Both of these scopes have reflex-sight finders, **C**. The refractor has a right-angle diagonal, **D**, that allows for more comfortable viewing (not necessary for Newtonian reflectors).

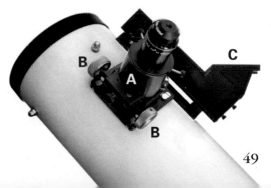

**Reflector Telescope**

# Using Your Telescope

For refractors, grab the area around the focusing knobs to move the scope. As with any scope, it is a good idea to be familiar with your mount because its tension, that is, its stiffness or ease of movement, is sometimes controlled by hand-tightened nuts or bolts.

If your telescope did not come equipped with a finderscope or reflex-sight finder, then you will need to purchase one before you can effectively use your scope (see page 53). After you have moved your scope by hand, use the finder to pinpoint the spot you wish to view, most likely after consulting a star chart.

Non-motorized telescopes have to be nudged continually to keep an object in the eyepiece. The higher the magnification, the more nudging you have to do.

### Finding the planets and other fainter objects

There is no doubt about it, but after you have viewed the Moon, the most challenging aspect of observational astronomy will be trying to find/identify the planets and other fainter objects. When I first started, I was on my own, so I took it slow and easy. I learned to identify some of the major constellations from charts in *Sky & Telescope* magazine and then I pointed my telescope, using the finderscope, to easy, visible objects like the Great Nebula in Orion and the Pleiades. I then ventured out to find objects that weren't conspicuous. For these, I carefully studied star charts, which are the same as road maps, and using these, pointed my telescope to the approximate vicinity of the object I wanted to view. I then moved my telescope slowly around this area to spot the object. Sometimes I was successful, other times

I wasn't. However, the more I tried, the better I got. I enjoyed those evenings of discovery because they gave me a sense of triumph in conquering the Universe firsthand. Like riding a bike, once learned, the skills of knowing and using the sky for your purposes will become automatic.

### Take down

If you are observing at home, you might want to leave the telescope's tripod and mount set up for successive nightly observing, but I recommend bringing the telescope inside. Cover your mount with a waterproof tarp to avoid dew and rain, but bring it inside if you will not use it within a few days. Always put the lens or dust covers on your telescope after each use, and never leave your telescope outside unprotected.

## German Equatorial Mounted Telescopes

The German equatorial mount came into use around 1820 and along with its variations, became the mainstay at every professional observatory until the 1970s, due to the advent of computer technology. The German equatorial mount is still used extensively today but is reserved for "smaller" professional and amateur telescopes. You can find it on telescopes selling for as little as a few hundred dollars.

Telescope on one end of the Declination axis, weights on the other

**Anatomy of the German Equatorial Mount.** These mounts may look intimidating (at least they did initially to me) but their operation is straightforward. If you have a telescope with a German equatorial mount, familiarize yourself with its operation during the day and preferably indoors. All German equatorial mounts are similar to each other, no matter the cost.

There are two axes, the Polar, **P** and Declination, **D**. These two axes are perpendicular to one another, allowing the telescope to turn at both **C**s and point anywhere in the sky. The biggest clue that a mount is a German equatorial is that it has weights, **W** at one end of the declination axis (the telescope is at the other end).

The Polar Axis is adjusted so it points to a celestial pole. In the Northern Hemisphere, this would be the North Celestial Pole, **P**, which is close to the North Star or *Polaris*. This is a two-step process. First, pick the whole mount up and point it due north (due south in the southern hemisphere). Second, adjust for altitude, unloosen the tightening bolt **E**, and turn the altitude adjuster **F** until your latitude is indicated at **G**. Retighten **E**.

Many German equatorial mounts have setting circles (**Dec** and **RA**). These are graduated scales used to find objects by their celestial coordinates. The **Dec**lination of an object is analogous to latitude, while its **R**ight **A**scension is analogous to longitude.

The telescope is grossly moved by grabbing its tube and pushing or pulling on it. Once an object is in the eyepiece, the slow motion controls, **SR** and **SD**, are used to smoothly move the telescope in order to keep an object in view. The knobs at the end of these cables can be seen in the pictures at the bottom of the next page. On more expensive mounts, there are motors, instead of knobs to perform these tasks.

Once an object is in view, only the slow motion control **SR** has to be turned to keep the object in the eyepiece. This "single movement" is the advantage of a manual equatorial mount over alt-az mounts.

This mount was and is important for astrophotography. Amateurs need some form of an equatorial mount to take long exposures of celestial objects (see more on page 112).

Professional observatories have discontinued using these mounts on the largest telescopes because of size and cost considerations. Today, the largest telescopes are mounted on computerized alt-azimuth mounts, like those used on SCTs.

### Equatorial vs. other mounts

An obvious difference between the German equatorial mount and others is that it uses weights to balance the telescope around one of its axes. All mounts have two axes, allowing the telescope to point in any direction. One of the axes on an equatorial mount, called the Polar Axis, points to a celestial pole — the North Celestial Pole in the Northern Hemisphere, which is close to the star *Polaris*. A slow-moving motor, matching the rotation of the Earth is often attached to this axis, allowing the telescope to follow celestial objects as they move across the sky. Only one motor is required for equatorial mounts to follow objects, whereas two motors are required for the normal setup of SCTs (one on each axis).

**German Equatorial Mount Movements.** **A** through **D** show various positions of a telescope on a German equatorial mount to provide a feel for this mount's movements. View these pictures as if you were positioned south of the mount looking north. The back of the Polar Axis is visible and is angled upward, pointing toward a celestial pole (near *Polaris* in the northern hemisphere).

**A** and **B** show movement of the telescope around the Polar Axis as if following a star from east to west. This is the only movement needed to keep an object in the eyepiece. **C** and **D** show movement around the Declination Axis for positioning north and south.

In all these pictures, the eyepiece is awkwardly positioned for observing. In each case, the right-angle diagonal can be swiveled to a more comfortable viewing position by loosening and then retightening its lock screw.

You move this telescope about by grabbing the area around the focuser (not the eyepiece or diagonal) and then pull or push it around its axes. These mounts have some built-in tension that keeps them in place once you let go.

A slow-moving motor can be attached to the Polar Axis to allow this mount to automatically follow stars. The mechanical tolerances on this mount are adequate for visual observation, but are not sufficient for astrophotography.

## GO TO Schmidt-Cassegrains

Over the past 35 years, telescope technology has dramatically unfolded. When I began assembling my own telescopes at the end of the 1960s, no one had ever dreamed of the advances to take place. We've experienced a golden age of scientific and technological growth. Fortunately, telescope manufacturers took advantage of this quickly growing body of knowledge to bring us the best telescopes ever.

Celestron's 8-inch GPS GO TO telescope is the most advanced SCT available. I also consider it the best value for your money.

### The motorized GO TO* computer telescopes

What exactly is a GO TO* computerized telescope? It is not the telescope that is computerized, but the motorized mount; however, it is simpler to refer to the GO TO mount and telescope as one unit. A motorized GO TO computer telescope will automatically move to and follow any celestial object chosen through a hand controller.

Once a GO TO telescope is aligned to two bright stars, a process which I will discuss below, it is set to go. Okay, what are the hitches? There are only two minor ones. The first is that after you have physically set up the telescope, you have to spend 3 to 5 minutes (probably longer the first few times) aligning the telescope to two bright stars. To help you with this process, the

*GO TO is often written GOTO, but I have separated the words for clarity.

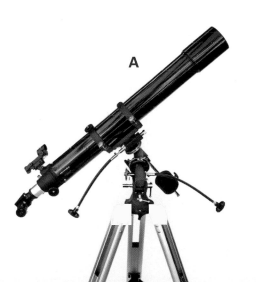

**A**

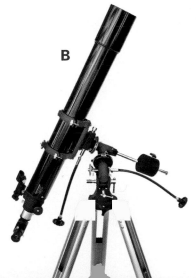

**B**

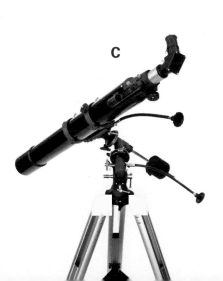

**C**

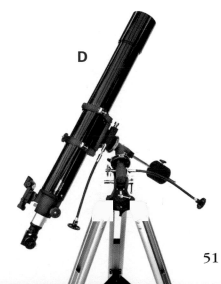

**D**

# Using Your Telescope

hand controller walks you through the steps. The second is that you must understand a little about how celestial objects are cataloged in order to enter them in the hand controller. But you can get around this by letting the telescope take you on a tour of the best objects in your sky. Most GO TO telescopes have a tour option.

I have manual, partial and fully computerized GO TO mounts, but I have to admit that I enjoy the GO TO mounts the most. They allow me to spend my time looking at objects instead of spending most of it on the tedious task of finding and identifying them.

### Hand controllers

The hand controller is your command center. They are not difficult to use, but like those for TVs, VCRs or DVD players, require some familiarity. I would say that using a GO TO hand controller is easier than programming a VCR. I strongly recommend that you practice using and exploring the options on your GO TO system during the day, in the comfort of your home, before venturing out at night.

### GPS GO TO telescope setup

Celestron International was the first company to produce a GO TO telescope incorporating GPS (Global Positioning System) technology. It only takes two steps and two stars to align the telescope so that it can automatically find and track objects. Here they are:

**1** Set your tripod and telescope in a convenient location for observing. Ideally, place it where you have the greatest expanse of visible sky. Adjust the legs of the tripod so that the base of the telescope is approximately level. This will take 10 to 15 minutes and is the longest part of the process.

**2** Turn the power to the telescope ON and press ALIGN on the keypad. The GPS system, using location satellites orbiting the Earth, determines the date, time and location of the telescope. It then uses this information to automatically move and point in the direction of the first bright star that is needed for a 2-star alignment. Center the star in the eyepiece using the directional buttons on the hand controller. Press ALIGN and the telescope moves to the second bright star. Center this star in the eyepiece and press ALIGN.

The focuser, **A** on a SCT is to the side of the eyepiece holder, **B**. Amateurs like to upgrade their instruments. This focuser is a two-speed micro-focuser (gold end) and the eyepiece diagonal is inserted into a VirtualView, **C**, which allows the diagonal to be rotated for comfortable viewing, without hassling with a tightening screw. Both upgrade accessories are by Starizona.

This hand controller conveniently stores in the arm of this mount, but comes out for easier use. The numerical buttons provide access to catalogs of celestial objects

This base of this SCT has several plugs for interfacing with a computer and to provide advanced control for astrophotography. When you get started, you don't have to worry about these but they are there if you need them. This is one of the reasons why I say that SCTs are the most versatile telescopes available.

The telescope is ready to use and can now find more than 10,000 objects in its database, accessed through the hand controller.

### GO TO objects

Almost every GO TO telescope offers a plethora of objects which it can find by commands from the hand controller. For the SCT's pictured, the "1" button has an M for the Messier objects, a catalog of 110 of the brightest objects visible from the northern hemisphere. The CALD (Caldwell) catalog on the "2" button offers another 109 objects and the NGC (New General Catalogue) on button "4" accesses nearly 8,000 objects. If you are new to astronomy, these catalogs may seem a bit overwhelming, so let the computer take you on a TOUR, button "0," of the brightest objects in your sky — no knowledge of catalogs required. Star charts and catalogs of objects are available at telescope stores. See more about these catalogs on page 105.

### SCT Roundup

Here are a few other SCT considerations:

**Susceptibility to dew.** The front corrector plate is susceptible to condensation from dew during times of high humidity. Dew shields, like those on refractors, are available to curtail dew formation. There are also electric warmers to eliminate condensation.

**Reducer/corrector.** The focal ratio (page 56) of most SCTs is around f/10, which yields high magnifications and narrow fields of view. A reducer/corrector, which is a special type of lens placed inline with the eyepiece holder, lowers the f-ratio to f/6.3, providing lower magnifications and greater fields of view. This accessory also makes the stars more pinpoint.

**Astrophotography.** A tripod wedge is needed if you wish to use your SCT for astrophotography. This allows tilting of the telescope and mount so that it can be pointed to one of the celestial poles (see page 113). In essence, this converts this mount into an equatorial (similar to the German equatorial mount described on page 50), allowing it to rotate with the stars. If you try to take long time-exposure photographs without a wedge, your photos will show what is called "field rotation," that is, the stars will appear elongated, especially around the edges of the photo.

# Finders

## Traditional finderscopes

Have you ever tried to point a telescope at a star or planet? It can be difficult to do this even if you use an eyepiece providing low magnification. So, telescopes have traditionally been outfitted with small, low powered (5x to 10x) "finderscopes" that sport a large field of view (page 54), making them easier to aim. Often, finderscopes have cross reticles for centering, like those used on rifle scopes.

A finder-type device is so important that almost every telescope sold comes with one. Otherwise, it is the *first* accessory that is purchased.

## The 21st century reflex sight

Today, most amateurs use what are called reflex sights to aim their telescopes, instead of traditional finderscopes. The major drawbacks of finderscopes are that they provide "unnatural" magnified and upside-down images of the sky. This combination makes it confusing to identify the area of the sky you are pointing to, especially in areas where there are no bright reference stars.

Reflex sights "project" a red dot or concentric circles "onto" the night sky for guiding the telescope (they actually just reflect a pattern off a piece of glass). There is no magnification, and you look directly at the sky, usually through a piece of plain glass. These are wonderful because they allow quick and natural pointing of the telescope to a specific spot in the night sky without having to deal with the modified imagery from finderscopes. Reflex sights come in several designs and sizes, but the most popular is the Telrad, which projects a series of concentric circles. Although this instrument lacks "looks," it performs well.

## Adjusting finders

In order for a finder to work, it and the telescope must be aligned to point in the same direction. Finders have several adjusting screws or knobs. Telrads have three screwheads at the back. The finderscope pictured below uses just three screws but some have six (a set of 3 in the front and 3 in back). Finderscopes can be aligned during the day, but it is easiest to align reflex sights immediately before dark because the red dots or concentric circles that they project can be difficult to see in bright daylight. To align either, point the telescope to something far away like a mountaintop or distant pole, and use the adjusting screws to center the same view in the finder. Finders keep their alignment fairly well. This alignment should provide good pointing accuracy for lower telescope magnifications, but not for the highest magnifications. Most finderscopes can also be focused by turning the eyepiece until the stars appear at their sharpest.

## Finders for binoculars

It is easy to point binoculars during the daytime, but it is a little harder to point to the stars at night. Although binoculars are like a finderscope, where they are pointed is not always obvious, especially in areas where there are no bright reference stars. Many amateurs attach one of the smaller reflex sights to their binoculars (see photo on page 44) to help with pointing. Most reflex sights can be detached from their small permanent base, so storing the binoculars afterwards is not a problem.

## Finders, and observing the Sun

**WARNING**: When observing the Sun with your telescope, cover up or better yet, remove your finderscope or reflex sight. Not doing so can cause serious personal injury, including accidental eye damage and burns from the finderscope, or damage to your reflex sight. The reflex sight is like a reverse optical system, with its focus point on an internal reticle that can be heated and burned if pointed towards the Sun.

**Left.** The Teldrad reflex-sight finder. To use, place your eye a foot or so behind the unit and look through the slanted glass to the sky. These units detach from a permanently mounted base.
**Above.** A bird's-eye view, looking through a Telrad. The series of concentric circles are helpful because they correspond to arc-degrees used on star charts. The brightness of the red circles can be adjusted.

**Right.** A traditional finderscope, that is, a small, low-powered telescope. Note the three adjusting screws used for aligning this little scope so that it points to the same view as the telescope.

# Eyepieces

Eyepieces control the magnification of the telescope. One eyepiece usually provides just one magnification and since most telescopes generally come with just one eyepiece, you must purchase more to achieve a range of magnifications.

Eyepieces fit into the focuser of telescopes, located at the back end of refractors and SCTs* (Schmidt-Cassegrain Telescopes) and the front end of Newtonian reflectors.

**Don't underestimate the value of quality eyepieces. The telescope is an optical *system* consisting of the objective lens or primary mirror *and* the eyepiece. Low quality eyepieces render poor quality images despite the quality of your primary optics.**

## Eyepiece Designs

Plössl

Orthoscopic

"Typical" Specialty

### Standard quality eyepieces

The Plössl eyepiece, which is the name of a specific lens design, is the standard quality eyepiece. Although there are many eyepiece lens designs, Plössls are the most popular because they represent a balance between price, features and quality. The cost of an individual Plössl eyepiece ranges from $50 to $130. Another lens design, called the Orthoscopic, was the eyepiece of choice for years. They are not widely available today but provide sharper imagery than Plössls. Their only drawback is having a smaller field of view and shorter eye relief (see below). Some advanced amateurs prefer Orthoscopics over *all* other eyepieces.

### Magnification & eyepiece focal length

Magnification of the telescope is governed by the focal length of the eyepiece. And, other than its optical design, an eyepiece is chiefly identified by its focal length, which is always expressed in millimeters (mm) and imprinted on the exterior of the eyepiece. Focal lengths range from about 2.5mm to 55mm (0.16 inches to 2.16 inches). Shorter focal length

eyepieces, that is, those with smaller numbers, provide higher magnifications. Often, beginners have "high magnification fever." Outside of viewing the planets, the average magnification used is about 100x. For beginners, I recommend staying in the eyepiece range of 6 to 40 millimeters. How do you compute the magnification of your telescope system? See Computing Telescope Magnification on page 56. Also read The Myth of Telescope Magnification on page 58.

### Eyepiece characteristics

**Eye relief.** Eye relief determines your viewing comfort more than any other characteristic. In simple terms, eye relief dictates how close you must place your eye to the eyepiece to fully see the image. Specified in millimeters, eye reliefs range from about 5mm to 40mm, where 10mm or more is comfortable for non-eyeglass wearers and 20mm or more is comfortable for eyeglass wearers. Unfortunately, eye relief is not marked on eyepieces and often, this specification is not even provided. Generally, shorter focal length eyepieces have shorter eye reliefs. I say generally, because this has changed with some modern lens designs. A 6mm eyepiece that I bought in 1970 has an eye relief of 1.5mm, and I literally have to shove my eye against it to see anything. Modern 6mm focal length specialty eyepieces can have 20mm of eye relief (see Specialty Eyepieces below). If possible, try out eyepieces for viewing comfort before you buy.

**Field of view.** One of the biggest differences (but not the only one) between Plössls and more expensive specialty eyepieces is the field of view. Field of view determines how much of the sky you see at one time through the eyepiece. It is analogous to the difference between looking through a small porthole and a large window. Eyepiece fields of view are specified in angular degrees and range from about 42° for Orthoscopics to 53° for Plössls, and on to 82° for

**Top center.** A barlow lens is a popular eyepiece accessory because it can be used to double the magnification of any eyepiece. Eyepieces slide into the top and are secured by a thumbscrew that cannot be seen in this picture. The barlow (with eyepiece) is inserted into the focuser. See more on page 55.

**Right.** Plössl eyepieces are a present-day standard. They provide good performance at a reasonable price. The large 55mm has a 2-inch diameter barrel and will only fit focusers that accept 2-inch eyepieces.

*SCTs do not technically have eyepiece focusers, they have eyepiece holders; however, it is easier to refer to the holder as a focuser.

specialty eyepieces. These numbers indicate the angular view of the lens design and not the angular degrees of the sky seen through the telescope. When looking through eyepieces that have the widest fields of view (82°), you actually have to look around to see where the image ends. These show an *area* three times greater than Plössls.

**Barrel diameter.** The *standard* eyepiece barrel diameter is 1.25 inches. Some inexpensive telescopes use eyepieces that have barrel diameters of 0.965 inches (about an inch), but very few eyepieces are available in this smaller barrel size. Additionally, the optics of the smaller barrel eyepieces are often poor. Ninety percent of all eyepieces have the standard 1.25-inch barrel. There is a larger 2-inch barrel size that is necessary for some eyepiece lens designs. Many telescopes have focusers that accept 2-inch eyepieces (2-inch focusers come with an adapter for 1.25-inch eyepieces). As a general rule, don't buy a telescope whose focuser and eyepieces are 0.965 inches because these telescopes and their included eyepieces are usually of poor optical quality.

**Rubber eye guards.** I like the rubber eye guards on eyepieces because they provide for warmer and softer viewing, protect eyeglasses, as well as help in blocking stray light, but not every eyepiece incorporates them into their design. Rubber eye guards can be purchased for eyepieces that don't have them. Avoid the winged eye guards (one side is higher than the other to cup the side of the head) because you can easily poke your eye with the high side. I use my eyepieces "as is" and don't add eye guards if they don't have them.

**Eyepiece sets.** Manufacturers usually design a set of eyepieces that share similar optical and physical characteristics. The Vixen Lanthanums series totals about 11 eyepieces, while there are about 9 Tele Vue Radians. Many amateurs like myself don't buy complete sets, but instead pick and choose among them.

**Above.** A specialty zoom eyepiece that can be varied in focal length from 3 to 6mm. The rubber eye guard incorporated into many eyepieces can often be folded back (left) to better accommodate eyeglass wearers. **Below.** Filters screw into the bottom of eyepieces. Colored filters are generally used to *subtly* enhance planetary detail. The *most* important filter is the neutral density (or two polarizing filters) which is used when observing the Moon to reduce its brightness.

## Modern, specialty eyepieces

In recent years, there has been a proliferation of modern-designed eyepieces that address "issues" of standard eyepieces. Three of these issues are: 1) short eye relief for short focal length eyepieces, 2) in general, narrow fields of view, and 3) stars not pinpointed across the entire field of view.

Several manufacturers have designed a new generation of eyepieces that address these issues. The leader and innovator has been Tele Vue, owned by Al Nagler. Tele Vue is synonymous with quality, and their specialty eyepieces provide you with breathtaking viewing experiences. They accomplish their feats by using six to eight lens elements (some made of exotic glass), compared to the four in Plössls. Eyepieces of this class perform extremely well but are pricey, since they *start* at around $150 each.

## Barlows:
## Double your fun & magnification

A barlow lens is used in conjunction with an eyepiece to double its magnification. A barlow looks like a long eyepiece that fits into the focuser. Regular eyepieces are then inserted into the barlow. A barlow is a convenient and relatively inexpensive way to expand your magnification selection by a factor of two. One barlow effectively doubles the number of achievable magnifications, or as it is sometimes said, "doubles the numbers of your eyepieces."

Modern-day quality barlows do not degrade the performance of eyepieces, though there was a time when this was not true. Prices for a quality 2x barlow start at around $80. Although there are barlows that can triple or quadruple the magnification of your eyepiece, I do not recommend them for beginners.

(Continued on next page)

**Left to right.** Orthoscopic eyepieces perform as well as specialty eyepieces, they just don't have a wide field of view or generous eye relief. Vixen's Lanthanum series (second from the left) and Tele Vue's Radian eyepieces are specialty eyepieces particularly suited to eyeglass wearers because they have long eye relief. The 23mm Axiom eyepiece is one of Celestron's specialty eyepieces. There are many eyepiece lens designs on the market. The König lens design has been around for years and is similar to the Plössl but features sharper imagery at the edge of its field. Note: Barrels on two of the eyepieces are undercut (indented band) to positively capture a tightening thumbscrew that is on most focusers. This prevents them from falling out when you are repositioning the telescope.

# Eyepieces

## Viewing with and without eyeglasses

If possible, observe without your eyeglasses because it will make your observing easier and more comfortable. If you are unsure as to whether or not you can, give it a try! I observe without my glasses but have to put them back on to write notes or look at star charts. If you must use glasses, remember that some eyepieces have a rubber guard that can be folded back to get closer to the lens for better viewing. Also, some eyepieces, like the Vixen Lanthanum series or Tele Vue Radians, have long eye reliefs, which make them easier for eyeglass wearers to use.

## Focusing and parfocal

Each time you place a different eyepiece into the focuser, you must refocus. Also, every observer will need to refocus for their eyes. The amount of refocusing between observers can be considerable (if you wear glasses, compare the focus with and without your glasses). The barrels on some sets of eyepieces are machined to be "parfocal," that is, once you focus with one of the eyepieces of the parfocal set, all the others eyepieces will be very close to focus when inserted into the focuser.

## Are you confused?

Does all this have your head spinning? Take some time to let it digest. If possible, visit a telescope store and try out various eyepieces to experience all the differences. Better yet, if you are an astronomy club member, have other members walk you through the differences.

## Eyepiece Recommendations

**Optical design:** Plössl is the current standard design. Orthoscopics provide the highest quality imagery for the least amount of money. Specialty designs, like Tele Vue Naglers, are superb but expensive.

**If your telescope did not come with an eyepiece:** A good starter set for many telescopes would be 20mm and 30mm eyepieces and a barlow lens.

**If your telescope came with one eyepiece:** Consider buying a quality barlow lens first (around $80). Your second eyepiece should then have a focal length of either 1.5 or 0.75 times that of your other eyepiece in order to avoid duplicating magnifications when using the barlow.

**Try before you buy:** Always try out eyepieces before you buy, on a telescope similar to yours. If you must purchase by mail order, check the return policy.

**Avoid high magnification:** Stick with eyepieces that are comfortable to use, so stay in the range of 6mm to 40mm.

## Computing Telescope Magnification

Focal Length of TELESCOPE ÷ Focal Length of EYEPIECE = Magnification

*NOTE: For any calculation, ALL focal lengths must be expressed in the same units of length — usually millimeters.*

### EXAMPLE 1

You know that the focal length of your 8-inch SCT is 2032mm because it is in the owner's manual. What are the magnifications achieved with 6mm, 8mm, 15mm and 20mm eyepieces?

2032mm ÷ 6mm = 339x       2032mm ÷ 15mm = 135x
2032mm ÷ 8mm = 254x       2032mm ÷ 20mm = 102x

### EXAMPLE 2

What magnification will you achieve using a 20mm eyepiece with a 4-inch f/6 telescope?

1. Compute focal length of the telescope.
   4-inch x 6 (f/6) = 24-inch focal length
2. Change 24-inch focal length into millimeters.
   24 x 25.4 (conversion factor) = 610mm focal length
3. Compute Magnification.
   610mm ÷ 20mm = 31x

## f/numbers or Focal Ratios

What are all those f/numbers about? The f/numbers (e.g. f/4, f/5.4, f/8) associated with telescopes indicate the ratio of the telescope focal length to the aperture. In other words, the focal length of a telescope, divided by the diameter of the objective lens or primary mirror, gives you the f/number. For example, if your telescope has a focal length of 21.5 inches (540mm) and an objective lens diameter of 4 inches (100mm), then your f/number is f/5.4 (21.5 inches ÷ 4 inches = 5.4 *or* 540mm ÷ 100mm = 5.4). Telescopes with f/numbers of 5 or lower are considered rich-field telescopes (RFT) because they provide lower magnifications and wider fields of view (that is, you can see more of the sky in an eyepiece). Most often, telescope f/numbers range from f/4 to f/11. The f/number is also referred to as the focal ratio.

# Collimation of Newtonian Reflectors

## Aligning the mirrors of Newtonian reflectors for good imagery

Newtonian telescopes provide excellent imagery; however, the optics must be properly aligned or "collimated," to achieve this result. Collimating Newtonians is the bane of these instruments and to make matters worse, the process may seem difficult and confusing at first; but it is easily accomplished after you have performed it a few times.

Generally, the optics in Newtonian reflectors stay aligned, but they can get out of alignment with transport or the occasional bump received during setup and take down. Normally, collimation is accomplished by making only minor adjustments. However, if you purchased a telescope requiring assembly, or if you are reinstalling your mirrors after cleaning, you will have to perform the full basic collimation as described with the pictures numbered 1 through 5.

Collimation is achieved by turning adjusting screws/nuts on the secondary mirror holder and the primary mirror cell. The secondary mirror beneath the eyepiece focuser is adjusted first, followed by the primary mirror.

## Precision collimation

Here on this page is the *basic* collimation process that has been the standard practice for years. However, you can purchase other "tools" for fine-tuning collimation, ranging from eyepiece-type devices to lasers. For many Newtonian reflectors, the basic collimation will provide good imagery, but telescopes with faster focal ratios, like those around f/5 or lower (see previous page), can benefit from fine-tuning. Precision collimation is beyond the scope of this book, but it involves marking the center of the primary mirror with a dot or circle (using a marker or piece of round tape) and using a special eyepiece-type device called a Cheshire eyepiece. This allows you to tweak a basic collimation into a precision collimation. Laser collimators that fit into eyepiece focusers are also available and make basic and precision collimation easy to perform, but quality units start at around $100.

**1**

**2**

View through eyepiece focuser

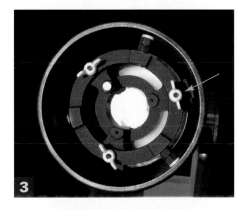

**3**

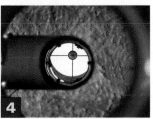

**4**

View through eyepiece focuser

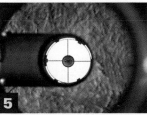

**5**

View through eyepiece focuser

## Basic collimation process

**Must Do First • Aligning the Secondary Mirror.**
The secondary mirror is the smaller mirror (usually oval) located beneath the eyepiece focuser. Start by extending the eyepiece focuser all the way out. Keep it in this position throughout the collimation process. Also, when you look through the eyepiece focusing tube, keep your eye centered. This helps provide for better alignment. You can purchase an eyepiece sighting tube, that is, an "eyepiece" which has a small centered hole instead of lenses, to keep your eye centered.

**Picture 1.** Examine the secondary mirror holder from the top of the tube to determine the tools required for adjustment — usually a small screwdriver, but sometimes a wrench. Adjust the secondary mirror holder by rotating it (YELLOW arrow), and/or tilting it up and down — usually accomplished by turning three screws (RED arrow pointing to one of the screws), so that you can see the whole primary mirror centered in the secondary mirror when you look through the eyepiece focuser, as in **Picture 2**. The PINK arrows indicates the outline of the primary mirror, which is what you want to see in the secondary mirror. For now, ignore the *reflection* of the primary mirror indicated by the ORANGE arrow.

Depending on the design of the secondary mirror holder, this alignment may require fiddling, especially with the final tightening. Be patient and loosen/tighten the three screws a little at a time. If it gets frustrating, set it aside and come back to it later. This process is not difficult, but may seem so if you have never done anything similar. Aligning the secondary mirror is usually the hardest part of the collimation process.

**Aligning the Primary Mirror.** At the back-end of the tube is the primary mirror cell, in **Picture 3**. There are usually three nuts or screw heads that can be turned for adjusting. On some telescopes, the adjusting nuts or screw heads stick out from the back, and on others, the whole assembly may be set a few inches inside the tube. The mirror, pictured, is adjusted by turning the three white wingnuts (BLUE arrow). Experiment with tightening and loosening one adjusting nut/screw at a time to get a feel for what happens to the view through the eyepiece focuser. The goal here is to adjust the primary mirror so that the secondary mirror appears centered in the *reflection* of the primary mirror when you look through the eyepiece focuser. In other words, make your adjustments so that all the images appear centered. You want to go from **Picture 2** to **Picture 5**. This is a good time to enlist the help of another person. Adjusting the primary is tedious if done alone because you have to go back and forth between the eyepiece focuser and primary mirror. With an assistant, you can direct them to adjust the mirror as you watch through the focuser. *Once a telescope has been collimated, future adjustments should be infrequent and minor. Full collimation, as described above, is usually only necessary after the mirrors have been removed and replaced for cleaning.*

# Buyer Beware

## Low cost, poor quality telescopes

Once, I received a call from a complaining dad who had purchased a telescope from a major nature retailer. "The telescope would have to be good if they put their name on it," he exclaimed. Well, he was disappointed with every aspect of it. His thoughts of enjoying time looking at the stars with his son vanished. He returned the scope and was so bitter that he did not purchase another one.

A poorly performing telescope is the quickest way to dampen, if not extinguish, initial enthusiasm towards observational astronomy. The only way to avoid this is to become an informed consumer.

Optically, today's poorest performing telescopes are better than anything Galileo used back in the early 1600s. However, this is not an argument to say that poor quality telescopes are acceptable. Adults and children base optical quality on their views through binoculars and cameras. Nowadays, the quality of these instruments is quite high. Any telescope that doesn't meet these standards will certainly cause concern and disappointment. With consumers inundated with quality optics, it would behoove telescope manufacturers to offer higher optical quality. Such telescopes would cost more, but customer satisfaction would be much higher.

Price is what drives the sale of poor optical quality telescopes. It is based on the misconceived notion that $65 to $150 should buy a quality telescope, especially if it is for a child.

When the performance of a telescope is less than that of an average pair of binoculars, the telescope stands a good chance of not being used. Why not spend a little more and make the telescope a family purchase? This can prevent your telescope from becoming what is commonly known as a closet, basement or garage scope.

## The myth of telescope magnification

Magnification is the least important factor in choosing a telescope! But, unfortunately, the selling and marketing of many telescopes (especially those sold in department, chain or toy stores) has often been based on magnification.

Technically, it is possible to get any magnification out of any optical system, but there are practical limits.

Don't buy a telescope that looks like this! This imported telescope is made overseas but all the major telescope manufacturers and retailers sell it with their name printed on it. The attraction of this "entry level" telescope is price. Although it provides marginal views of the Moon and planets, it is not suitable for astronomy. Far worse than the optics is its mount, which does not work as expected and provides jerky movement, making it very difficult and frustrating to follow celestial objects as they move through the sky. A telescope like this will disappoint whoever uses it. There are other telescopes that I would not recommend, but this telescope is by far the most ubiquitous. For the record, there are many quality imported telescopes.

## Magnification rule of thumb

Useful magnification for most observing, independent of objective lens or primary mirror size, is from 30x to 250x. The average magnification used is about 100x. Higher magnifications can be useful for the planets and Moon, but only on the best of nights.

The "rule of thumb" is that a quality telescope can support about 50x per aperture inch. For example, an 8-inch diameter telescope can comfortable achieve 400x (50 x 8). Larger diameter telescopes *can* support higher magnifications better than smaller diameter telescopes.

## Will it ever end?

The practice of selling high magnification does not seem to go away, despite the repeated efforts of professional and amateur astronomers to stamp out this idea. Within the last months of finishing this book, the major manufacturer of telescopes in the US had a ridiculous magnification claim printed on the outside of one of their telecope boxes. They should know better!

### Informed Consumer Suggestions

★ Beware of purchasing a telescope from a department store, no matter what the price.

★ Beware of the lowest priced telescopes from the major manufacturers and larger retailers. Many of these are imported products of poor quality priced to appeal to your pocketbook.

★ If possible, stop at a local telescope store for advice and purchasing. Prices on telescopes vary little from store to store. Local service and support are more valuable than saving a few dollars.

★ Buy one of the popular monthly astronomy magazines and look at ads to get a feel for pricing, selection and dealers if there are no telescope stores in your area.

★ Instead of buying a telescope for a single family member, spend a little more on a quality telescope as a gift for the whole family. These start at around $350 dollars.

★ Visit internet sites that review telescopes (listed in the Appendix).

# Telescope Summary/Comparison

**Ratings**
**1** Low to **5** High
**Y** Yes
**N** No
**S** Some(times)

## Refractors

| | | Adult Starter Scope | Family with Children Scope | Child Scope | Used by Advanced Amateurs | Overall Ease of Use + Setup | Sky-Knowledge Required | Overall Versatility | Planets, Moon, Sun | Clusters, Nebulae, Galaxies | Convenient Terrestrial Viewing | Mount Included | Mount Motorized | Overall Craftsmanship | Overall Optical Quality | Astrophotography See Notes | Maintenance/Collimating | Price Range | $ per Aperture Inch | Overall Value |
|---|---|---|---|---|---|---|---|---|---|---|---|---|---|---|---|---|---|---|---|---|
| Basic Quality | 2" to 3" | N | Y | Y | N | 5 | Y | 1 | 1 | 1 | Y | Y | N | 1 | 1 | N | 1 | $300-$500 | 4 | 1 |
| Good Quality | 2" to 3" | Y | Y | N | Y | 5 | Y | 3 | 2 | 2 | Y | S | S | 3 | 3 | Y | 1 | $700-$1500 | 4 | 3 |
| | 4" to 6" | Y | N | N | Y | 3 | Y | 3 | 3 | 3 | Y | S | S | 3 | 3 | Y | 1 | $1500-$2000 | 4 | 3 |
| Best Quality (APOs) | 2" to 3" | Y | Y | N | Y | 5 | Y | 3 | 3 | 2 | Y | N | – | 5 | 5 | Y | 1 | $1000-$2200 | 5 | 3 |
| | 4" to 6" | Y | N | N | Y | 3 | Y | 4 | 4 | 3 | Y | N | – | 5 | 5 | Y | 1 | $2500-$9000 | 5 | 3 |

**Refractor Notes:** Refractors are almost maintenance free. The highest quality APOs provide the best imagery of all telescopes but are very expensive. Refractors rarely exceed 6" in diameter, so they are not the best for observing fainter objects like galaxies. They are excellent for astrophotography but must be mounted on motorized German equatorial mounts because the motorized mounts that come with them are often not suitable for extended astrophotography.

## Newtonian Reflectors

| | | Adult Starter Scope | Family with Children Scope | Child Scope | Used by Advanced Amateurs | Overall Ease of Use + Setup | Sky-Knowledge Required | Overall Versatility | Planets, Moon, Sun | Clusters, Nebulae, Galaxies | Convenient Terrestrial Viewing | Mount Included | Mount Motorized | Overall Craftsmanship | Overall Optical Quality | Astrophotography | Maintenance/Collimating | Price Range | $ per Aperture Inch | Overall Value |
|---|---|---|---|---|---|---|---|---|---|---|---|---|---|---|---|---|---|---|---|---|
| Dob or Equatorial | 4.5" | N | Y | Y | N | 5 | Y | 3 | 2 | 2 | N | Y | N | 3 | 3 | N | 5 | $200-$375 | 2 | 3 |
| Dobsonian | 6" | Y | Y | Y | Y | 5 | Y | 3 | 3 | 3 | N | Y | N | 3 | 4 | N | 5 | $350-$400 | 1 | 4 |
| | 8" | Y | Y | N | Y | 5 | Y | 3 | 4 | 4 | N | Y | N | 3 | 4 | N | 5 | $500-$600 | 1 | 4 |
| | 10" | Y | N | N | Y | 4 | Y | 3 | 5 | 5 | N | Y | N | 3 | 4 | N | 5 | $600-$700 | 1 | 4 |

**Reflector Notes:** Newtonian reflectors require the most maintenance. Amateur reflectors reach around 36 inches in diameter. Newtonians classified as Dobsonians come on simple mounts that are normally not motorized. A computer locating system can often be attached to these mounts to help find objects, but you must still move the scope by hand.

## Hybrids

| | | Adult Starter Scope | Family with Children Scope | Child Scope | Used by Advanced Amateurs | Overall Ease of Use + Setup | Sky-Knowledge Required | Overall Versatility | Planets, Moon, Sun | Clusters, Nebulae, Galaxies | Convenient Terrestrial Viewing | Mount Included | Mount Motorized | Overall Craftsmanship | Overall Optical Quality | Astrophotography | Maintenance/Collimating | Price Range | $ per Aperture Inch | Overall Value |
|---|---|---|---|---|---|---|---|---|---|---|---|---|---|---|---|---|---|---|---|---|
| SCTs (GO TO) | 5" | Y | Y | N | Y | 4 | S | 3 | 3 | 3 | Y | Y | Y | 4 | 4 | Y | 3 | $1000-$1500 | 3 | 3 |
| SCTs (GPS GO TO) | 8" | Y | Y | N | Y | 4 | N | 5 | 4 | 4 | Y | Y | Y | 4 | 4 | Y | 3 | $2000-$2500 | 3 | 5 |
| | 10" to 12" | N | N | N | Y | 3 | N | 5 | 5 | 5 | Y | Y | Y | 4 | 4 | Y | 3 | $3000-$4000 | 3 | 5 |
| Maksutovs-Cassegrains | 3" to 5" | Y | Y | N | Y | 4 | Y | 3 | 3 | 3 | Y | S | S | 4 | 3 | Y | 2 | $250-$1000 | 3 | 3 |

**Hybrid Notes:** I consider the 8" GO TO SCT to be the best valued telescope because you get the most features and versatility for your money. Also, the size and weight are reasonable. A "wedge" accessory (see page 113) is needed to take long time-exposure photos with SCTs. Larger Maksutovs are starting to become available, so keep an eye on the market if this type of scope interests you.

**General Notes:** Although telescopes are not difficult to operate, they all require familiarity. Not every scope comes with eyepieces, so be prepared to purchase a few. Most people should eventually own a barlow lens which doubles the magnification of any eyepiece. If your scope is equipped with a traditional finderscope, I strongly recommend replacing it with a reflex-sight finder, like a Telrad, as soon as possible.

# Using the Star Charts

This set of 10 star charts is complete and covers the entire celestial sphere, that is, all the stars and constellations of the northern and southern hemispheres. All 88 constellations are indicated. The charts are, however, orientated for those residing in the northern hemisphere and only need to be turned upside down if you travel south of the equator.

**Star clusters, nebulae, galaxies and catalogs**
Over 100 deep sky objects, that is, star clusters, nebulae and galaxies, are indicated and described. Many of these objects are easy to find and observe, while others will be downright challenging. These 100 objects should be plenty to keep you busy for a few seasons. *A lengthy discussion on finding and observing deep sky objects, as well as explanations of the "M" and "NGC" catalog numbers, begins on page 103.*

**Object sizes ★ Arc size or diameter**
The size of objects as they appear in the sky is noted in arc minutes. It will take some orientation to get a feel for these figures. Keep in mind that the Moon is about 30 arc minutes in diameter (30').

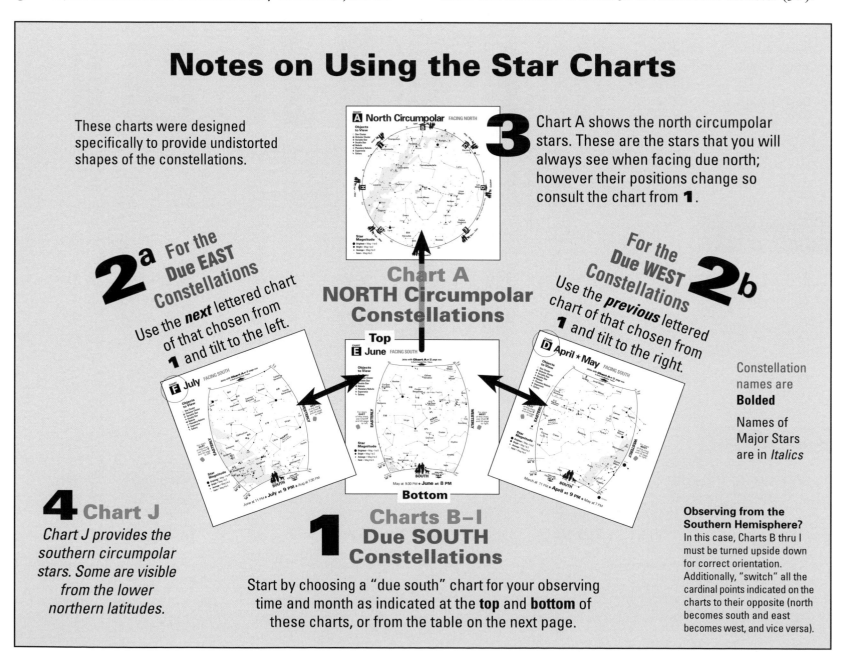

## Notes on Using the Star Charts

These charts were designed specifically to provide undistorted shapes of the constellations.

**3** Chart A shows the north circumpolar stars. These are the stars that you will always see when facing due north; however their positions change so consult the chart from **1**.

**Chart A**
**NORTH Circumpolar Constellations**

**2a For the Due EAST Constellations**
Use the *next* lettered chart of that chosen from **1** and tilt to the left.

**For the Due WEST Constellations 2b**
Use the *previous* lettered chart of that chosen from **1** and tilt to the right.

Constellation names are **Bolded**

Names of Major Stars are in *Italics*

**4 Chart J**
*Chart J provides the southern circumpolar stars. Some are visible from the lower northern latitudes.*

**1 Charts B–I Due SOUTH Constellations**
Start by choosing a "due south" chart for your observing time and month as indicated at the **top** and **bottom** of these charts, or from the table on the next page.

**Observing from the Southern Hemisphere?**
In this case, Charts B thru I must be turned upside down for correct orientation. Additionally, "switch" all the cardinal points indicated on the charts to their opposite (north becomes south and east becomes west, and vice versa).

## Double stars

There are about 60 double stars indicated on the charts. A double star is really two or more stars that are so "close" to each another that they appear as a single star, but with the proper magnification, they separate into two or more stars. Double stars are either optical doubles, that is, where two stars are simply in the same line of sight, or truly binary stars, where they revolve around one another. About half of all stars are true binary stars.

Observing double stars is a historic pastime for amateurs. They are interesting for different reasons. For some, it is the pure "challenge" of separating a pair of stars that are particularly close or contrasted in magnitudes. For others, it is the sight of two beautiful colored jewels side by side. Probably most of all, it is simply the magical joy of seeing what looks like a single star suddenly appear as two or more shining suns.

Most of the double stars indicated on charts A through J do not have descriptions, so each will be a surprise. All can be viewed easily, that is, separated into two or more stars with magnifications ranging from 50x to 200x. Most can be separated with a magnification of about 100x. About ten of them will separate into 3 or 4 stars.

## Heavenly coordinates

Outside of the constellation patterns, how are the positions of stars and objects indicated? In astronomy, a coordinate system of "right ascension" and "declination" is used that is analogous to longitude and latitude on Earth. Declination uses a similar nomenclature as latitude; however, right ascension uses the 24 hours of the day instead of the 180° east or west longitude.

It is not necessary to know this heavenly coordinate system in order to enjoy or find objects, but I briefly bring it up because I have included some coordinate markings on the charts. Along the right hand edges of charts B through I, the declination (Dec) is indicated. This ranges from +90° for the North Celestial Pole to 0° at the Celestial Equator, reversing to –90° for the South Celestial Pole. Right ascension is listed at the top of charts B through I. These numbers range from 0h to 23h and represent the hours of the day. The small "h" indicates the hour "angle." As you observe the sky, the hours of right ascension "march by" as the Earth rotates on its axis.

## Constellation lore

Ancient myths and legends were actual beliefs of early civilizations. These stories were the religions that helped make sense of nature and human behavior. Our western culture is most familiar with the mythology of the Greeks because therein lie the roots of modern western civilization. If you have a thirst for more lore, I recommend *The New Patterns in the Sky, Myths and Legends of the Stars,* by Julius D. W. Staal or any of Edith Hamilton's books. The "king" of Greek mythology, Robert Graves, wrote, *The Greek Myths,* which is an incredible work, but a more difficult read.

## Black stars on a white background

These charts have black stars printed on a white background. This is the preferred format for amateur and professional astronomers because it is easier to read, but more importantly, easier to use when exploring the sky and matching stars.

**Star Chart Instructions**

---

## Star Magnitude ★ Scale of Brightness

Star magnitude is a light intensity scale for comparing the relative brightness of the stars and other celestial objects. This scale ranges, at its brightest, from –27 for the Sun to over +30 for the faintest galaxies.

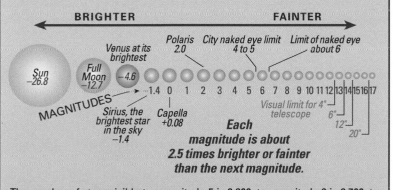

The number of stars visible to magnitude 5 is 2,800; to magnitude 6 is 8,700; to magnitude 7 is 27,000 and about one million to magnitude 11. The five brightest stars are Sirius (–1.44), Canopus (–0.62), Rigil Kent (–0.28), Arcturus (–0.05) and Vega (+0.03). The major planets at their brightest are Venus (–4.6), Mars (–2.8), Jupiter (–2.5), Mercury (–1.9) and Venus (–0.4).

---

## Extra-Hour Star Chart Guide

Consult this table to determine which star chart to use for hours other than those listed at the bottom of each chart. Refer to the instructions on these charts for the correct orientation of the A & J polar charts.

| | 6 pm | 8 pm | 10 pm | 12 Midnight | 2 am | 4 am | 6 am |
|---|---|---|---|---|---|---|---|
| **January** | Chart I | Chart B | Chart B | Chart C | Chart D | Chart E | Chart E |
| **February** | Chart B | Chart B | Chart C | Chart D | Chart E | Chart E | Chart F |
| **March** | Chart B | Chart C | Chart D | Chart E | Chart E | Chart F | Chart G |
| **April** | Chart C | Chart D | Chart E | Chart E | Chart F | Chart G | Chart G |
| **May** | Chart D | Chart E | Chart E | Chart F | Chart G | Chart G | Chart H |
| **June** | Chart E | Chart E | Chart F | Chart G | Chart G | Chart H | Chart I |
| **July** | Chart E | Chart F | Chart G | Chart G | Chart H | Chart I | Chart I |
| **August** | Chart F | Chart G | Chart G | Chart H | Chart I | Chart I | Chart B |
| **September** | Chart G | Chart G | Chart H | Chart I | Chart I | Chart B | Chart B |
| **October** | Chart G | Chart H | Chart I | Chart I | Chart B | Chart B | Chart C |
| **November** | Chart H | Chart I | Chart I | Chart B | Chart B | Chart C | Chart D |
| **December** | Chart I | Chart I | Chart B | Chart B | Chart C | Chart D | Chart E |

# CHART **A** North Circumpolar FACING NORTH

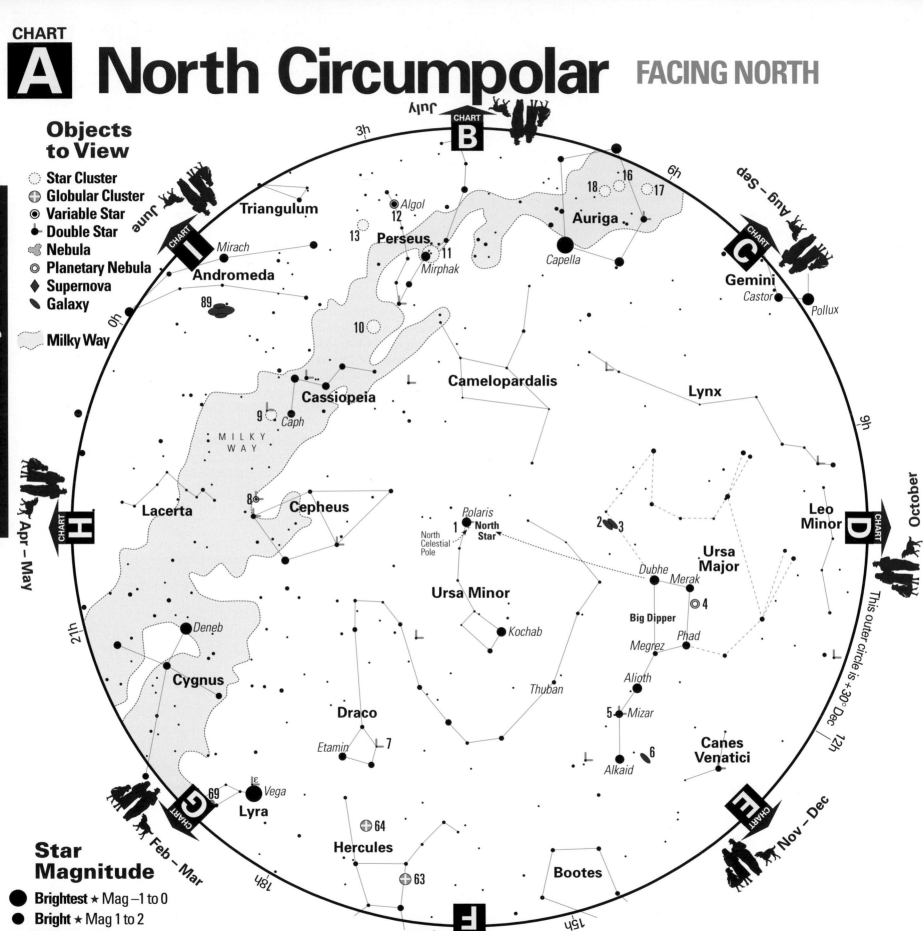

## Objects to View

- ◯ Star Cluster
- ⊕ Globular Cluster
- ◉ Variable Star
- • Double Star
- ✹ Nebula
- ◎ Planetary Nebula
- ◆ Supernova
- ◗ Galaxy

Milky Way

## Star Magnitude

- ⬤ **Brightest** ★ Mag −1 to 0
- ● **Bright** ★ Mag 1 to 2
- • **Average** ★ Mag 2 to 3
- · **Faint** ★ Mag 4 to 5

July

CHART **B**

3h

6h

Aug – Sep

Triangulum

Algol
12

13

Perseus

11
Mirphak

Auriga

18  16
17

Capella

CHART **C**

Gemini

Castor
Pollux

June

CHART **I**

Mirach

Andromeda

89

10

0h

Cameleopardalis

Lynx

9h

Cassiopeia

9  Caph

MILKY WAY

Leo Minor

CHART **D**

October

Lacerta

8

Cepheus

Polaris
**North Star**

North Celestial Pole

1

2  3

Dubhe  Merak

**Ursa Major**

This outer circle is +30° Dec

Apr – May

CHART **H**

21h

**Ursa Minor**

Kochab

**Big Dipper**

◎ 4

Deneb

Cygnus

Thuban

Megrez  Phad

Alioth

Draco

Etamin  7

5  Mizar

6

**Canes Venatici**

Alkaid

12h

Nov – Dec

CHART **E**

ε
69  Vega

Lyra

⊕ 64

Hercules

⊕ 63

Bootes

Feb – Mar

CHART **G**

18h

CHART **F**

January

15h

62

## Constellation Lore

**Ursa Major** and **Ursa Minor**, respectively the "Big Bear" and "Little Bear," are better known as the Big and Little Dippers. In Greek mythology they represent a mother, Callisto and her son, Arcas sent to the sky because of a misdeed by Jupiter and his wife Juno's jealousy. Jupiter came upon the beautiful Callisto, daughter of King Lycaon of Arcadia, when he was on Earth, inspecting carnage caused by Phaethon, son of Helios, who had arrogantly tried to ride the Sun Chariot across the sky. Jupiter took favor upon Callisto, and against her will, fathered her son Arcas. Juno discovered her husband's escapade and turned Callisto into an ugly bear. Later, when Arcas had grown up and was hunting, he encountered a bear running towards him. Not knowing that it was his mother, he aimed an arrow to kill it but Jupiter took sympathy and intervened, turning Arcas into a bear and hurling both into the sky as restitution for all the agony he caused.

**Cepheus** and **Cassiopeia** were the king and queen of Ethiopia and parents of a daughter, **Andromeda**. The gods became angry at Cassiopeia because of she boasted that she and her daughter were more beautiful than the Nereids mermaids, whose protector was Poseidon. To appease the gods for Cassiopeia's disrespect, Cepheus had to sacrifice his daughter to the Sea Monster, **Cetus**. About this same time, **Perseus**, the son of Jupiter, had cut off Medusa's head as a wedding gift, and was heading back from a journey. He noticed Andromeda chained to a sea cliff, and instantly fell in love. He saw her parents watching in agony and they agreed to him rescuing her for marriage. So, before the sea monster devoured Andromeda, he chopped its head off with the sickle he had used on Medusa. At the wedding, a prior suitor showed up and the royal parents then reneged on their promise to Perseus. A fight ensued, and Perseus was almost overpowered but was saved by Medusa's head, for all who looked upon her face turned to stone. Afterwards, the royal couple was banished to the heavens by Poseidon for their misdeeds.

**Cassiopeia** the constellation is also known as the celestial W or M, depending on its orientation in the sky; and because one side of the figure is lazy, it is often thought of as the throne or chair of the queen.

**Draco** the Dragon was one of the many monsters fighting along with the great Titans against the Olympians, commanded by Jupiter. Near the climax of a battle, the dragon opposed the goddess of Wisdom, Minerva, who in turned flung it into the heavens where it froze twisted, after landing so close to the frigid North Celestial Pole.

**Camelopardalis**, the Giraffe, **Lacerta**, the Lizard and the **Lynx** are faint constellations that were added in the 1600's.

## Distance to Named Stars

| | |
|---|---|
| Alioth | 81 l.y. |
| Alkaid | 101 l.y. |
| Caph | 54 l.y. |
| Dubhe | 124 l.y. |
| Etamin | 148 l.y. |
| Kochab | 126 l.y. |
| Megrez | 81 l.y. |
| Merak | 79 l.y. |
| Mirphak | 630 l.y. |
| Mizar | 78 l.y. |
| Phad | 84 l.y. |
| Polaris | 316 l.y. |
| Thuban | 310 l.y. |

## Binocular & Telescope Objects

**1** All the constellations revolve around *Polaris*, the North Star. This star appears stationary because the Earth's axis is pointed in its direction. This has not and will not always be the case. Five thousand years ago, the Earth's axis was pointed towards *Thuban* in Draco, and 12,000 years from now it will be pointing close to *Vega* in Lyra. The Earth's axis slowly "wobbles" around a great circle in the sky every 25,800 years, because of tugs from the Moon and Sun.

**2 & 3** GALAXIES M81 & M82 respectively. Visible in the same eyepiece view at low power, they are separated by about one Moon's diameter. M82 is pictured on page 22 and is the one that looks like a cigar. Distances: 4.5 million l.y. & 17 million l.y.. Diameters: 37,000 l.y. & 54,000 l.y.. Arc lengths in sky: 28' & 11'. Mag: 6.9 & 8.4. **Favorites. A little challenging to locate, but easy to spot even in mildly polluted skies. Need TELESCOPE, start at 50x.**

**4** "Owl" PLANETARY NEBULA M97. Larger, fainter planetary that needs dark skies. In photographs, looks like the face of an owl. Dist: 1,630 l.y.. Diameter: 1.3 l.y.. Arc diameter in sky: 2.8'. Mag: 10. **Difficult to see. Needs dark skies. Use TELESCOPE at 50x to 100x.**

**5** A famous DOUBLE STAR. *Alcor* is the "bright" star next to *Mizar* that can be seen with good eyes or binoculars. With a telescope, you can see the much closer, actual binary that takes 10,000 years to revolve around *Mizar*. **A favorite. Alcor just visible with the NAKED EYES, but need TELESCOPE with at least 60x to easily see the actual binary star very close to *Mizar*.**

**6** GALAXY M51 is known as the Whirlpool Galaxy. The "bright" knot off to one side that appears to be interacting with an outer arm is actually a galaxy farther away. Dist: 15 million l.y.. Diameter: 50,000 l.y.. Arc size in sky: 11' x 7'. Mag: 8.4. **TELESCOPE object that comes alive in dark skies. Easy to find. 50x to 100x**

**7** Known as *Nu (ν) Draconis*, this is a good example of an *easy* DOUBLE STAR. **Single star to the EYES, two with BINOCULARS.**

**8** A historically famous VARIABLE STAR that helped establish a means to measure distances to stars (see page 32). The magnitude of *Delta (δ) Cephei* varies from 4.4 to 3.5 every 5.4 days. **EYES only. Star changes brightness by 1 magnitude.**

**9** Pretty CLUSTER NGC 7789. Many equal brightness stars make a faint sprinkle. In our skies, it has an arc diameter of 16', or 1/2 the Moon's width. **A little challenging, but worth it. Need TELESCOPE at 50x.**

(Continued on next chart)

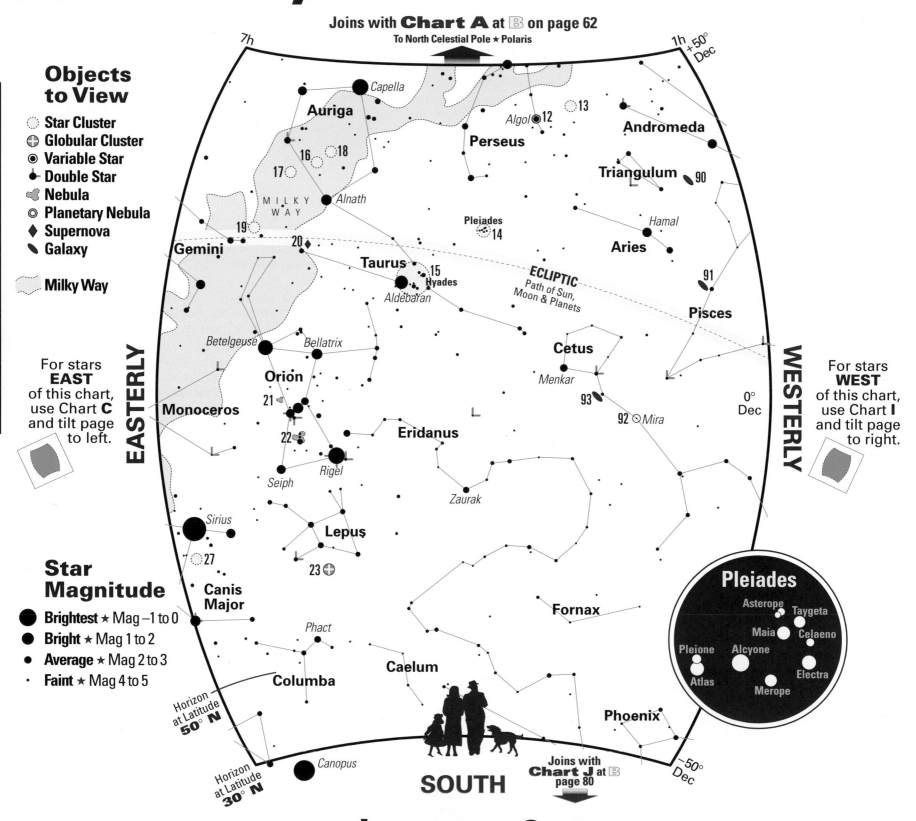

Joins with **Chart A** at Ⓑ on page 62

To North Celestial Pole ★ Polaris

**Objects to View**

- ◌ Star Cluster
- ⊕ Globular Cluster
- ⊙ Variable Star
- •⊸ Double Star
- ✺ Nebula
- ◎ Planetary Nebula
- ◆ Supernova
- ◥ Galaxy
- ⬚ Milky Way

**EASTERLY**

For stars **EAST** of this chart, use Chart **C** and tilt page to left.

**WESTERLY**

For stars **WEST** of this chart, use Chart **I** and tilt page to right.

7h

Capella
Auriga
16  18
17
MILKY WAY
19
Gemini
Alnath
20
Taurus
Aldebaran
Betelgeuse  Bellatrix
Orion
21
Monoceros
22
Seiph  Rigel
Eridanus
Zaurak
Sirius
Lepus
27
23 ⊕
Canis Major
Phact
Columba
Caelum

Algol ⊙ 12  ◌ 13
Perseus
Andromeda
Triangulum  ◥ 90
Pleiades
14
Hamal
Aries
91
Pisces
Cetus
Menkar
93 ◥
92 ⊙ Mira
0° Dec
Fornax
Phoenix

1h +50° Dec

**ECLIPTIC**
Path of Sun,
Moon & Planets

15
Hyades

**Star Magnitude**

- ⬤ Brightest ★ Mag −1 to 0
- ● Bright ★ Mag 1 to 2
- • Average ★ Mag 2 to 3
- · Faint ★ Mag 4 to 5

Horizon at Latitude **50° N**

Horizon at Latitude **30° N**

Canopus

−50° Dec

Joins with **Chart J** at Ⓑ page 80

**SOUTH**

**Pleiades**

Asterope  Taygeta
Maia  Celaeno
Pleione  Alcyone
Atlas  Merope  Electra

Dec at 11 PM ★ **January** at **9 PM** ★ Feb at 7 PM

# Constellation Lore

**Eridanus** is a meandering connection of stars that were recognized by various cultures as a river. In Egypt, it represented the Nile. In Greek mythology, its water was used by Hercules to help clean the stables of King Augeas, as one of his twelve labors. Phaethon (see Chart A & G) fell into this river after being thrown from the Sun Chariot. Although Eridanus is not near the Milky Way, it is sometimes associated with it.

**Cetus** was an ugly, evil Sea Monster that lived deep in the ocean and personified everything bad. It almost devoured Andromeda, but Perseus chopped its head off before it reached her (more in Chart A). Sometimes referred to as a Whale.

In illustrations, **Auriga** the charioteer or wagoneer, is often seen holding a goat, represented by the star *Capella*, and two kids. One of the charioteer's responsibilities was supervising the royal livestock, used for food. One legend has it that the milk from the goat Amaltheia was fed to Jupiter when he was a child. Another has Jupiter placing the chariot in the sky as an appeasement for causing the physical disability of his offspring Hephaestus, whose son inherited the disability, but invented the chariot to move about more easily.

The **Pleiades** or Seven Sisters are the daughters of Atlas and Pleione. They were changed into doves and sent into the heavens as stars to avoid the amorous clutches of Orion. Thus, the Seven Sisters always rise before Orion, forever escaping him. One Native American legend is that there were Seven Sisters who longed to wander among the stars, lost their way home and huddled together so as not to get separated. The seventh star is difficult to see and in both stories it is said that crying blurs its brightness.

The **Hyades** are piglets and the half-sisters of the Pleiades, all having Atlas as their father. Together, they make up the 14 Atlantides which reside in Taurus.

There are two stories related to **Taurus**, the Bull. Jupiter's wife, Juno, turned the beautiful Io, the daughter of the river god Inachos, into a white heifer to stop Jupiter's affair with her. In another story, Jupiter fell in love with the beautiful Europe, daughter of Agenor, King of Sideon. To lure her away, he changed himself into a mighty white bull and stood among her father's cattle. She went to see the white bull and was captivated by its friendliness. After getting on its back for a ride, Jupiter rode off with her to Crete. Later she bore a son, Minos, who became King of Crete.

**Fornax**, the Furnace and **Caelum**, the Engraver's Tool have no lore, since they were added in the 1600's.

The **Phoenix** is a great bird that lives for 500 years and can regenerate itself from its own ashes. At the end of its life, it builds a nest and lays until the noon sunlight strikes it, setting it aflame. From the ashes comes forth a worm that transforms into a new Phoenix.

**Columba** the Dove was set aflight by Jason to see how it would fare between the dangerous rocks of a channel. It returned safely, providing Jason with a good omen to sail his ship Argo through the same waters. The god of wisdom, Minerva, placed the bird in the sky as a reward for its helpful role.

# Distance to Named Stars

| | |
|---|---|
| Algol | 93 l.y. |
| Aldebaran | 65 l.y. |
| Alnath | 131 l.y. |
| Capella | 42 l.y. |
| Hamal | 66 l.y. |
| Menkar | 220 l.y. |
| Mira | 200 l.y. |
| Zaurak | 170 l.y. |

# Binocular & Telescope Objects

**10** Favorite DOUBLE CLUSTER, NGC 869 & NGC 884, that spans two Moon diameters. Must-see object! NGC 869 has the higher concentration of stars at its center. Clusters are about 7,300 l.y. away and each spans 70 l.y. **A favorite. Best with TELESCOPE at about 50x.**

**11** Nice open CLUSTER that can be seen as a haze with the naked eyes. About 150 l.y. away. **A favorite. Easy & best with BINOCULARS.**

**12** The "Demon Star" VARIABLE that dips in brightness by over 1 magnitude for two hours every 2.87 days. Consult the popular monthly astronomy magazines for times. Dip is caused by a fainter orbiting star passing in "front." **EYES only. Star changes brightness by over 1 magnitude for 2 hours.**

**13** CLUSTER M34 with fairly bright members totaling 60 stars. Dist: 1,450 l.y.. Diameter: 10 l.y.. Arc width in sky: 25'. Mag: 5.2. **Easy object for BINOCULARS or TELESCOPE at low power.**

**14** Well-known "Pleiades" CLUSTER M45 is comprised of 100 stars. There is some nebulosity surrounding these stars but it is difficult to see. Dist: 407 l.y.. Width: 14 l.y.. Arc width in sky: 2°. Mag: 1.5. **Wonderful and best with BINOCULARS.**

**15** The "Hyades" CLUSTER is 20 l.y. across and 150 l.y. away. It is the brightest, closest cluster in our skies, spanning over 8° or 16 Moons. **EYES and BINOCULARS.**

**16, 17 & 18** CLUSTERS M36, M37 & M38 respectively. In the sky, each is about magnitude 6 and half a Moon's diameter in size. M37 is generally the favorite, housing a red star. They are 4,100, 2,200 & 4,200 l.y. away, spanning 12 l.y. with 60 stars, 19 l.y. with 2,000 stars and 18 l.y. with 120 stars. **Easy to find. Best with TELESCOPE starting at 50x.**

**19** This favorite CLUSTER M35 contains about 200 stars spanning 20 l.y. at a distance of 2,800 l.y. Covers an area the size of the Moon. Mag: 5. Look for a smaller cluster, NGC 2158, a Moon's diameter away. **TELESCOPE object. Fairly easy to find and nice at 50x. Look for a smaller and fainter cluster nearby.**

**20** "Crab Nebula" SUPERNOVA remnant, M1. Needs dark skies away from light population. Shaped like a flame. Dist: 6,500 l.y.. Length: 14 l.y.. Arc size in sky: 6' x 4'. Mag: 8.4. **Need TELESCOPE with dark skies. 50x to 100x.**

(Continued on next chart)

# **C** February ★ March FACING SOUTH

Joins with **Chart A** at Ⓒ on page 62

**To North Celestial Pole ★ Polaris**

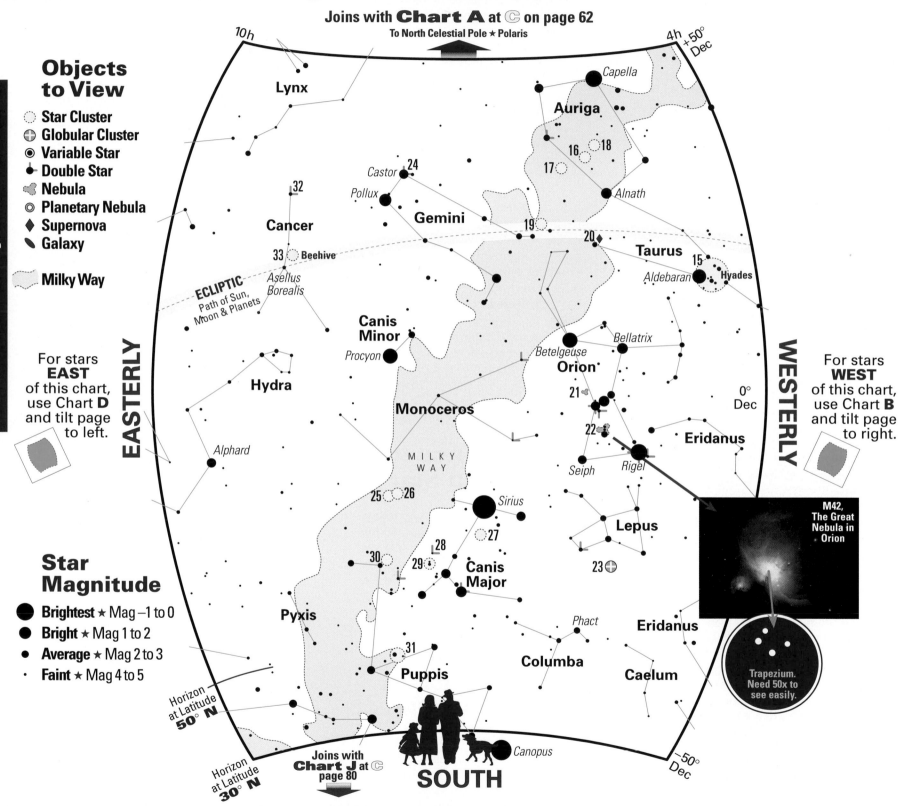

10h

4h +50° Dec

## Objects to View

- ⊙ **Star Cluster**
- ⊕ **Globular Cluster**
- ◉ **Variable Star**
- •– **Double Star**
- ☁ **Nebula**
- ◎ **Planetary Nebula**
- ♦ **Supernova**
- ◖ **Galaxy**

**Milky Way**

**Chart C Objects 21-31**

Lynx

*Capella*

**Auriga**

16  18

17

*Castor* 24
*Pollux*

32

**Cancer**

**Gemini**

19

20 ♦

*Alnath*

**Taurus**

15

33 ⊙ Beehive

**ECLIPTIC**
Path of Sun, Moon & Planets

*Asellus Borealis*

*Aldebaran*   **Hyades**

**Canis Minor**

*Procyon*

*Bellatrix*

*Betelgeuse*   **Orion**

**EASTERLY**

For stars **EAST** of this chart, use Chart **D** and tilt page to left.

**Hydra**

21 •–

22

*Seiph*   *Rigel*

**Eridanus**

0° Dec

**WESTERLY**

For stars **WEST** of this chart, use Chart **B** and tilt page to right.

**Monoceros**

*Alphard*

MILKY WAY

25 ⊙ 26

*Sirius*

**Lepus**

M42, The Great Nebula in Orion

## Star Magnitude

- ⬤ **Brightest ★** Mag –1 to 0
- ● **Bright ★** Mag 1 to 2
- • **Average ★** Mag 2 to 3
- · **Faint ★** Mag 4 to 5

30  28

29 ⊙

**Canis Major**

27 ⊙

23 ⊕

*Trapezium. Need 50x to see easily.*

**Pyxis**

31

**Puppis**

*Phact*

**Columba**

**Eridanus**

**Caelum**

Horizon at Latitude **50° N**

Horizon at Latitude **30° N**

Joins with **Chart J** at Ⓒ page 80

**SOUTH**

*Canopus*

–50° Dec

Jan at Midnight ★ **February** at **9:30 PM** ★ Mar at 8 PM

# Chart C

Chart C Objects 21-31

## Constellation Lore

**Gemini** the Twins, represented by the stars *Castor* and *Pollux,* were warlike heroes who protected seafarers from pirates. Allegedly, Pollux was immortal but Castor was not and was eventually killed in a quarrel. Pollux then asked Jupiter for death so he could be with his twin, but immortals cannot be killed. Jupiter allowed him to live alternately one day with the gods and the other in Hades with his brother. Thus, the stars Castor and Pollux take turns in rising and setting.

**Orion**, the Hunter was the handsomest man alive. He was the son of Neptune and the nymph Euryale. When he visited the island Hyria, he fell in love with Merope, daughter of Oenopion, who promised her to him in marriage if Orion rid the island of dangerous wild beasts. Oenopion kept Orion hunting long past his commitment because he favored his daughter to the point of wanting her for himself. One night, in his grief, Orion drank wine and was given even more until he fell asleep. Oenopion then put out both of his eyes and threw him on the shore. An oracle pronounced that he could regain his sight if he traveled east and gazed with his sockets at the place where Helios rises from the ocean. He did, and then returned for revenge, but he could not find Oenopion anywhere. During his pursuit, he met up with Artemis, sister of Apollo, who persuaded him to forget his revenge and to hunt with her. But Apollo did not favor Orion and arranged to have Mother Earth send Scorpio, a giant scorpion, after Orion to prevent him from taking advantage of his sister. During the scorpion's pursuit, Apollo tricked Artemis into killing Orion with her arrow. She pleaded with Apollo's son Asclepius to revive him, but Jupiter struck him down before he got the chance. Artemis then sent Orion's image into the stars because his spirit had already descended to the Underworld. So, as the constellation Orion sets, **Scorpius** is rising for the chase.

**Lepus** the Hare is quiet at Orion's feet, waiting to spring if discovered. **Canis Major** and **Canis Minor** are respectively Orion's loyal Greater and Lesser Dogs.

**Monoceros** the Unicorn was the ultimate prize for any hunter, even just to catch a glimpse of it. Its horn is said to have had magical powers that could protect from evil.

The three stars, *Sirius*, *Procyon* and *Betelgeuse* are commonly known as the **Winter Triangle**. The "Dog Days of Summer" refers to the fact that the bright dog star *Sirius* rises and sets with the Sun during the summer.

## Distance to Named Stars

| | |
|---|---|
| Bellatrix | 1,400 l.y. |
| Betelgeuse | 1,400 l.y. |
| Castor | 52 l.y. |
| Phact | 180 l.y. |
| Pollux | 34 l.y. |
| Procyon | 11 l.y. |
| Rigel | 1,400 l.y. |
| Seiph | 78 l.y. |
| Sirius | 8.6 l.y. |

## Binocular & Telescope Objects

**21** NEBULA M78 almost looks like the head of a comet. Dist: 1,630 l.y.. Length: 4.8 l.y.. Arc size in sky: 8' x 6'. Mag: 8. **Fairly easy with a TELESCOPE at 50x. Darker skies helpful.**

**22** Great "Orion" NEBULA, M42, is the brightest stellar nursery in the sky. Even a small telescope shows considerable detail. Lit up by four central stars known as the Trapezium. Dist: 15,000 l.y.. Length: 39 l.y.. Arc size in sky: 1.5° x 1°. Mag: 3.7. **Favorite, beautiful and bright. Use TELESCOPE from 50x to 100x. Look for Trapezium starting at 50x. See inset on chart.**

**23** GLOBULAR CLUSTER M79. Only globular visible in the winter sky. Dist: 43,000 l.y.. Diameter: 75 l.y.. Arc diameter in sky: 6'. Mag: 7.7. **TELESCOPE object fairly easy to find because it is below the two bright stars in Lepus. Start at 50x.**

**24** *Castor* is a favorite DOUBLE STAR, somewhat challenging to split because the separation is just 4 arc seconds. These 2nd and 9th magnitude white stars are true binaries that revolve about each other in 467 years. **Classical favorite. Easy to find but need TELESCOPE at 150x to separate easily.**

**25 & 26** CLUSTERS M46 and M47 respectively are 1.5° apart, less than two eyepiece views at 50x. M47 has bright members while those of M46 are fainter. With averted vision, look for a faint planetary nebula in M47. Distances: 5,300 l.y. & 1,550 l.y.. Widths: 31 l.y. & 11 l.y.. Arc widths in sky: 20' & 25'. Mag: 6.1 & 5. **Favorites. Fairly easy with a TELESCOPE at 50x.**

**27** "Little Beehive" CLUSTER M41. This sprinkle of stars pops out because it is in an area where stars are sparse. Dist: 2,100 l.y.. Width: 24 l.y.. Arc width in sky: 40'. Mag: 4.5. **Fairly easy with a TELESCOPE at 50x because it "pops out."**

**28** Pretty orange and blue DOUBLE STAR similar to *Albireo* in Cygnus (object #79), thus sometimes called the "Winter Albireo." Known as *145 Canis Majoris*, it is a true binary. **TELESCOPE object. Start at 50x.**

**29** A beautiful CLUSTER, NGC 2362. A bright star surrounded by a triangle of fainter ones. **TELESCOPE object that is fairly easy to find. Start at 50x.**

**30** CLUSTER M93 is a nice cluster of about 80 stars. Dist: 3,600 l.y.. Width: 24 l.y.. Arc width in sky: 10'. Mag: 6.2. **Best with TELESCOPE. Pops out. Start at 50x.**

**31** CLUSTER NGC 2451 plus surrounding stars. Lower in the sky, but easy to spot with binoculars because it is large with many bright members, including one red. **Nice and easy with BINOCULARS. Pops out.**

(Continued on next chart)

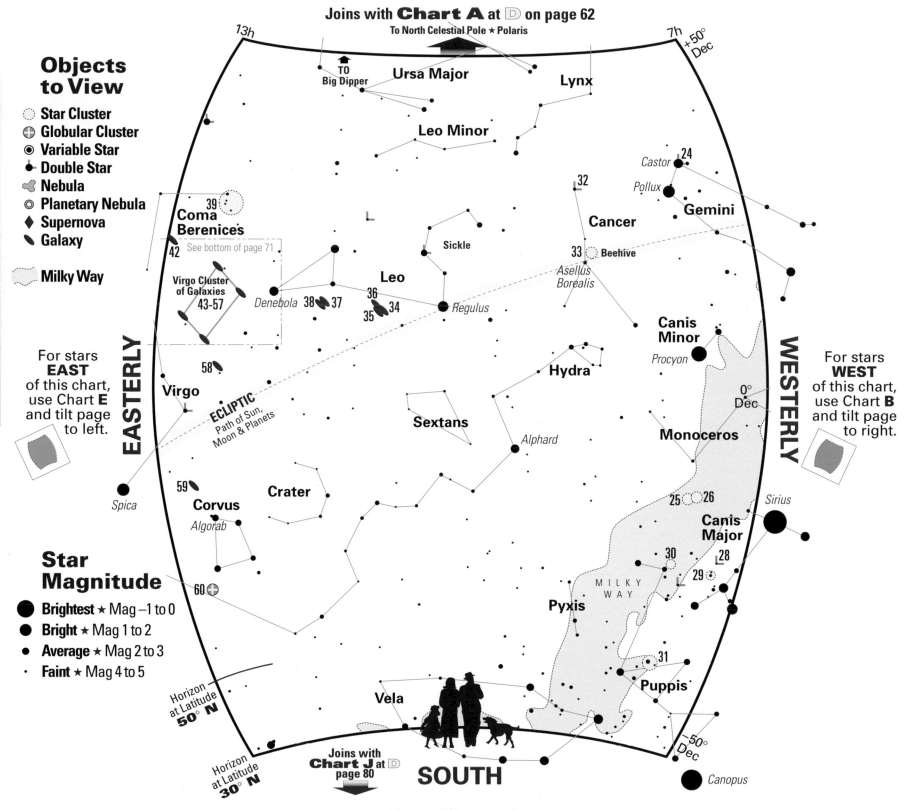

**Chart D  Objects 32-57**

Joins with **Chart A** at Ⓓ on page 62
To North Celestial Pole ★ Polaris

13h

7h +50° Dec

**Objects to View**

- ◌ **Star Cluster**
- ⊕ **Globular Cluster**
- ◉ **Variable Star**
- • **Double Star**
- ☁ **Nebula**
- ◎ **Planetary Nebula**
- ◆ **Supernova**
- ◗ **Galaxy**

◌ **Milky Way**

TO Big Dipper

Ursa Major

Lynx

Leo Minor

Castor 24
Pollux 32
Gemini

39
**Coma Berenices**

See bottom of page 71

Cancer

Sickle

33 ◌ Beehive

Asellus Borealis

42

**Virgo Cluster of Galaxies 43-57**

Denebola 38 37 36 34
35
**Leo**
Regulus

For stars **EAST** of this chart, use Chart **E** and tilt page to left.

58

**Canis Minor**
Procyon

**EASTERLY**

**Virgo**

**ECLIPTIC**
Path of Sun, Moon & Planets

**Hydra**

0° Dec

**WESTERLY**

For stars **WEST** of this chart, use Chart **B** and tilt page to right.

**Sextans**

Alphard

**Monoceros**

59

**Crater**

**Corvus**
Algorab

25 ◌◌ 26

Sirius

**Star Magnitude**

- ● **Brightest** ★ Mag −1 to 0
- ● **Bright** ★ Mag 1 to 2
- • **Average** ★ Mag 2 to 3
- · **Faint** ★ Mag 4 to 5

60 ⊕

**Canis Major**

30
28
29

MILKY WAY

**Pyxis**

31

**Puppis**

Horizon at Latitude **50° N**

**Vela**

Horizon at Latitude **30° N**

Joins with **Chart J** at Ⓓ page 80

**SOUTH**

−50° Dec

Canopus

March at 11 PM ★ **April at 9 PM** ★ May at 7 PM

## Constellation Lore

Around 150 AD, **Leo** the Lion extended eastward to **Cancer** and westward to **Coma Berenices**. Its whiskers were the Beehive (object #33) and its tail ended up in the cluster of stars at the top of Coma Berenices. *Regulus*, the brightest star in Leo, has been identified with the birth of Christ. Its name implies King, Mighty, Great, Center or Hero, depending on the culture. The planet Jupiter, named after the king of the gods, was in close conjunction with *Regulus* in 3 BC (that is, Jupiter and *Regulus* were next to each other in the sky) and at two other times in 2 BC. Was this interpreted by the Magi as the sign of the birth of Christ? (See illustration on page 93.)

There is no classical mythology for **Leo Minor**, because this constellation was created in the 1600s. **Cancer** the Crab was sent to prevent Hercules from killing the Hydra. However, Hercules trampled the crab and succeeded in killing the Hydra anyway. The **Hydra** had nine heads and if one was chopped off, two grew back in its place. Hercules had to burn each stub to prevent the heads from growing back. **Corvus** was a bird placed in the heavens on Hydra's back by Apollo for being slow in bringing him water and lying about his tardiness. **Crater** represents the container of water that is always out of reach of Corvus. **Puppis** refers to the stern (poop) of Jason's ship *Argo*, and **Vela**, its sail.

## Distance to Named Stars

| | |
|---|---|
| Algorab | 88 l.y. |
| Alphard | 177 l.y. |
| Asellus Borealis | 136 l.y. |
| Castor | 52 l.y. |
| Denebola | 36 l.y. |
| Pollux | 34 l.y. |
| Procyon | 11 l.y. |
| Regulus | 78 l.y. |
| Sirius | 8.6 l.y. |

## Binocular & Telescope Objects

**32** Pretty orange and blue optical DOUBLE STAR that is also the "top" star in Cancer. Easy to separate in a telescope at low power. The challenge here is to spot the 5th magnitude top star with your unaided eyes. The distance to the brighter star is 188 l.y. **TELESCOPE object that is a little challenging to locate with your unaided eyes. Start at 50x.**

**33** "Beehive" CLUSTER M44, also known as the *Praesepe*. This is a wonderful cluster seen best with binoculars. It is similar in size to the Pleiades but its members are not as bright, so binoculars are needed to bring them to life. M44 is often found by scanning the area halfway between Regulus and Pollux. Dist: 515 l.y.. Width: 11 l.y.. Arc width in sky: 1.2°. Mag: 3.1. **A favorite. Easy & best with BINOCULARS.**

**34, 35 & 36** GALAXIES M95, M96 and M105 respectively. All three visible within two eyepiece views at low power. M95 & 96 are spirals, while M105 is an elliptical. Distances: 27 million l.y., 27 million l.y. & 26 million l.y.. Diameters: 57,000 l.y., 59,000 l.y. & 41,000 l.y.. Arc sizes in sky: 7' x 5', 8' x 5' & 5' x 5'. Mags: 9.5, 9.2 & 9.3. **Fairly easy with a TELESCOPE at 50x.**

**37 & 38** Spiral GALAXIES M65 & M66 respectively. Visible in the same eyepiece view at low power, they are separated by about one Moon's diameter. Distances: 24 million l.y. & 21.5 million L.y.. Diameters: 68,000 l.y. & 57,000 l.y.. Arc sizes in sky: 10' x 3' & 9' x 4'. Mag: 9 & 9. **Favorites. Fairly easy with a TELESCOPE at 50x.**

**39** CLUSTER of stars in Coma Berenices that can be seen as a haze with the naked eyes. Big loose group best with binoculars. **Easy & pops out with BINOCULARS.**

**40** GLOBULAR CLUSTER M3. Bright, plump cluster. Dist: 32,000 l.y.. Diameter: 177 l.y.. Arc diameter in sky: 19'. Mag: 6+. **TELESCOPE object a little challenging to find but worth it. Start at 50x.**

**41** GLOBULAR CLUSTER M53. Smaller and fainter than the nearby M3. Dist: 56,000 l.y.. Diameter: 212 l.y.. Arc diameter in sky: 13'. Mag: 8. **TELESCOPE object a little challenging to find. Start at 50x.**

**42** GALAXY M64 is by far the biggest and brightest looking galaxy in the area. Known as the "Black-Eye Galaxy," for its resemblance to a black eye. Dist: 13.5 million l.y.. Width: 35,000 l.y.. Arc size in sky: 10' x 5'. Mag: 8.5. **TELESCOPE object that does better in darker skies. Start at 50x.**

**43-57** "VIRGO" CLUSTER of GALAXIES totalling about 2,500 galaxies. Our Local Group of 40 galaxies, which includes the Andromeda Galaxy, is linked to this cluster and others to form the Local Supercluster. The galaxies in the Virgo cluster are on average 55 million l.y. years away and are centered around M87, an elliptical galaxy with a diameter of 133,000 l.y. and a mass estimated at 800 billion of our Suns. Although M87 appears as a featureless, round fuzzy star (see bottom left photo on page 22 & 37), it has an active nucleus, fueled by a supermassive black hole with a mass estimated at 3 billion Suns. All of the 15 Messier galaxies in this area appear

(Continued on next chart)

Object #59: The Sombrero Galaxy, M104, in Virgo.

**Joins with Chart A** at Ⓖ on page 62

To North Celestial Pole ★ Polaris

22h

16h +50° Dec

## Objects to View

◌ Star Cluster
⊕ Globular Cluster
◉ Variable Star
⊢ Double Star
☁ Nebula
◎ Planetary Nebula
◆ Supernova
◣ Galaxy

〰️ Milky Way

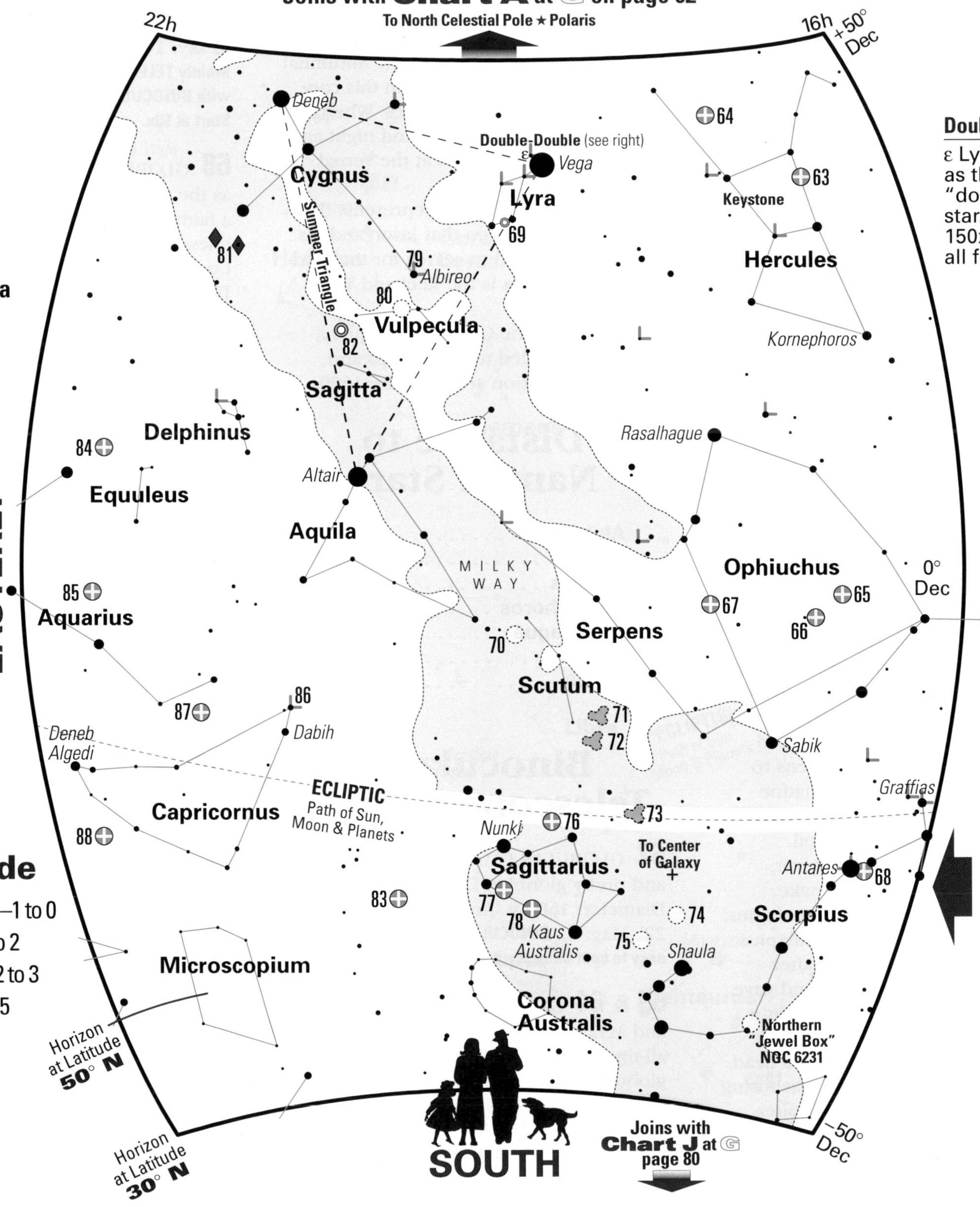

**Double-Double**

ε Lyrae is known as the challenging "double-double" star. Need about 150x to easily see all four stars.

**Double-Double** (see right)
ε
*Vega*
**Cygnus**
*Deneb*
**Lyra**
64 ⊕
63 ⊕
**Keystone**
**Hercules**
69
79
*Albireo*
80
*Kornephoros*
81
Summer Triangle
82
**Vulpecula**
**Sagitta**
*Rasalhague*

**Delphinus**
84 ⊕
**Equuleus**
*Altair*
**Aquila**
0° Dec
**Ophiuchus**
MILKY WAY
85 ⊕
**Aquarius**
67 ⊕
65 ⊕
66 ⊕
**Serpens**
70
**Scutum**
86
87 ⊕
*Dabih*
71
72
*Sabik*
*Deneb Algedi*
88 ⊕
ECLIPTIC
Path of Sun, Moon & Planets
73
*Graffias*
**Capricornus**
76 ⊕
*Nunki*
To Center of Galaxy
*Antares*
68 ⊕
83 ⊕
77 ⊕
78
74
**Scorpius**
75
*Kaus Australis*
*Shaula*
**Microscopium**
**Corona Australis**
Northern "Jewel Box" NGC 6231

**For stars EAST** of this chart, use Chart **H** and tilt page to left.

**EASTERLY**

**WESTERLY**

**For stars WEST** of this chart, use Chart **F** and tilt page to right.

## Star Magnitude

● Brightest ★ Mag –1 to 0
● Bright ★ Mag 1 to 2
• Average ★ Mag 2 to 3
· Faint ★ Mag 4 to 5

**Milky Way Viewing Splendor**

Don't miss viewing the brightest and thickest part of the Milky Way Band, around the constellation Sagittarius. In the northern hemisphere, it comes out of the southern horizon and stretches overhead. **Observed best with naked eyes in dark skies.**

Horizon at Latitude **50° N**

Horizon at Latitude **30° N**

**SOUTH**

**Joins with Chart J** at Ⓖ page 80

July at 11:30 PM ★ **Aug at 9:30 PM** ★ Sep at 8 PM

# Constellation Lore

**Cygnus** the Swan is widely recognized as the beautiful Northern Cross amidst the Milky Way. Cycnus was friends with Phaethon, son of Helios, who unsuccessfully rode the Sun Chariot across the sky. After Phaethon was thrown into the river Eridanus, Cycnus diligently dove in to retrieve all his bones so he could ensure his friend a proper afterlife in the Underworld. For this consideration, Jupiter transformed Cycnus into Cygnus, a swan and placed him in the Milky Way river.

**Lyra**, the Lyre, was invented by Mercury as he sat on a shore, playing around with a tortoise shell. Apollo took a liking to this marvelous instrument and passed it to his son Orpheus. Orpheus mastered the lyre and when he played, its music could stop arrows and knives midair if thrown at him. The lyre was placed in the heavens by Jupiter after Orpheus was killed by jealous women who became enamored with him through his enchanted music.

**Aquila** the Eagle was Jupiter's bird who carried out various tasks for the supreme god. Hercules killed Aquila with **Sagitta**, the Arrow, because Jupiter had ordered the bird to daily eat the liver of Prometheus, one of the Titans, while he was chained to a mountain. His liver grew back each day.

**Delphinus** the Dolphin was placed in the sky by Neptune in return for helping him find and win over the woman he loved, Amphitrite, daughter of Oceanus.

**Scutum** the Shield was a constellation added in the 1600s.

**Sagittarius** the Archer is usually represented by a centaur, a warlike hunter distinctly different from Centaurus, representing Chiron the educator.

I have fond memories of **Scorpius**, the Scorpion, because it was the first constellation that my daughter learned to recognize. In the sky, the scorpion's tail lies over a dark part of the Milky Way, signifying a crevice leading to the Underworld from which it came. One version of Orion's story has him boasting about killing all the animals on Earth. For this reason Mother Earth, Gaia, sent a giant scorpion to kill him, and it bit him in the heel. The healer Ophiuchus, who stands above Scoripus in the sky, brought Orion back to life, and keeps the scorpion at bay under his feet.

**Corona Australis**, the Southern Crown, was placed into the sky by Bacchus, the god of Wine, in honor of his mother Semele who was accidentally destroyed by the trickery of Juno because of her affair with Jupiter.

# Distance to Named Stars

| | |
|---|---|
| Albireo | 380 l.y. |
| Altair | 16 l.y. |
| Dabih | 560 l.y. |
| Deneb | 1,500 l.y. |
| Kaus Australis | 76 l.y. |
| Nunki | 170 l.y. |
| Vega | 25 l.y. |

# Binocular & Telescope Objects

**72** Favorite M17 "Omega" or "Swan" NEBULA that looks similar to the body and neck of a swan. Dist: 4,890 l.y.. Width: 57 l.y.. Arc width in sky: 40'. Mag: 6. **A favorite. Best in a TELESCOPE because the body of the swan shows up well and makes it easy to spot. Brightest nebulae in the area. Start at 50x. Move the telescope due north to bump into M16 (object #71).**

**73** Favorite M8 "Lagoon" NEBULA and star cluster. Large and easy to find because it is off Sagittarius. Dist: 5,200 l.y.. Width: 136 l.y.. Arc width in sky: 90'. Mag: 4.5. **A favorite. BINOCULARS or TELESCOPE object. Although this nebula is large, it is fainter than you might expect. In binoculars, it looks like a large patch of the Milky Way. Start at 50x.**

**74 & 75** Star CLUSTERS M6 & M7 respectively. Both are visible to the naked eye as patches but M7 is the lower, larger and brighter one. M6 contains about 330 stars and M7 only 80. Dist: 1,585 l.y. & 780 l.y.. Widths: 9 l.y. & 18 l.y.. Arc widths in sky: 20' & 1° 20'. Mags: 4.2 & 3. **Favorites. BINOCULARS and TELESCOPE objects that are easy to find. M7 will fill any eyepiece field of view.**

**76** Large GLOBULAR CLUSTER M22 is one of my favorites. Some of the stars are resolvable, that is, they can be seen individually in a small scope. Dist: 10,100 l.y.. Diameter: 97 l.y.. Arc diameter in sky: 33'. Mag: 5.2. **BINOCULARS AND TELESCOPE object that is easy to locate. Nice in a telescope at 50x to 75x. Also look for a much fainter and smaller globular, NGC 6642, one degree northwest of M22.**

**77 & 78** GLOBULAR CLUSTERS M54 and M70 are more typical of globulars. Distances: 23,400 & 25,400 l.y.. Diameters: 143 & 103 l.y.. Arc diameters in sky: 21' & 14'. Mag: 5+ & 6.5. **TELESCOPE objects, start at 50x. M70 is easy to find because it is halfway between a line drawn from the "end" stars. M54 is on the same line but within two degrees of one end.**

**79** Favorite pretty blue and gold DOUBLE STAR *Albireo*. There is some question as to whether this is an actual pair of stars revolving around each other or just two stars near one another. Both stars appear to be about 380 l.y. away. **Easy and very pretty TELESCOPE object. Start at 50x.**

**80** "Coathanger" CLUSTER comprised of 10 stars shaped like a bar-type coathanger. It spans about 2° and its stars may be about 150 l.y. away. Actual name is Brocchi's Cluster. **BINOCULARS object. From the northern hemisphere, it looks like an upside down bar-type coathanger.**

**81** "Veil" SUPERNOVA remnants. East and west arcs of nebulosity indicated. East arc (NGC 6992) is brightest but west (NGC 6960) has a fairly bright star near its middle. The explosion occurred about 5,000 years ago and it is about 1,500 l.y away. Both arcs stretch about 1°. **TELESCOPE object better viewed with larger scopes of 8-inch diameters or more, and dark skies. Arcs are large and faint. Start with 50x.**

(Continued on next chart)

# CHART I

**Nov ★ Dec** FACING SOUTH

**Chart I Objects 89-93**

Joins with **Chart A** at ▯ on page 62

To North Celestial Pole ★ Polaris

## Objects to View

◌ Star Cluster
⊕ Globular Cluster
◉ Variable Star
•─ Double Star
☁ Nebula
◎ Planetary Nebula
◆ Supernova
✎ Galaxy

▨ Milky Way

**EASTERLY**

For stars **EAST** of this chart, use Chart **B** and tilt page to left.

**WESTERLY**

For stars **WEST** of this chart, use Chart **H** and tilt page to right.

## Star Magnitude

● **Brightest ★ Mag −1 to 0**
● **Bright ★ Mag 1 to 2**
• **Average ★ Mag 2 to 3**
· **Faint ★ Mag 4 to 5**

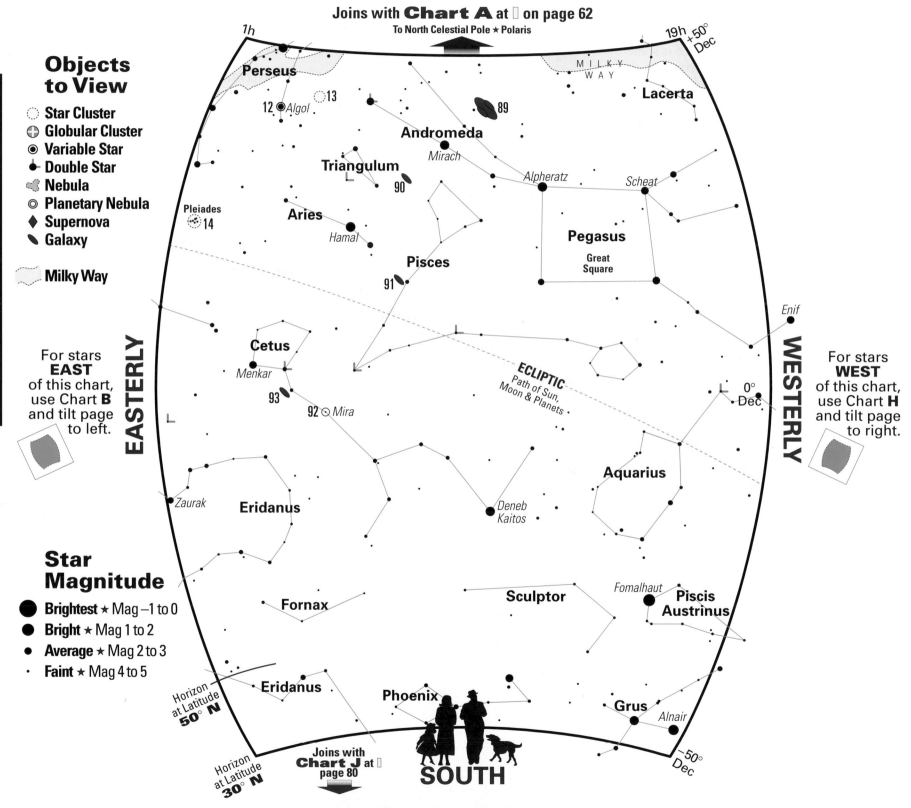

Perseus
12 ◉Algol  ◌13
Andromeda
*Mirach*
89
Lacerta
MILKY WAY

Triangulum
90
*Alpheratz*
*Scheat*

Pleiades
◌14
Aries
*Hamal*
Pisces
91

Pegasus
**Great Square**

Cetus
*Menkar*
93
92 ◉ *Mira*

**ECLIPTIC**
*Path of Sun, Moon & Planets*

*Enif*

0° Dec

*Zaurak*
Eridanus

Aquarius

*Deneb Kaitos*

Fornax
Sculptor
*Fomalhaut*
Piscis Austrinus

Eridanus
Phoenix
**SOUTH**
Grus
*Alnair*

Horizon at Latitude **50° N**
Horizon at Latitude **30° N**

Joins with **Chart J** at ▯ page 80

−50° Dec

Oct at 11:30 PM ★ **Nov at 9:30 PM** ★ Dec at 8 PM

# Chart I

## Constellation Lore

**Triangulum** the Triangle is believed to have represented the mathematical accomplishments of ancient Greece.

   **Aries** is the Ram with the golden fleece. King Athamas had two children by Nephele, the goddess of the Nebulous Cloud. After Nephele returned to Olympus (gods usually don't stay with mortals for long), Athamas took another wife, Ino, who disliked his children. She blamed a crop failure on them and convinced Athamas that the gods were angry at his children and that they had to be sacrificed for appeasement. The King was taken aback, but Ino had even convinced the local priests that this was necessary. Of course, the goddess Nephele saw all this from Olympus and planned a rescue for her children, Phrixos and Helle. A ram with a curly golden fleece would appear at the moment of sacrifice. They were to jump on and hold tight, for it was to fly them to safety. Nephele specified that the only thing they could not do while on the ram was to look down. Unfortunately, Helle did, and fell to the ocean. The place where she landed is now called Hellespont.

   **Pisces** represents the Fishes, transformations of Venus, the goddess of Love and Beauty, and Cupid, the god of Love. One day, Venus and Cupid were startled by Typhon, the monster-dragon who could live in fire but not water. To escape, they changed themselves into fishes and dove into the sea. To stay together, they tied themselves to a long line. The constellation represents two fishes connected by a v-shaped line.

   This section of the sky is inundated with water-related constellations. Eridanus, Cetus, Pisces, Aquarius and Capricornus are all next to each other. It is ironic that the constellations on or near the Milky Way are not water-related.

   To the Greeks and Romans, the stars were lights from the fires of the god's palaces shining through many holes in the fabric of the sky. Meteors were embers the gods threw down for amusement.

## Distance to Named Stars

| | |
|---|---|
| Alpheratz | 100 l.y. |
| Deneb Kaitos | 96 l.y. |
| Hamal | 66 l.y. |
| Menkar | 200 l.y. |
| Mira | 200 l.y. |
| Mirach | 170 l.y. |
| Fomalhaut | 22 l.y. |
| Scheat | 220 l.y. |

## Binocular & Telescope Objects

**89** GALAXIES M31, M32 and M110. M31 is the legendary Andromeda Galaxy, a sister to our own Milky Way Galaxy. It is the only galaxy that can be seen easily with the naked eyes (not counting the Small and Large Magellanic Clouds in the southern hemisphere). When you view M31 with binoculars or a telescope, what you actually see is the glow of the core. M32 and M110 are small elliptical companion galaxies next to M31. M32 is easy to spot and is not far for M31's core. On the "opposite" side of the core from M32 is the much fainter M110. See the photo on page 20 which shows all three galaxies. In pictures of M31, M32 overlaps onto the outer edge (arms) of the galaxy. However, visually through a telescope, *only* the core can be seen, so M32 appears as a fuzzy spot detached from the core. To the eyes, M31 appears as a very pale spot, often better seen using averted vision. It can be glimpsed in some light polluted skies. Distance to all three: 2.3 million l.y.. Diameters: 120,000 l.y., 6,000 l.y. & 15,000 l.y.. Arc sizes in sky: 3° x 2°, 9' & 22'. Mags: 3.4, 8 & 8. **M31 is a NAKED EYE, BINOCULARS and TELESCOPE object. The bright oval core is apparent but the surrounding arms are generally not seen. M32 appears brighter and closer to the core of M31 than M110. Both M32 and M110 appear as though they are on opposite sides of the core. Some advanced amateurs like using larger Newtonians (16-inch or larger) to find the brightest globular clusters around this galaxy.**

**90** Spiral GALAXY M33 is sometimes referred to as the Pinwheel Galaxy because it is almost "face on," so its arms look like the petals of a pinwheel. I have always had a hard time seeing this galaxy in a telescope, while others report no problems. Since it is almost face-on, its luminosity is low and spread over a large area. Dist: 2.3 million l.y.. Diameter: 47,500 l.y.. Arc diameter in sky: 1° 11' x 42'. Mag: 5.7. **TELESCOPE object that requires dark skies. Its location in the sky is easy to find but if you are like me, you may pass it by several times looking for a brighter object. It is a large object with very low luminosity. Start at 30x to 50x, no higher.**

**91** GALAXY M74, like M33 above, is a faint face-on spiral galaxy. Some have nicknamed this one "The Phantom" because of its elusiveness. Dist: 32 million l.y.. Diameter: 102,000 l.y.. Arc diameter in sky: 11'. Mag: 9. **Challenging TELESCOPE object. This faint galaxy is easy to locate because it is slightly more than a degree away from a "bright" star making up Pisces, but it is more difficult to see because its surface brightness is very low. Needs dark skies. Use 50x to 75x.**

**92** The famous VARIABLE STAR *Mira* was one of the first stars recognized to change in brightness by ancient civilizations. This long-term variable star has a cycle averaging 332 days. It stays faint, at magnitude 9, for most of the time and then flares up to magnitude 3.5 or brighter for a week or so. Consult astronomy periodicals for predicted flare-ups. **NAKED EYE monitoring.**

**93** GALAXY M77 is within one degree of the star *Delta (δ) Ceti* so it shares a placement similar to galaxy M74 above (object #91). Dist: 47 million l.y.. Diameter: 95,000 l.y.. Arc diameter in sky: 7'. Mag: 8.9. **Somewhat challenging TELESCOPE object. This face-on galaxy is brighter than M74. It is within one degree of a "bright" star making up Cetus. M77 appears as two "stars," with nebulosity around one, which actually is the galaxy's core, while the other is a star in our Milky Way Galaxy. Needs dark skies. Start with magnifications from 50x to 75x.**

(Continues and wraps to **Chart B**)

Chart I   Objects 89-93

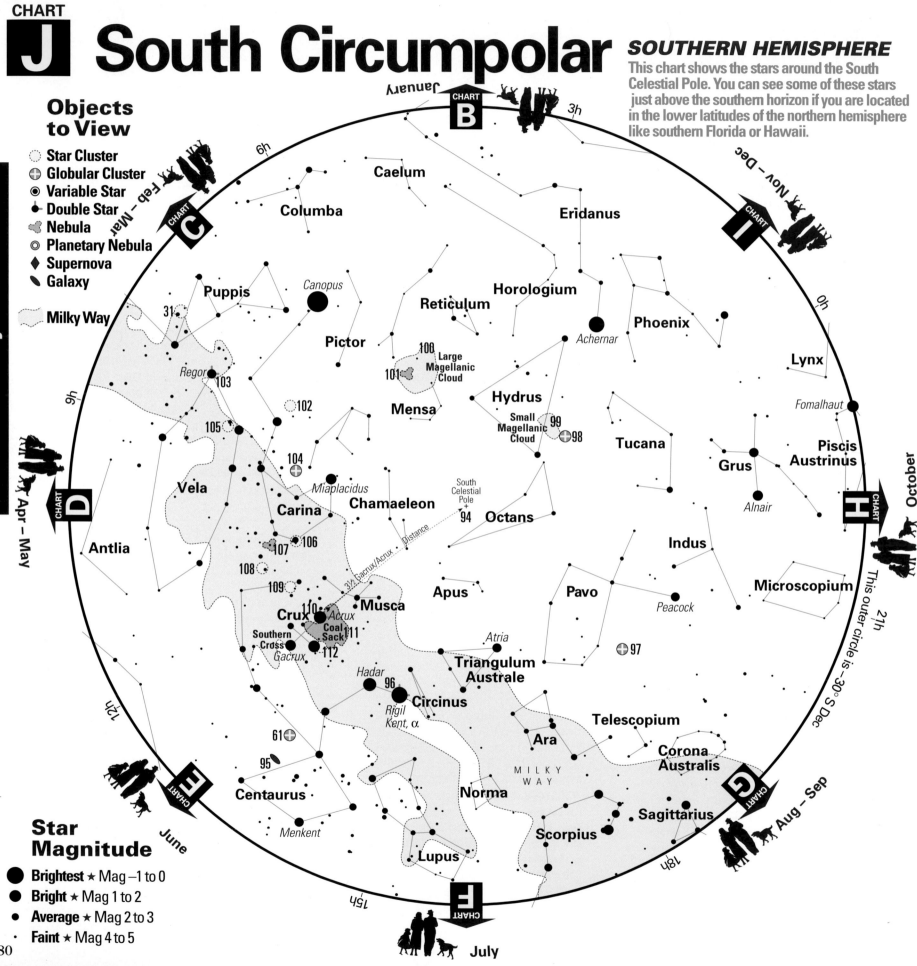

# CHART J South Circumpolar

## SOUTHERN HEMISPHERE

This chart shows the stars around the South Celestial Pole. You can see some of these stars just above the southern horizon if you are located in the lower latitudes of the northern hemisphere like southern Florida or Hawaii.

### Objects to View

- ○ Star Cluster
- ⊕ Globular Cluster
- ◉ Variable Star
- ● Double Star
- Nebula
- ◎ Planetary Nebula
- ◆ Supernova
- Galaxy
- Milky Way

**Chart J  Objects 94–112**

### Star Magnitude

- ● Brightest ★ Mag –1 to 0
- ● Bright ★ Mag 1 to 2
- • Average ★ Mag 2 to 3
- · Faint ★ Mag 4 to 5

January

CHART B

CHART C  Feb – Mar

CHART D  Apr – May

CHART E  June

CHART F  July

CHART G  Aug – Sep

October

CHART H

CHART I  Nov – Dec

3h

6h

9h

12h

15h

18h

21h

0h

This outer circle is –30° S. Dec

Caelum

Columba

Eridanus

Puppis

Canopus

Pictor

Reticulum

Horologium

Phoenix

Achernar

Lynx

31

Regor

103

Large Magellanic Cloud

100

101

Mensa

Hydrus

Small Magellanic Cloud

99

98

Tucana

Fomalhaut

Piscis Austrinus

102

105

Vela

104

Miaplacidus

Carina

Chamaeleon

South Celestial Pole

94

Octans

Grus

Alnair

Antlia

106

107

108

109

Apus

Indus

Microscopium

Pavo

Peacock

Musca

Crux

Acrux

110

Coal Sack

111

Southern Cross

Gacrux

112

Atria

Triangulum Australe

97

Hadar

96

Circinus

Rigil Kent, α

Telescopium

Corona Australis

61

Ara

95

Norma

Centaurus

Scorpius

Sagittarius

Menkent

Lupus

MILKY WAY

Distance

3½ Gacrux/Acrux

80

## Constellation Lore

There is no classical Greek and Roman mythology for the stars around the south celestial pole because the empires of these civilizations resided mostly in the mid-latitudes of the northern hemisphere, hence they never got to see these stars.

Obviously, the people of South America and southern Africa had lore associated with the stars in this area, but the patterns that prevailed were those drawn by early European explorers.

The Large and Small Magellanic Clouds, which are companion galaxies to our Milky Way Galaxy, were named in honor of Magellan for his voyage around the world that began in 1519. In 1596, Dutch explorer Pieter Dirckszoon Keyser constructed a dozen constellations, mostly named after animals and using brighter stars. Keyser's only inanimate constellation was Triangulum Australe. During the 1600s, Frenchman Augustin Royer created Cruz, the "Southern Cross," by breaking off part of the constellation Centaurus. Then in the 1750s, Frenchman Nicolas Louis de Lacaille, while on a respite at the Cape of Good Hope, constructed fourteen new constellations mostly based on scientific instruments and mainly using faint stars. Lacaille's patterns were the last to be recognized and many consider his to be clutter. His constellations were kept in recognition of contributions he made to astronomical cataloging.

## Distance to Named Stars

| Star | Distance |
|---|---|
| Achemar | 144 l.y. |
| Acrux | 510 l.y. |
| Alnair | 57 l.y. |
| Atria | 110 l.y. |
| Canopus | 74 l.y. |
| Fomalhaut | 22 l.y. |
| Gacrux | 120 l.y. |
| Hadar | 320 l.y. |
| Menkent | 50 l.y. |
| Miaplacidus | 111 l.y. |
| Peacock | 150 l.y. |
| Regor | 1,500 l.y. |
| Rigil Kent | 4 l.y. |

## Binocular & Telescope Objects

**94** There is no bright star at the SOUTH CELESTIAL POLE like there is in the north. Extend the longest length of Cruz, the "Southern Cross," 3.5 times to get close to the "down under" celestial pole.

**(61)** GLOBULAR CLUSTER, NGC 5139, is the largest in our galaxy and brightest in the sky. Designated and called *Omega (ω) Centauri*. To the naked eye, this looks like a faint 5th magnitude star and was identified as such by the ancient Egyptians. In the sky, it has an arc size of 53', almost two Moon diameters. It is estimated to contain a million stars. Dist: 18,000 l.y.. Diameter: 281 l.y.. **Beautiful sight in BINOCULARS or TELESCOPE! Easy to find, but very low in northern hemisphere skies. Start at 50x.**

**95** "Centaurus A" GALAXY, NGC 5128. Dist: 23 million l.y.. Diameter: 120,000 l.y.. Arc width in sky: 18'. Mag: 7. **Use TELESCOPE starting at 50x. Big & round.**

**96** *Rigil Kent*, at magnitude –0.3, is the closest, brightest star in the sky, at a little more than 4 l.y. away. **NAKED EYE.**

**97** GLOBULAR CLUSTER, NGC 6752. Dist: 17,000 l.y.. Diameter: 208 l.y.. Arc width in sky: 42'. Mag: 5. **Use BINOCULARS or TELESCOPE starting at 50x.**

**98** Well-known *47 Tucanae* GLOBULAR CLUSTER, NGC 104. Dist: 16,000 l.y.. Diameter: 205 l.y.. Arc width in sky: 44'. Mag: 5. **Use BINOCULARS or TELESCOPE. Large & bright, start at 50x.**

**99 & 100** SMALL and LARGE MAGELLANIC CLOUDS (SMC & LMC respectively) are nearby companion galaxies to ours. Dist: 195,000 & 160,000 l.y.. Span: 14,000 & 18,000 l.y.. Arc widths in sky: 4° & 6.5°. **NAKED EYE, BINOCULARS or TELESCOPE objects.**

**101** "Tarantula" NEBULA, NGC 2070. Distance: 160,000 l.y.. Width: 1,860 l.y.. Arc width in sky: 40'. Magnitude: 5. **Use BINOCULARS or TELESCOPE.**

**102** Large open CLUSTER of stars, NGC 2516. Dist: 1,300 l.y.. Width: 11 l.y.. Arc width in sky: 30'. Mag: 3.8. **Use BINOCULARS or TELESCOPE.**

**(31)** Large open CLUSTER, NGC 2477. Dist: 4,200 l.y.. Width: 33 l.y.. Arc width in sky: 27'. Mag: 6. **Use BINOCULARS or TELESCOPE.**

**103** *Regor* is actually 4 stars. **Use TELESCOPE starting at 50x.**

**104** GLOBULAR CLUSTER, NGC 2808. Dist: 30,000 l.y.. Diameter: 166 l.y.. Arc width in sky: 19'. Mag: 6. **Use BINOCULARS or TELESCOPE starting at 50x.**

**105** Large naked-eye CLUSTER, IC 2391. Dist: 600 l.y.. Spans: 21 l.y.. Arc size in sky: 2°. Mag: 2.5. **NAKED EYE, BINOCULARS or TELESCOPE.**

**106** "Southern Pleiades" CLUSTER, IC 2602. Fainter version of northern counterpart. Dist: 480 l.y.. Spans: 8 l.y.. Arc size in sky: 60'. Mag: 1.9. **Use BINOCULARS or TELESCOPE.**

**107** Favorite *Eta Carinae* STAR & NEBULA, NGC 3372. Dist: 6,000 l.y.. Spans: 210 l.y.. Arc size in sky: 2°. Mag: 3. **Use BINOCULARS or TELESCOPE.**

**108** CLUSTER, NGC 3532, pretty sprinkle of stars. Dist: 1,300 l.y.. Spans: 11 l.y.. Arc width in sky: 30'. Mag: 3. **Use BINOCULARS or TELESCOPE.**

**109** CLUSTER, NGC 3766. Dist: 5,500 l.y.. Spans: 19 l.y.. Arc size in sky: 12'. Mag: 5. **Use BINOCULARS or TELESCOPE.**

**110** TRIPLE STAR *Acrux*. The two brightest are very close, third much fainter and farther away. **Use TELESCOPE starting at 50x.**

**111** "Coal Sack" DARK NEBULA extends over 7° or 14 Moon diameters. **NAKED EYE, BINOCULARS or TELESCOPE.**

**112** Southern "Jewel Box" CLUSTER, NGC 4755 with a red star. Dist: 7,600 l.y.. Spans: 22 l.y.. Arc size in sky: 10'. Mag: 4. **Use TELESCOPE starting at 50x.**
*Note: The northern Jewel Box, indicated on charts F & G, is in the constellation Scorpius.*

# Observing the Moon

Although we still can't book flights to the Moon, it's possible to experience the rush of flying over its surface! You can accomplish this on a night when the Moon is less than full and using maximum telescope magnifications — anywhere from 200x to 400x depending on your scope and atmospheric conditions. View the area around the "line" that separates the lighted from the dark side. I guarantee that you will feel like you are there, looking down into craters. The picture on page 13, of the Moon's craters with Earth floating above provides a realistic view of what you can expect from a telescope.

## The Moon can be seen during the day!

When I drove around with my two year old daughter during the day, I often pointed the Moon out to her, visible as a white phase against the blue daytime sky. Regularly after that, and to my surprise, she would stretch out her arm, point her finger, and say as only a two-year-old can, "Moooon." Her ability to find the Moon during the day became uncanny. Once, I told her, "No, that's not the Moon"; but on closer inspection, I realized that she was right.

When you start noticing the Moon during the day, you will see it there often. In fact, about the only time you cannot see the Moon during the day is around New and Full Moon. From New Moon to Full Moon, the Moon trails the Sun. From Full Moon to New Moon, it precedes the Sun.

## Front and back sides

Why does the same side of the Moon always face the Earth? Because the Moon's rotation on its axis is synchronized with its revolution around the Earth. This is not a coincidence. Tidal and other forces have "locked in" one side of the Moon so it always faces the Earth. What's on the other side? The "back" side of the Moon is almost completely covered with craters. There are a few small maria (dark plains), but they are indistinct. The Earth-facing side is *by far* the more interesting side.

## Name calling

There is probably more lore associated with the Moon than any other celestial body. Every culture has its myths and traditions; however, the Moon's most important

impact has been the division of the year into months.

In the past, the Full Moon was given 12 nicknames (see table on next page), one for each month of the year. Today, only one is widely known — the "Harvest Moon" which is the Full Moon closest to the Autumnal Equinox (about September 23). What makes this Full Moon special? At one time it had significance to farmers who needed extra time (light) for harvesting crops (go outside around Full Moon and see how much the Moon lights up the night). During this time of the year, the Moon's orbit has a shallow angle to the horizon, so its rising time on consecutive nights is only 25 minutes later each day compared to an average of 50 minutes. This allows for a Full or near Full Moon to rise at nearly the same time over successive nights, providing convenient light for outdoor work. Although this phenomenon offers little benefit to modern society, it is one of the few remaining links to our immediate past.

The origin of the phrase "Once in a Blue Moon" is uncertain, but it means "very seldom." The modern-day definition of a Blue Moon refers to the occurrence of two Full Moons in a month. This happens about once every three years. In the past, when the Moon had 12 nicknames, "Blue Moon" was the name given to the third Full Moon in a season (winter, spring, fall or summer) that had four Full Moons. A season, which spans three months, normally has three Full Moons. On average, there are 12 Full Moons in a year, but because the lunar cycle is 29 days, which is less than most months, occasionally there are years that squeeze in 13 Full Moons. Our farming ancestors were attuned to the seasons, so a year with 13 Full Moons meant that one of the seasons would get a fourth Full Moon. For some unknown reason, they settled on calling the third Full Moon the Blue Moon instead of the fourth one.

What about the Man in the Moon? The darker plains (maria) and the lighter cratered areas (terrae) have given rise to people seeing a host of figures on its surface. These include a rabbit, donkey, jack-o'-lantern, woman, man, and a girl reading. Let me note that seeing these figures or any other requires a bit of imagination, so let your mind go!

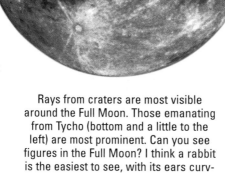

Rays from craters are most visible around the Full Moon. Those emanating from Tycho (bottom and a little to the left) are most prominent. Can you see figures in the Full Moon? I think a rabbit is the easiest to see, with its ears curving back along the left outer edge.

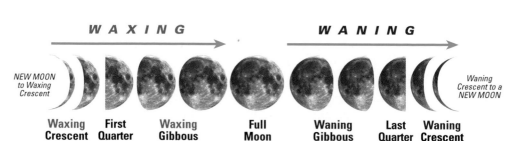

*WAXING*

*WANING*

NEW MOON to Waxing Crescent

Waning Crescent to a NEW MOON

| Waxing Crescent | First Quarter | Waxing Gibbous | Full Moon | Waning Gibbous | Last Quarter | Waning Crescent |

## OBSERVING the Moon, Generally

### Phases

The Moon cycles through phases as it orbits Earth every 29 days. When we see a phase, we are viewing nothing more than its day and night sides at the same time. Like Earth, the Moon always has a day and a night side (even when full). And because the Moon revolves around the Earth, we get to see it from angles that allow us to view both sides at once.

The **First Quarter Moon** rises at noon and sets at midnight. It trails the Sun and can be seen during the day from noon to sunset.

The **Full Moon** rises at sunset and sets at sunrise. It cannot be seen in the daytime.

The **Last or Third Quarter Moon** rises at midnight and sets at noon. It precedes the Sun and is visible during the day from sunrise to noon.

The **New Moon** is not visible at night, nor during the day. Use this time to take advantage of the dark sky and observe star clusters, nebulae and galaxies.

### Through a telescope

The best time to observe the Moon is when it is not full, but during its waxing and waning phases. Waxing means "adding on" and waning means "subtracting from." The terminator, the "line" separating the lighted side from the dark side (the day side from the night side) is present when the Moon is waxing and waning. Craters appear at their best or sharpest when near the terminator because the contrast from shadows make them more pronounced. Magnifications from 40x to 250x or higher are recommended. The Moon is disappointing to observe around Full Moon because its entire surface gets "washed out" from direct sunlight. However, at this time, the rays of craters are most pronounced, especially Tycho's which stretch halfway across the surface.

Want to observe the dark or night side of the Moon? This side of the Moon is slightly lighted by reflected light from Earth, called earthshine. Some features on the dark side are visible in a telescope, especially when the Moon is a crescent. Try it — it's a pretty sight!

**Moon beams**. Any telescope concentrates lots of light when focused on the Moon, which can easily strain your eye unless you use an eyepiece filter (these screw into threads at the bottom of the barrel) to reduce the intensity. A common practice is to purchase two polarizing filters, **A**, which are rotated against each other to vary the amount of light passing through, **B** and **C**. Or you can purchase a neutral density filter, **D** that cuts down light transmission by a specified amount. Note: Some inexpensive eyepieces are not threaded to accept filters.

## Major Moon features

The Moon's surface has brighter cratered highlands called terrae and smoother darker plains known as maria. Most of the Moon's craters were formed from meteoroid or cometary impacts during its early history, from 3.8 to 4 billion years ago. The maria are a result of lava flow and appear darker than the terrae because of higher iron content. They are a little more than three billion years old. The Moon is no longer geologically active.

**Craters.** Huge bowl-like depressions on the Moon. All of the craters on the Moon were formed from meteoroid or cometary impact. Most of these impacts occurred during the early history of the solar system.

**Rays.** Bright streaks that radiate from some craters. They result from the ejection of reflective material during the formation of craters (from a cometary or meteoroid impact). They are most pronounced around the Full Moon. The crater Tycho has the longest rays, spanning one-quarter of the globe. It is estimated that rayed craters are less than one billion years old because the rays of older craters have been eroded by micrometeorites (sand-size meteoroids).

**Maria.** A term coined by Galileo meaning "seas." Maria are the darker, smoother areas of the Moon and represent 16% of its surface. Almost all of the maria are on the hemisphere facing Earth. They are on average 500 to 600 feet thick. The maria are the result of impacts from large asteroids or comets creating fractures to the once molten interior and releasing basalt lava, which flowed upward and outward to create the great plains.

**Rille.** A long cliff or split in the maria, up to hundreds of miles in length. Rilles are easy to see in a telescope. They are the result of cracks, fractures or collapses in the maria.

**Terminator.** The border or "line" separating the lighted side from the dark side. The terminator is absent during Full Moon. Craters appear at their sharpest near the terminator.

**Regolith.** A fine grained "soil" that covers the surface of the Moon. Created from the bombardment of the surface by micrometeorites, the regolith varies in depth from 6 to 26 feet in the maria, and to a possible 50 feet in the highlands. The micrometeorites that bombard Earth, however, burn up in the atmosphere.

| Monthly Moon Names | | |
|---|---|---|
| | *Recent Almanac* | *Other Names* |
| **January** | Wolf | Old, Moon After Yule |
| **February** | Snow | Hunger, Storm |
| **March** | Worm | Crust, Chaste, Crow |
| **April** | Pink | Seed, Awakening |
| **May** | Flower | Hare, Milk |
| **June** | Strawberry | Rose |
| **July** | Buck | Mead, Hay, Thunder |
| **August** | Sturgeon | Corn, Lightening |
| **September** | Harvest | Barley, Fruit |
| **October** | Hunter's | Blood |
| **November** | Beaver | Snow, Frosty |
| **December** | Cold | Moon Before Yule |

# Observing the Moon

## Named Craters

| | | |
|---|---|---|
| 1 Abenezra | 31 Capella | 61 Godin |
| 2 Abulfeda | 32 Cassini | 62 Guericke |
| 3 Agrippa | 33 Catharina | 63 Gutenberg |
| 4 Albategnius | 34 Cepheus | 64 Hainzel |
| 5 Alexander | 35 Cichus | 65 Halley |
| 6 Aliacensis | 36 Clavius | 66 Hell |
| 7 Almanon | 37 Cleomedes | 67 Hercules |
| 8 Alpetragius | 38 Colombo | 68 Herschel |
| 9 Alphonsus | 39 Copernicus | 69 Hipparchus |
| 10 Anaxagoras | 40 Cuvier | 70 Hommel |
| 11 Anaximenes | 41 Cyrillus | 71 Horrocks |
| 12 Apianus | 42 Delambre | 72 Huggins |
| 13 Archimedes | 43 Democritus | 73 Isidorus |
| 14 Aristarchus | 44 Deslandres | |
| 15 Aristillus | 45 Dionysius | |
| 16 Aristoteles | 46 Endymion | |
| 17 Arzachel | 47 Epigenes | |
| 18 Atlas | 48 Eratosthenes | |
| 19 Azophi | 49 Eudoxus | |
| 20 Ball | 50 Fermat | |
| 21 Barrow | 51 Fernelius | |
| 22 Bianchini | 52 Firmicus | |
| 23 Blancanus | 53 Flammarion | |
| 24 Bonpland | 54 Fracastorius | |
| 25 Boscovich | 55 Franklin | |
| 26 Buch | 56 Gassendi | |
| 27 Bullialdus | 57 Gauricus | |
| 28 Bürg | 58 Geber | |
| 29 La Caille | 59 Geminus | |
| 30 Campanus | 60 Goclenius | |

## Maria ★ Oceans, Seas, Lakes & Channels

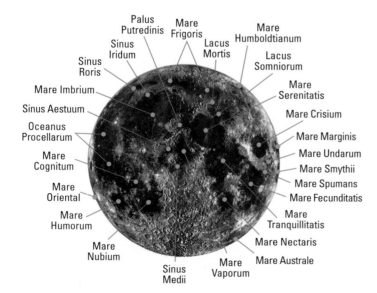

Palus Putredinis
Mare Frigoris
Sinus Iridum
Lacus Mortis
Mare Humboldtianum
Sinus Roris
Lacus Somniorum
Mare Imbrium
Mare Serenitatis
Sinus Aestuum
Mare Crisium
Oceanus Procellarum
Mare Marginis
Mare Cognitum
Mare Undarum
Mare Smythii
Mare Oriental
Mare Spumans
Mare Humorum
Mare Fecunditatis
Mare Tranquillitatis
Mare Nubium
Mare Nectaris
Sinus Medii
Mare Vaporum
Mare Australe

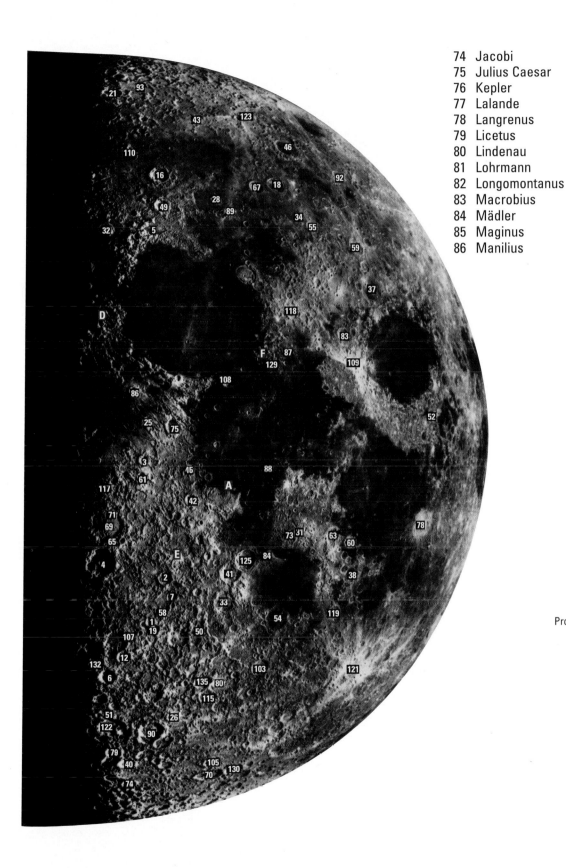

## Named Craters

| | | | | | |
|---|---|---|---|---|---|
| 74 | Jacobi | 87 | Maraldi | 116 | Regiomontanus |
| 75 | Julius Caesar | 88 | Maskelyne | 117 | Rhaeticus |
| 76 | Kepler | 89 | Mason | 118 | Römer |
| 77 | Lalande | 90 | Maurolycus | 119 | Santbech |
| 78 | Langrenus | 91 | Mercator | 120 | Saussure |
| 79 | Licetus | 92 | Mercurius | 121 | Stevinus |
| 80 | Lindenau | 93 | Meton | 122 | Stöfler |
| 81 | Lohrmann | 94 | Moretus | 123 | Strabo |
| 82 | Longomontanus | 95 | Mösting | 124 | Thebit |
| 83 | Macrobius | 96 | Murchison | 125 | Theophilus |
| 84 | Mädler | 97 | Nasireddin | 126 | Timocharis |
| 85 | Maginus | 98 | Nonius | 127 | Triesnecker |
| 86 | Manilius | 99 | Orontius | 128 | Tycho |
| | | 100 | Parrot | 129 | Vitruvius |
| | | 101 | Parry | 130 | Vlacq |
| | | 102 | Philolaus | 131 | Walter |
| | | 103 | Piccolomini | 132 | Werner |
| | | 104 | Pitatus | 133 | Wilhelm |
| | | 105 | Pitiscus | 134 | Wurzelbauer |
| | | 106 | Plato | 135 | Zagut |
| | | 107 | Playfair | | |
| | | 108 | Plinius | | |
| | | 109 | Proclus | | |
| | | 110 | Protagoras | | |
| | | 111 | Ptolemaeus | | |
| | | 112 | Purbach | | |
| | | 113 | Pythagoras | | |
| | | 114 | Pytheas | | |
| | | 115 | Rabbi Levi | | |

## Landing Sites

A  Apollo 11 • July 1969
B  Apollo 12 • Nov 1969
C  Apollo 14 • Feb 1971
D  Apollo 15 • July 1971
E  Apollo 16 • Apr 1972
F  Apollo 17 • Dec 1972

## Mountain Ranges & Associated Features

Montes Recti *"Straight Range"*
Promontorium Laplace
Promontorium Heraclides
Montes Alpes
Montes Teneriffe
Montes Spitzbergensis
Montes Jura
Montes Apenninus
Montes Caucasus
Montes Harbinge
Montes Taurus
Montes Carpatus
Montes Haemus
Montes Rook
Rupes Altai
Montes Riphaeus
Rupes Recta *"Straight Wall"*
Vallis Snellius
Vallis Rheita

# Moon Phases 2002 to 2017

The following tables indicate the dates of Moon phases based on Mountain Standard Time. Overall, these dates are accurate for all North American time zones, but a few dates could be off by one day if you reside in a time zone east of Mountain. Additionally, the appearance of First Quarter, Full and Last Quarter Moons may vary slightly from month to month because the actual moment of a phase can occur at different times of the day. For example, if the actual time of a phase is 1 A.M., you may not view it until 8 P.M. that day, which is 19 hours later. This can cause a quarter Moon to look a little more or less like a half phase.

Eclipses can happen only at the New Moon or Full Moon. See the table on page 91 for dates of these events.

## 2002

| | Jan | Feb | Mar | Apr | May | Jun | Jul | Aug | Sep | Oct | Nov | Dec |
|---|---|---|---|---|---|---|---|---|---|---|---|---|
| New ● | 13 | 12 | 13 | 12 | 12 | 10 | 10 | 8 | 6 | 6 | 4 | 4 |
| First Qtr. ☽ | 21 | 20 | 21 | 20 | 19 | 17 | 16 | 15 | 13 | 12 | 11 | 11 |
| Full ○ | 28 | 27 | 28 | 26 | 26 | 24 | 24 | 22 | 21 | 21 | 19 | 19 |
| Last Qtr. ☾ | 5 | 4 | 5 | 4 | 4 | 2 | 2 | 1/30 | 29 | 28 | 27 | 26 |

## 2003

| | Jan | Feb | Mar | Apr | May | Jun | Jul | Aug | Sep | Oct | Nov | Dec |
|---|---|---|---|---|---|---|---|---|---|---|---|---|
| New ● | 2 | 1 | 2 | 1 | 1/30 | 29 | 29 | 27 | 25 | 25 | 23 | 23 |
| First Qtr. ☽ | 10 | 9 | 11 | 9 | 9 | 7 | 6 | 5 | 3 | 2/31 | 30 | 30 |
| Full ○ | 19 | 18 | 16 | 18 | 15 | 14 | 13 | 11 | 10 | 10 | 8 | 8 |
| Last Qtr. ☾ | 25 | 23 | 24 | 23 | 22 | 21 | 21 | 19 | 18 | 18 | 16 | 16 |

## 2004

| | Jan | Feb | Mar | Apr | May | Jun | Jul | Aug | Sep | Oct | Nov | Dec |
|---|---|---|---|---|---|---|---|---|---|---|---|---|
| New ● | 21 | 20 | 20 | 19 | 18 | 17 | 17 | 15 | 14 | 13 | 12 | 11 |
| First Qtr. ☽ | 28 | 27 | 28 | 27 | 27 | 25 | 24 | 23 | 21 | 20 | 18 | 18 |
| Full ○ | 7 | 6 | 6 | 5 | 4 | 2 | 2/31 | 29 | 28 | 27 | 26 | 26 |
| Last Qtr. ☾ | 14 | 13 | 13 | 11 | 11 | 9 | 9 | 7 | 6 | 6 | 4 | 4 |

## 2005

| | Jan | Feb | Mar | Apr | May | Jun | Jul | Aug | Sep | Oct | Nov | Dec |
|---|---|---|---|---|---|---|---|---|---|---|---|---|
| New ● | 10 | 8 | 10 | 8 | 8 | 6 | 6 | 4 | 3 | 3 | 1 | 1/31 |
| First Qtr. ☽ | 16 | 15 | 17 | 16 | 16 | 14 | 14 | 12 | 11 | 10 | 8 | 8 |
| Full ○ | 25 | 23 | 25 | 24 | 23 | 21 | 21 | 19 | 17 | 17 | 15 | 15 |
| Last Qtr. ☾ | 3 | 2 | 3 | 1/30 | 30 | 28 | 27 | 26 | 24 | 24 | 23 | 23 |

## 2006

| | Jan | Feb | Mar | Apr | May | Jun | Jul | Aug | Sep | Oct | Nov | Dec |
|---|---|---|---|---|---|---|---|---|---|---|---|---|
| New ● | 29 | 27 | 29 | 27 | 26 | 25 | 24 | 23 | 22 | 21 | 20 | 20 |
| First Qtr. ☽ | 6 | 4 | 6 | 5 | 4 | 3 | 3 | 2/31 | 30 | 29 | 27 | 27 |
| Full ○ | 14 | 12 | 14 | 13 | 13 | 11 | 10 | 9 | 7 | 6 | 5 | 4 |
| Last Qtr. ☾ | 22 | 21 | 22 | 20 | 20 | 18 | 17 | 15 | 14 | 13 | 12 | 12 |

## 2007

| | Jan | Feb | Mar | Apr | May | Jun | Jul | Aug | Sep | Oct | Nov | Dec |
|---|---|---|---|---|---|---|---|---|---|---|---|---|
| New ● | 18 | 17 | 18 | 17 | 16 | 14 | 14 | 12 | 11 | 10 | 9 | 9 |
| First Qtr. ☽ | 25 | 24 | 25 | 23 | 23 | 22 | 21 | 20 | 19 | 19 | 17 | 17 |
| Full ○ | 3 | 1 | 3 | 2 | 2/31 | 30 | 30 | 28 | 26 | 25 | 24 | 23 |
| Last Qtr. ☾ | 11 | 10 | 11 | 10 | 9 | 8 | 7 | 5 | 3 | 3 | 1 | 1/31 |

## 2008

| | Jan | Feb | Mar | Apr | May | Jun | Jul | Aug | Sep | Oct | Nov | Dec |
|---|---|---|---|---|---|---|---|---|---|---|---|---|
| New ● | 8 | 6 | 7 | 5 | 5 | 3 | 2 | 1/30 | 29 | 28 | 27 | 27 |
| First Qtr. ☽ | 15 | 13 | 14 | 12 | 11 | 10 | 9 | 8 | 7 | 7 | 5 | 5 |
| Full ○ | 22 | 20 | 21 | 20 | 19 | 18 | 18 | 16 | 15 | 14 | 12 | 12 |
| Last Qtr. ☾ | 29 | 28 | 29 | 28 | 27 | 26 | 25 | 23 | 21 | 21 | 19 | 19 |

## 2009

| | Jan | Feb | Mar | Apr | May | Jun | Jul | Aug | Sep | Oct | Nov | Dec |
|---|---|---|---|---|---|---|---|---|---|---|---|---|
| New ● | 26 | 24 | 26 | 24 | 24 | 22 | 21 | 20 | 18 | 17 | 16 | 16 |
| First Qtr. ☽ | 4 | 2 | 4 | 2 | 1/30 | 29 | 28 | 27 | 25 | 25 | 24 | 24 |
| Full ○ | 10 | 9 | 10 | 9 | 8 | 7 | 7 | 5 | 4 | 3 | 2 | 2/31 |
| Last Qtr. ☾ | 17 | 16 | 18 | 17 | 17 | 15 | 15 | 13 | 11 | 11 | 9 | 8 |

## 2010

| | Jan | Feb | Mar | Apr | May | Jun | Jul | Aug | Sep | Oct | Nov | Dec |
|---|---|---|---|---|---|---|---|---|---|---|---|---|
| New ● | 15 | 13 | 15 | 14 | 13 | 12 | 11 | 9 | 8 | 7 | 5 | 5 |
| First Qtr. ☽ | 23 | 21 | 23 | 21 | 20 | 18 | 18 | 16 | 14 | 14 | 13 | 13 |
| Full ○ | 29 | 28 | 29 | 28 | 27 | 26 | 25 | 24 | 23 | 22 | 21 | 21 |
| Last Qtr. ☾ | 7 | 5 | 7 | 6 | 5 | 4 | 4 | 2 | 1/30 | 30 | 28 | 28 |

## 2011

| | Jan | Feb | Mar | Apr | May | Jun | Jul | Aug | Sep | Oct | Nov | Dec |
|---|---|---|---|---|---|---|---|---|---|---|---|---|
| New ● | 4 | 2 | 4 | 3 | 2 | 1 | 1/30 | 28 | 27 | 26 | 24 | 24 |
| First Qtr. ☽ | 12 | 11 | 12 | 11 | 10 | 8 | 7 | 6 | 4 | 3 | 2 | 2/31 |
| Full ○ | 19 | 18 | 19 | 17 | 17 | 15 | 14 | 13 | 12 | 11 | 10 | 10 |
| Last Qtr. ☾ | 26 | 24 | 26 | 24 | 24 | 23 | 22 | 21 | 20 | 19 | 18 | 17 |

## 2012

| | Jan | Feb | Mar | Apr | May | Jun | Jul | Aug | Sep | Oct | Nov | Dec |
|---|---|---|---|---|---|---|---|---|---|---|---|---|
| New ● | 23 | 21 | 22 | 21 | 20 | 19 | 18 | 17 | 15 | 15 | 13 | 13 |
| First Qtr. ☽ | 30 | 29 | 30 | 29 | 28 | 26 | 26 | 24 | 22 | 21 | 20 | 19 |
| Full ○ | 9 | 7 | 8 | 6 | 5 | 4 | 3 | 1/31 | 29 | 29 | 28 | 28 |
| Last Qtr. ☾ | 16 | 14 | 14 | 13 | 12 | 11 | 10 | 9 | 8 | 8 | 6 | 6 |

## 2013

| | Jan | Feb | Mar | Apr | May | Jun | Jul | Aug | Sep | Oct | Nov | Dec |
|---|---|---|---|---|---|---|---|---|---|---|---|---|
| New ● | 11 | 10 | 11 | 10 | 9 | 8 | 8 | 6 | 5 | 4 | 3 | 2 |
| First Qtr. ☽ | 18 | 17 | 2/31 | 19 | 17 | 18 | 15 | 14 | 12 | 11 | 9 | 9 |
| Full ○ | 26 | 25 | 27 | 25 | 24 | 23 | 22 | 20 | 19 | 18 | 17 | 17 |
| Last Qtr. ☾ | 4 | 3 | 4 | 2 | 2/31 | 29 | 29 | 28 | 26 | 26 | 25 | 25 |

## 2014

| | Jan | Feb | Mar | Apr | May | Jun | Jul | Aug | Sep | Oct | Nov | Dec |
|---|---|---|---|---|---|---|---|---|---|---|---|---|
| New ● | 1/30 | – | 1/30 | 28 | 28 | 27 | 26 | 25 | 23 | 23 | 22 | 21 |
| First Qtr. ☽ | 7 | 6 | 8 | 7 | 6 | 5 | 5 | 3 | 2 | 1/30 | 29 | 28 |
| Full ○ | 15 | 14 | 16 | 15 | 14 | 12 | 12 | 10 | 8 | 8 | 6 | 6 |
| Last Qtr. ☾ | 23 | 22 | 23 | 22 | 21 | 19 | 18 | 17 | 15 | 15 | 14 | 14 |

## 2015

| | Jan | Feb | Mar | Apr | May | Jun | Jul | Aug | Sep | Oct | Nov | Dec |
|---|---|---|---|---|---|---|---|---|---|---|---|---|
| New ● | 20 | 18 | 20 | 18 | 17 | 16 | 15 | 14 | 12 | 12 | 11 | 11 |
| First Qtr. ☽ | 26 | 25 | 27 | 25 | 25 | 24 | 23 | 22 | 21 | 20 | 18 | 18 |
| Full ○ | 4 | 3 | 5 | 4 | 3 | 2 | 1/31 | 29 | 27 | 27 | 25 | 25 |
| Last Qtr. ☾ | 13 | 11 | 13 | 11 | 11 | 9 | 8 | 6 | 5 | 4 | 3 | 3 |

## 2016

| | Jan | Feb | Mar | Apr | May | Jun | Jul | Aug | Sep | Oct | Nov | Dec |
|---|---|---|---|---|---|---|---|---|---|---|---|---|
| New ● | 9 | 8 | 8 | 7 | 6 | 4 | 4 | 2 | 1/30 | 30 | 29 | 28 |
| First Qtr. ☽ | 16 | 15 | 15 | 13 | 13 | 12 | 11 | 10 | 9 | 8 | 7 | 7 |
| Full ○ | 23 | 22 | 23 | 21 | 21 | 20 | 19 | 18 | 16 | 15 | 14 | 13 |
| Last Qtr. ☾ | 1/31 | – | 1/31 | 29 | 29 | 27 | 26 | 24 | 23 | 22 | 21 | 20 |

## 2017

| | Jan | Feb | Mar | Apr | May | Jun | Jul | Aug | Sep | Oct | Nov | Dec |
|---|---|---|---|---|---|---|---|---|---|---|---|---|
| New ● | 27 | 26 | 27 | 26 | 25 | 23 | 23 | 21 | 19 | 19 | 18 | 17 |
| First Qtr. ☽ | 5 | 3 | 5 | 2 | 2 | 1/30 | 30 | 29 | 27 | 27 | 26 | 26 |
| Full ○ | 12 | 10 | 12 | 10 | 10 | 9 | 8 | 7 | 6 | 5 | 3 | 3 |
| Last Qtr. ☾ | 19 | 18 | 20 | 19 | 18 | 17 | 16 | 14 | 12 | 12 | 10 | 10 |

# Safely Observing the Sun

Observing the Sun can be fun and rewarding, but strict safety precautions must be taken to avoid eye and other injuries, because there may be no cure for these!

## SAFELY OBSERVING the Sun with SOLAR FILTERS

There is only one safe way to view the Sun with a telescope, and that is to use a solar filter that completely covers the front of the telescope. *All other types of filters or methods are dangerous.*

Solar filters can be purchased at your local telescope store or through retailers that advertise in the popular monthly astronomy magazines. DO NOT attempt to make your own filter. Solar filters transmit about 1/100,000 of the Sun's light and filter out harmful rays. The photo to the right shows a telescope properly fitted with a solar filter for safely viewing the Sun.

Once the filter is fastened securely to the front of the telescope, use the telescope in a normal fashion. **IMPORTANT**: Remember to cover up your finderscope or reflex-sight finder — better yet, remove it! These also present viewing hazards and/or can be damaged by the Sun if they are not covered. To point the telescope at the Sun, use the telescope's shadow as your guide. Move the telescope until the shadow of its tube is smallest. The Sun should then be in or near your eyepiece view.

## Observing the Sun

The Sun emits so much energy that many of its features are overpowered by its brilliance. With a regular, white-light solar filter, only the photosphere and sunspots are visible. A special hydrogen-alpha filter is required to view prominences.

**Sunspots.** Sunspots are plainly visible with a regular, white-light solar filter (priced less than $100 for smaller telescopes). These spots form, grow and dissipate, rotating with the Sun, changing their position and appearance daily. The inner and darkest part of a sunspot is called the umbra, while the surrounding lighter area is called the penumbra. Sunspots often appear in groups composed of many larger and smaller spots.

About every 11 years, there is a period of heightened sunspot activity; however, the period of this cycle can vary by a few years. The first peak of the 21st century occurred in the year 2000.

**Prominences.** In order to view prominences, telescopes must be fitted with a special hydrogen-alpha filter. Unfortunately, these filters are expensive, starting at about $1,000.

Hydrogen-alpha filters transmit only a very narrow range of light on the red end of the spectrum where prominences are visible. Prominences cannot be seen with regular white-light solar filters because they get "washed out" among all the other colors that these filters transmit. Without a hydrogen-alpha filter, prominences can sometimes be seen around the edge of the Moon during a total solar eclipse.

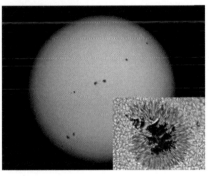

**Top left**. Sunspots are about 4,000°F cooler than the average surface temperature of 10,000°F. The pictured Sun is typical of the view through a small telescope using a white-light solar filter. The inset shows an enlargement of a single sunspot. **Top right**. A refractor telescope properly fitted with a white-light solar filter that completely covers the front lens. Note that the reflex-sight finder is covered with an orange plastic cap to avoid damage from the Sun.

The hydrogen-alpha filter provides incredible views of the Sun. Not only will you see prominences, but also the Sun's mottled surface. Changes in prominences can be seen in as little as 15 minutes. I highly recommend making inquires at your local planetarium or telescope store about the possibility of observing the Sun through a hydrogen-alpha filter. Some daytime astronomy events feature telescopes equipped with these filters.

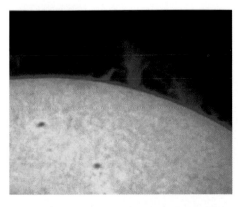

**Far left.** A telescope outfitted with a hydrogen-alpha filter manufactured by the leaders in the field, Coronado Instruments, located in Tucson, Arizona. This type of filter has front and rear parts.

**Left.** A picture of the Sun taken by Vincent Chan of Hong Kong through a Coronado Instruments hydrogen-alpha filter.

# Glorious Eclipses

A total solar eclipse is one of the most spectacular natural events to behold. Those who witness them consider themselves fortunate. They carry an indelible impression that is visual as well as emotional. It is disheartening that most people never experience one of the greatest astronomical and sensory events on our planet.

It is an incredible coincidence that the Sun and Moon appear to be the same size in the sky. It is even more amazing that our Moon gets the chance to perfectly eclipse the Sun. The odds of this coincidence are astounding when all the factors are taken into account. Out of over 100 moons in our solar system, all are either too large, small or oddly shaped to eclipse the Sun in precisely the same manner as ours.

Although I emphasize the glorious nature of the total solar eclipse, I don't want to underrate the beauty of a total lunar eclipse; however, visually, it is a very different type of event compared to a total solar eclipse.

## Overview of solar and lunar eclipses

Both solar and lunar eclipses involve an alignment of the Earth, Moon and Sun. A solar eclipse is the blocking of the Sun by the Moon, either partially or totally. A lunar eclipse is the blocking of the Moon's light (from the Sun) by Earth's shadow.

Solar eclipses can occur *only* at the time of a New Moon; lunar eclipses *only* at the time of a Full Moon. In order to see a total or annular solar eclipse, one must be on a narrow path that can stretch for a thousand miles or so over the Earth. Only those on the path will see the total or annular eclipse — those near it will see only a partial eclipse. On the other hand, lunar eclipses can be seen by almost everyone on the night side of the world.

## Umbra and penumbra shadows

These are the names of the shadows responsible for all eclipses. The umbra is the innermost and darkest shadow. The penumbra is a secondary shadow around the umbra. You will see a solar eclipse if you are in the Moon's umbra or penumbra shadow. Lunar eclipses occur when the Moon passes into Earth's umbra or penumbra shadow. Umbra and penumbra shadows are visible whenever it is sunny. If you look at the

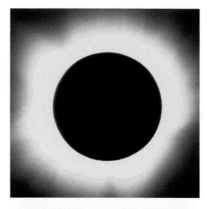

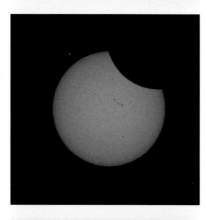

edge of an object's shadow, you will notice that it is fuzzy. This fuzzy edge is the penumbra and the main body of the shadow is the umbra.

## Solar eclipses

There are three types of solar eclipses: total, annular and partial which are pictured to the left and described below.

Why do annular eclipses occur? The Moon's orbit, like those of all orbiting bodies, is an oval ellipse; so the distance from the Moon to the Earth varies. Annular eclipses occur when the Moon is a little farther away in its orbit than usual, making its apparent size slightly smaller than that of the Sun. In these instances, the Moon is simply too small to totally block the Sun.

## Lunar eclipses

Lunar eclipses can be total, partial or penumbral; however, they do not share the characteristics of solar eclipses. Total lunar eclipses turn the Moon a dark red-orange color instead of turning it completely black. The red-orange color is caused by light refracted through the Earth's atmosphere and into its shadow. You see the same coloring at sunrise or sunset. Partial lunar eclipses may not be noticeable, except that an edge of the Moon may turn a little orange. Penumbral eclipses are usually not noticeable to the average observer.

## Why eclipses do not happen every month

Solar and lunar eclipses do not happen every month because the Moon's orbit is tilted 5.1° to Earth's orbit, placing the Moon above or below the Sun or Earth's shadow at the New and Full Moon most of the time. The Moon must be positioned exactly at the point where its orbit crosses the Earth's orbit for an eclipse to occur.

**From top to bottom. Total Solar Eclipse.** The Moon completely blocks the Sun. The irregularly shaped halo around the Moon is the Sun's corona, its outer atmosphere. **Annular Solar Eclipse.** The Moon moves completely in front of the Sun but is too small to completely cover it. **Partial Solar Eclipse.** The Moon only partially blocks the Sun. Those outside the path of a total or annular eclipse only see a partial eclipse. **Total Lunar Eclipse** turns the Moon burnt orange instead of black. Photo by Larry Moore.

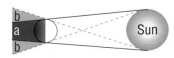

This exaggerated illustration depicts the formation of the **umbra** at **a** and the surrounding **penumbra** at **b**. The geometry of these shadows is a result of the Sun's diameter.

The Earth, Moon and Sun get perfectly aligned every 173 days, producing an eclipse somewhere on Earth.

## Frequency of eclipses: the Saros

Up to two eclipses can occur during a 173-day eclipse season: one lunar and one solar. Anywhere from two to seven lunar and solar eclipses can therefore occur in a year. Eclipses also repeat themselves in 18 year cycles called Saros (actually 18 years, 11 days, 8 hours). So, all of the eclipses that happen in the year 2000 will be repeated 18 years later, in 2018. However, the 2018 eclipses will advance by 11 days and 8 hours, placing them one-third farther around the world than their previous locations. There are 42 Saros series running concurrently, providing us with an on-going cycle of eclipses. The intensity of eclipses in a Saros (the ones that repeat every 18 years) waxes and wanes over time.

## OBSERVING solar eclipses

**Safely viewing an eclipse.** Safety of the eyes is of the utmost importance when viewing solar eclipses. Do not stare or even look directly at the Sun. Not only is this harmful to the eyes, but you cannot see a partially eclipsed Sun this way! I highly recommend using a solar or eclipse viewer/filter like the one pictured below. These inexpensive viewers are available at telescope shops, planetarium gift shops and from telescope dealers listed in the popular monthly astronomy magazines. During a solar eclipse, the Moon's progress can be viewed with a telescope that is properly fitted with a solar filter (see page 87).

There are also novel ways to view the progress of solar eclipses. My favorite is using trees. If you look at a tree's shadow (the tree must have leaves) during a solar eclipse, you will notice that mixed in with the shadow are hundreds of crescent Suns. A tree with leaves creates a multitude of pinholes that project the outline of the Sun. You will quickly realize that some trees work better than others.

## Partial and annular eclipses

Partial eclipses can last for several hours. They are not noticeable unless a substantial portion of the Sun is covered by the Moon. Even with half or more of the Sun eclipsed, you may not notice any appreciable difference in sunlight.

**Top.** Solar filters are required for looking at the Sun with your naked eyes. **Right.** If you have no means to view the progress of a solar eclipse, then look at the shadows of deciduous trees (trees with leaves). You will literally see hundreds of crescents from numerous pinholes created by the interweaving of the leaves.

## Solar Eclipses

**1 UMBRA.** The darkest part of the shadow where a total eclipse can be seen. On Earth, the umbra can be up to 170 miles (270 km) wide and travel one-third of the way around the world in a few hours.

**2 PENUMBRA.** The secondary shadow where only a partial eclipse of the Sun will be seen. The penumbra is thousands of miles wide and straddles the path of the umbra on the Earth's surface.

**3** Observers outside of the penumbra will not see the Sun eclipsed.

To observe an annular solar eclipse, consult the local media or popular monthly astronomy magazines for the location of the eclipse path. You cannot see the annular eclipse if you are not in its path. It will not get dark during an annular eclipse and the Moon will only be completely in front of the Sun for several minutes. A solar or eclipse viewer/filter is required to view the Sun during the *entire* partial or annular eclipse.

## Total solar eclipses & totality

Remember, to see a total solar eclipse, you must be on the eclipse path. Consult the local media or popular monthly astronomy magazines for details and locations of the path.

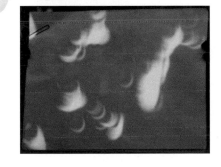

A total solar eclipse will last for several hours and is treated as a partial eclipse except for *totality*; that is, the time when the Moon completely blocks the Sun's light. During the one to five minutes of totality, no solar filter is required. Everyone stands and stares in wonder.

Many things happen during totality. The sky darkens a little (it does not get completely dark), and almost immediately, the white shimmering corona is seen surrounding the Moon. Around the Moon's edge, the thin red ring of the chromosphere may be visible along with prominences and flares protruding outward. If you look at the sky around the Moon, you will probably see a few stars and planets (usually Venus and Mercury), and if you

# Observing Eclipses

## Lunar Eclipses

**1** **TOTAL LUNAR ECLIPSES** occur when the Moon enters the Earth's umbra shadow. The Moon does not turn completely dark during a total lunar eclipse; instead, it turns a pretty red-orange color. A lunar eclipse is visible to almost half of the world.

**2** **PARTIAL LUNAR ECLIPSES** occur when only part of the Moon enters the Earth's umbra shadow. Partial lunar eclipses will show one edge of the Moon turning a slight orange color.

**3** **PENUMBRAL LUNAR ECLIPSES** occur when the Moon only enters the Earth's penumbral shadow. Penumbral lunar eclipses may not be noticeable.

scan the whole sky, you will see the umbra shadow circling the sky and extending almost to the horizon.

The sky near the horizon is still light but may have a red coloring like at sunset. The entire scene is incredible. There is nothing like it! No camera can capture the experience of totality, and everyone is touched differently. People clap, cheer, cry and pray. I recommend that everyone experience a total solar eclipse.

## Missed Eclipses

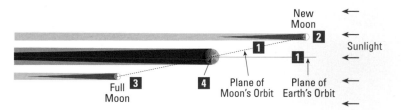

**1** The Moon's orbit is tilted 5.1° to the Earth's orbit. This slight tilt is enough to place the shadows necessary for eclipses out of reach of the Earth or Moon.

**2** The shadow of most New Moons falls either above or below the Earth.

**3** At Full Moon, the Moon is usually above or below the Earth's shadow.

**4** Eclipses occur when the Moon is either New or Full and the Moon crosses the plane of the Earth's orbit. This intersection happens every 173 days and this time interval is known as an eclipse season.

## OBSERVING lunar eclipses

No special equipment or caution is required to view lunar eclipses. Binoculars and telescopes can be used if you choose. Lunar eclipses are especially enjoyable when you can sit outside, talk with others and casually watch the event unfold.

For the most part, the Moon will turn a dark red-orange when it is completely in Earth's umbra shadow. Various hues of red and orange will dance slowly across the Moon's surface as it enters, passes through and exits the umbra. Since the umbra is considerably larger than the Moon, total lunar eclipses can last up to 3 1/2 hours. If the Moon crosses the umbra dead center, it takes about an hour for it to completely enter the umbra, stays within the umbra for about 1 1/2 hours, and finishes as it started, taking an hour to leave.

## 2002–2017 solar and lunar eclipse tables

The solar and lunar eclipse tables on the following pages summarize the locations and times of these events. Since the intensity of the event and the exact time vary considerably depending on your viewing location, please consult local media for details. The popular monthly astronomy magazines also provide details on eclipses; however, their articles appear several months before the event, so please be prepared to buy a copy in advance.

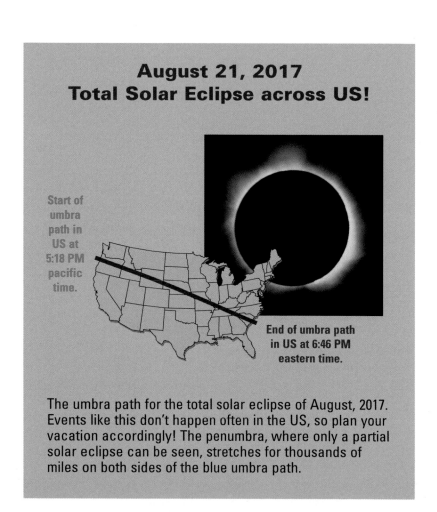

The umbra path for the total solar eclipse of August, 2017. Events like this don't happen often in the US, so plan your vacation accordingly! The penumbra, where only a partial solar eclipse can be seen, stretches for thousands of miles on both sides of the blue umbra path.

## Solar Eclipses 2002-2017

| | | |
|---|---|---|
| **TOTAL** | **Dec. 4, 2002** | **South-central Africa/Australia** |
| Annular | May 31, 2003 | Scotland/Greenland/Iceland |
| **TOTAL** | **Nov. 23, 2003** | **Antarctica** |
| Partial | April 19, 2004 | Southern Africa |
| Partial | Oct. 13/14, 2004 | Alaska/Japan/Siberia |
| **TOTAL*** | **Apr. 8, 2005** | **Panama/Northern South America** |
| Annular | Oct. 3, 2005 | Spain/Northeast Africa |
| **TOTAL** | **Mar. 29, 2006** | **Central Africa/Turkey** |
| Annular | Sep. 22, 2006 | Guyana thru French Guiani, South America |
| Partial | Mar. 19, 2007 | NE China/South Korea, Western Alaska |
| Partial | Sep. 11, 2007 | Southern South America |
| **TOTAL** | **Aug. 1, 2008** | **Central Russia/Northern Greenland** |
| Annular | Jan. 26, 2009 | Borneo/Sumatra (Indonesia) |
| **TOTAL** | **July 22, 2009** | **India thru China** |
| Annular | Jan. 15, 2010 | Mid-east Africa/Southern India thru China |
| **TOTAL** | **July 11, 2010** | **Southernmost South America** |
| Partial | Jan. 4, 2011 | Europe/Middle East/Southern Asia |
| Partial | Jun. 1, 2011 | Japan/Northern Alaska-Canada-Greenland |
| Partial | Nov. 25, 2011 | South Africa/New Zealand |
| Annular | May 20/21, 2012 | Southwest US/Japan/Eastern China |
| **TOTAL** | **Nov. 13, 2012** | **Northern Australia** |
| Annular | May 9/10, 2013 | North Australia/Papua New Guinea |
| **TOTAL*** | **Nov. 3, 2013** | **Central Africa** |
| Partial | Apr. 29, 2014 | Southern Australia (Annular in Antarctica) |
| Partial | Oct. 23, 2014 | US/Canada/Alaska |
| **TOTAL** | **Mar. 20, 2015** | **Arctic seas between Norway & Greenland** |
| Partial | Sep. 13, 2015 | Southern Africa |
| **TOTAL** | **Mar. 9, 2016** | **Borneo/Sumatra (Indonesia)** |
| Annular | Sep. 1, 2016 | Central Africa/Madagascar |
| Annular | Feb. 26, 2017 | Southern South America & Africa |
| **TOTAL** | **Aug. 21, 2017** | **ACROSS US! Oregon to South Carolina** |

*These eclipses start as annulars but change to total eclipses along their paths.

## Lunar Eclipses 2002-2017

| | | |
|---|---|---|
| Penumbral | May 26, 2002 | Pacific Ocean coastal areas |
| Penumbral | Jun. 24, 2002 | Asia/Europe/Africa |
| Penumbral | Nov. 20, 2002 | Europe/Western Africa, Eastern Americas |
| **TOTAL** | **May 16, 2003** | **Eastern North America/South America** |

| | | |
|---|---|---|
| **TOTAL** | **Nov. 8/9, 2003** | **Europe/Northwestern Africa, Eastern Americas** |
| **TOTAL** | **May 4, 2004** | **Central Asia/Africa** |
| **TOTAL** | **Oct. 28, 2004** | **Western Europe & Africa/South America, East & Central North America** |
| Penumbral | Apr. 24, 2005 | Western North America, New Zealand/Eastern Australia |
| Partial | Oct. 17, 2005 | Western Canada/Alaska/Northwest US, New Zealand/Australia |
| Penumbral | Mar. 14, 2006 | Europe/Africa/South America, Eastern North America |
| Partial | Sep. 7, 2006 | Western Australia/Central Asia, Eastern Africa |
| **TOTAL** | **Mar. 3, 2007** | **Western Europe & Africa/South America, Eastern & Central North America** |
| **TOTAL** | **Aug. 28, 2007** | **Pacific Ocean including West Coast of North America, Easternmost New Zealand/Australia** |
| **TOTAL** | **Feb. 21, 2008** | **Americas, Europe/Western Africa** |
| Partial | Aug. 16, 2008 | Asia/Eastern Europe/most of Africa |
| Penumbral | Feb. 9, 2009 | Alaska/Hawaii/Australia/Eastern Asia |
| Penumbral | July 7, 2009 | West half of North America/Hawaii, New Zealand/Eastern Australia |
| Penumbral | Aug. 6, 2009 | Europe/Africa |
| Partial | Dec. 31, 2009 | Europe/Africa/Australia/Asia |
| Partial | Jun. 26, 2010 | Hawaii/Western Alaska/Australia/ New Zealand/Eastern Malaysia & Asia |
| **TOTAL** | **Dec. 21, 2010** | **North America** |
| **TOTAL** | **Jun. 15, 2011** | **Eastern Africa/Southern Asia/W. Australia** |
| **TOTAL** | **Dec. 10, 2011** | **Australia/Eastern & Central Asia, Greenland/Northern Canada/Alaska** |
| Partial | Jun. 4, 2012 | Pacific Ocean including Coastal Areas |
| Penumbral | Nov. 28, 2012 | Alaska/Hawaii/New Zealand/Australia, most of Asia |
| Partial | Apr. 25, 2013 | Central Africa & Asia |
| Penumbral | May 25, 2013 | Americas/Western Europe/Africa |
| Penumbral | Oct. 18, 2013 | Europe/Africa/Western Asia |
| **TOTAL** | **Apr. 15, 2014** | **Most of North America/Canada, Western South America** |
| **TOTAL** | **Oct. 8, 2014** | **Western North America/Eastern Russia, Northern Greenland** |
| **TOTAL** | **Apr. 4, 2015** | **Western Alaska/Eastern Russia, Eastern Australia** |
| **TOTAL** | **Sep. 28, 2015** | **Western Europe & Africa, Eastern to Central North America/South America** |
| Penumbral | Mar. 23, 2016 | Pacific from Alaska to New Zealand and including Central Australia |
| Penumbral | Sep. 16, 2016 | Eastern Africa & Europe/Asia Eastern Australia |
| Penumbral | Feb. 11, 2017 | Atlantic touching New England and coasts of Europe and Africa |
| Partial | Aug. 7, 2017 | Australia/Central Asia |

# Observing the Planets

With our eyes, we can follow the movement of the planets through the constellations of the zodiac, but *the planets are best appreciated with the higher magnifications obtainable only by telescopes.*

If you have never observed a planet through a telescope, especially Jupiter and Saturn, I highly recommend that you seek out this experience. Seeing them "live" is a memorable event. If you don't have or plan to purchase a telescope, watch for public astronomy events hosted by national observatories or local astronomy clubs. The planets are always favorite targets.

The planets that are observed the most frequently with telescopes are, in order, Jupiter, Saturn and Mars: Jupiter for its cloud belts and moons, Saturn for its rings, and Mars, when nearby, for its polar caps and surface coloration. Becoming familiar with them beforehand will help you see subtleties that are otherwise missed.

## OBSERVING the Planets: Some Terminology

Here is some planet terminology that you will repeatedly encounter in monthly astronomy magazines and almanacs.

**Inferior and superior planets.** The inferior planets are Mercury and Venus, the two planets that have orbits inside Earth's. The superior planets are the six planets whose orbits lie beyond Earth's, namely: Mars, Jupiter, Saturn, Uranus, Neptune and Pluto.

**Inner and outer planets.** The asteroid belt is the dividing line for the inner and outer planets. The inner planets are Mercury through Mars, while the outer planets are Jupiter through Pluto.

**Elongation.** The arc angle distance in the sky that separates a planet from the Sun. This term is often applied to the inferior

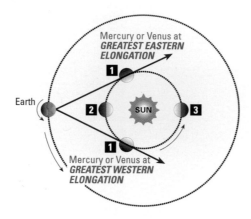

## Greatest Elongations, Inferior and Superior Conjunctions of Mercury & Venus

**1** **Greatest Eastern or Western Elongation** is the farthest that Mercury or Venus appears from the Sun in the sky.

**2** **Inferior Conjunction.** Neither Mercury nor Venus are visible at this time because they are in line with the Sun. Both rise and set with the Sun.

**3** **Superior Conjunction.** Neither Mercury nor Venus are visible at this time because they are in line with the Sun. Both rise and set with the Sun.

## Opposition of the Superior Planets

**4** The **superior planets** are Mars through Pluto. These planets are at **opposition** when they are directly opposite the Sun from Earth. At opposition, the planets appear at their largest and brightest. They rise in the east as the Sun sets in the west and are highest in the sky (sometimes overhead) at midnight.

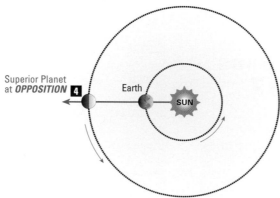

planets — Mercury and Venus. These planets are at their greatest eastern elongation or greatest western elongation when they appear, from Earth, the farthest away from the Sun. Elongation is a perspective view from the Earth.

**Opposition.** Refers to the superior planets, Mars through Pluto. A superior planet is at opposition if it is rising in the east as the Sun is setting; that is, it is on the opposite side of the Earth from the Sun. The superior planets are closest to the Earth at opposition; hence they will appear their largest in a telescope and be at their brightest. Opposition places a superior planet at its highest point in the sky, sometimes overhead, around midnight.

**Conjunction.** The "time" when two or more planets, a planet and the Moon/Sun or a planet and a bright star appear close to one another in the sky. Conjunctions are beautiful sights, as little can compare to the brilliant glow of Venus standing next to a crescent Moon. Conjunctions are a perspective "alignment" as viewed from Earth and do not represent celestial bodies physically getting close to one another.

**Retrograde motion.** An apparent backward movement of the superior planets, Mars through Pluto. Normally, these planets move slowly eastward against the stationary background stars because this is the direction of their orbits around the Sun. However, when the Earth comes around and "passes" them in their orbits, they appear to travel backwards or westward for several months before resuming their eastward course. This backward, retrograde motion is just a perspective view from Earth, a result of the Earth orbiting the Sun more quickly than the superior planets. This motion is similar to that seen from an automobile passing another.

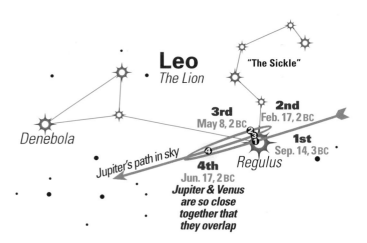

**Leo**
*The Lion*

"The Sickle"

**3rd**
May 8, 2 BC

**2nd**
Feb. 17, 2 BC

*Denebola*

**1st**
Sep. 14, 3 BC

*Jupiter's path in sky*

**4th**
Jun. 17, 2 BC

*Regulus*

***Jupiter & Venus
are so close
together that
they overlap***

## Retrograde Motion and Conjunctions

What was the star of Bethlehem? No one knows for certain but some scholars think that the Magi witnessed three conjunctions of Jupiter with *Regulus*, and a finale where Jupiter and Venus blended into one star, all within a span of 9 months. To many cultures, *Regulus* was the "regal" star while Jupiter was the king of the planets. What could be more propitious than these two royal bodies coming together? This event is an example of retrograde motion bringing about several conjunctions. The orange line in the illustration shows Jupiter's retrograde motion above Regulus (creating a crown) and ends in a rare conjunction where two planets overlap (not physically, but from a perspective view). This merging of the planets created a very bright apparition that truly represented a heavenly punctuation. Researchers have found no evidence of this 9-month event ever happening again. The Magi certainly realized that something rare and special occurred, even if it was only an astronomical event.

## OBSERVING the Planets: Some Considerations

**Binoculars.** Binoculars do not provide high enough magnification to reveal any details on the planets; however, with binoculars, you should be able to see the four Galilean moons of Jupiter and Venus (largest when crescent). Binoculars are helpful for locating Mercury and Uranus.

**Telescope magnification.** Useful magnifications for observing the planets are generally from 60x to 300x or higher. Depending on the size of your telescope, the quality of its optics and atmospheric conditions, magnifications of 150x or higher may not provide good images.

**Viewing/Seeing conditions.** Because of changing weather conditions, some nights are just better than others to view the planets. Observing as often as possible will increase your chance of encountering good seeing conditions.

**Moments of clarity and viewing near the horizon.** It is rare to observe a planet and see its features sharply. More often, the planets appear blurry because of Earth's atmospheric turbulence. However, there are moments of clarity when, just for a instant, you can clearly see details on the planets. These moments last just a fraction of a second, but occur frequently. These glimpses are important because they are often the best we can get.

Seeing conditions are poor near the horizon because light passes through more atmosphere and turbulence. Through a telescope, planets near the horizon look like they are bubbling, so wait until they get at least 30 arc angle degrees above the horizon (one-third of the way to the top of the sky).

**No dark-adapted eyes needed.** The planets are bright enough that dark-adapted eyes are not a requirement for viewing, so the Moon and outdoor lights will not readily interfere with observing these celestial objects.

**Size/Detail.** When I show the planets to others, a comment I often hear is, "It's pretty small." Don't expect any of the planets to appear "large" in telescopes. The amount of detail will also be limited. However, with repetitive viewing, the occasional crystal clear night, moments of clarity and familiarity, you will be able to see much more than you think. Of the superior planets, Jupiter appears the largest, and Saturn about one-half its size because it is twice as far away. Surface detail on Mars can only be studied every two years, around its opposition time, when it is closest to Earth.

## Arc Angle Sizes of Planets in the Sky

| Planet | Smallest / Largest Arc Angle Size |
|--------|-----------------------------------|
| **MERCURY** | 5" / 13" |
| VENUS | 10" / 64" |
| **MARS** | 4" / 25" |
| JUPITER | 31" / 50" |
| **SATURN** | Planet 15" / 21" |
| | Rings 35"/50" |
| URANUS | 3.4" / 4" |
| **NEPTUNE** | 2.2" / 2.4" |
| PLUTO | 0.16" / 0.28" |

**TABLE NOTES:** Sizes are based on the angle an object extends using the compass measurement of 360 arc degrees (360°) completing a circle. There are 60 arc seconds (") in an arc minute and 60 arc minutes (') in an arc degree. The Moon is very large in the sky compared to the planets and extends to an arc angle of about 1,800" (arc seconds) or 30' (arc minutes) which is 1/2 an arc degree. The planets appear their smallest when they are farthest away from Earth, on the other side of the Sun, and appear their largest near their inferior conjunction for Mercury and Venus, or at their opposition for Mars through Pluto.

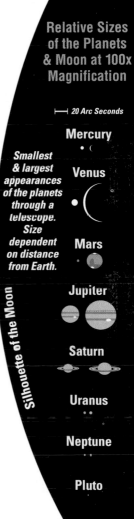

**Relative Sizes of the Planets & Moon at 100x Magnification**

├──┤ 20 Arc Seconds

**Mercury**

*Smallest & largest appearances of the planets through a telescope. Size dependent on distance from Earth.*

**Venus**

**Mars**

**Jupiter**

Silhouette of the Moon

**Saturn**

**Uranus**

**Neptune**

**Pluto**

# Observing Mercury

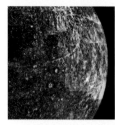

## Observing Mercury

Mercury is best viewed with the naked eye or binoculars and not with a telescope. It is only visible at dawn or dusk, near the horizon of a Sun that has just set or is about to rise. Unfortunately, this places Mercury in the most turbulent part of sky, making it look like a bubbling blob through a telescope. The farthest Mercury gets from the Sun is about 28°, less than one-third the distance from the horizon to the zenith. This makes it challenging to find, especially with obstructed horizons. For me, the most exciting part about observing Mercury is just finding it.

The little that was known about Mercury before *Mariner 10* visited this planet in 1975 was through telescopic observations made during the day. It is possible to observe, through a telescope, the brighter stars and planets during the day if you know where to look. During the day, Mercury can more easily be studied in a higher, steadier sky.

### Locating Mercury

**1** Consult the Mercury table to the right to find the best observing dates. This table lists the most favorable greatest eastern and western elongations, that is, when Mercury is farthest from the Sun and easiest to see. Mercury can be seen more often than indicated in this table, but these dates represent the times when almost everyone in North America has an opportunity to see this elusive first planet. Mercury's height above the horizon varies depending on your latitude, the Sun's inclination to the horizon and where Mercury is in its highly inclined orbit.

Mercury in the early eastern morning sky. On this day, Mercury was easy to spot because it was simply the brightest object in the area, but it can be missed easily if you are not looking directly at it. Sweeping the area with binoculars helps in locating this planet, but for safety reasons, use binoculars only when the Sun is below the horizon.

**2** Start your search for Mercury about one week prior to the dates in the table. The window of opportunity to see this planet is about one week on either side of a date. Low-lying clouds and an obstructed horizon can easily foil your attempt to locate this planet.

**3** For evening dates, search for Mercury low in the western sky. Start about 30 minutes after sunset. You will have about one-half hour to see Mercury.

**4** For morning dates, search for Mercury low in the eastern sky. Start about one hour and fifteen minutes prior to sunrise.

**5** Mercury will appear as bright as magnitude –2 above and near the sunrise/sunset point, so it may be the only "star" visible during twilight, making it difficult to confuse with anything else. At times Mercury is plainly visible to the naked eye, but more often, you will need binoculars to help locate it because it is easily missed unless you are looking directly at it. Mercury can be as much as a pencil length above the horizon when your arm is fully extended, but expect to see it lower.

### Observing Mercury

Since Mercury is always low in the sky where atmospheric turbulence is the greatest, it is not worthwhile to view it through a telescope where it will appear only as a bright, bubbling, color changing spot of light (pretty in its own right). Because of the turbulence, no disk or phase can be discerned.

> **CAUTION:** To prevent injury to the eyes, use binoculars to look for Mercury ONLY when the Sun is below the horizon.

## Most Favorable Dates to Observe Mercury

**Mercury is in the WESTERN sky in the Evening & the EASTERN sky in the Morning. Observe for one week on either side of these dates.**

| Year | Date | Time | Year | Date | Time |
|---|---|---|---|---|---|
| **2002** | **May 3** | **Evening** | **2010** | **April 8** | **Evening** |
| | **October 13** | **Morning** | | **September 19** | **Morning** |
| 2003 | April 16 | Evening | 2011 | March 22 | Evening |
| | September 26 | Morning | | September 2 | Morning |
| **2004** | **March 29** | **Evening** | | December 22 | Morning |
| | **September 9** | **Morning** | **2012** | **March 5** | **Evening** |
| | **December 29** | **Morning** | | **June 30** | **Evening** |
| 2005 | March 12 | Evening | | **August 16** | **Morning** |
| | August 23 | Morning | | **December 4** | **Morning** |
| | December 12 | Morning | 2013 | February 16 | Evening |
| **2006** | **February 23** | **Evening** | | June 12 | Evening |
| | **June 20** | **Evening** | | July 30 | Morning |
| | **August 6** | **Morning** | | November 17 | Morning |
| | **November 25** | **Morning** | **2014** | **January 31** | **Evening** |
| 2007 | February 7 | Evening | | **May 25** | **Evening** |
| | June 2 | Evening | | **November 1** | **Morning** |
| | November 8 | Morning | 2015 | May 6 | Evening |
| **2008** | **May 13** | **Evening** | | October 15 | Morning |
| | **October 22** | **Morning** | **2016** | **April 18** | **Evening** |
| 2009 | April 26 | Evening | | **September 28** | **Morning** |
| | October 5 | Morning | 2017 | April 1 | Evening |
| | | | | September 12 | Morning |

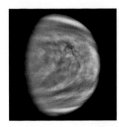

## Observing Venus

One cold, moonless, winter night in Milwaukee, I went outside to look at the stars. Snow covered the backyard and Venus was high and bright. Something that night seemed different. I suddenly noticed the shadows of lilac branches, plainly visible on the snow. Venus was casting shadows!

### Locating Venus

Venus is very easy to find in the sky because of its brightness and proximity to the rising or setting Sun. Reaching magnitude –4.6, it becomes a beacon, outshining all other stars and planets. For these reasons, it is often referred to as the morning or evening star. The table below indicates when Venus is at its greatest eastern and western elongations, that is, when it is farthest above the horizon or highest in the sky. Around these dates, it will appear at about half-phase. Venus will be visible in the sky a few months before and after these dates. If you see a bright star in the east or west, before sunrise or after sunset, it will most likely be Venus.

### Observing Venus

Through any telescope, Venus appears brilliantly white and featureless because of its thick cloud cover. And, since this planet orbits inside Earth's, it cycles through phases just like the Moon. However, unlike the Moon, it varies in size. Venus is at its largest and brightest near its crescent phase. This occurs about a month after greatest eastern elongation and a month before greatest western elongation. The crescent phase of Venus can just be seen in a good pair of well-focused binoculars. At greatest eastern or western elongation, Venus' phase is about half.

### When Venus is HIGHEST in the Sky

| Venus is in the WESTERN sky in the Evening and the EASTERN sky in the Morning | | | | | |
|------|------------|---------|------|------------|---------|
| 2002 | August 22 | Evening | 2010 | August 19 | Evening |
| 2003 | January 10 | Morning | 2011 | January 8 | Morning |
| 2004 | March 29 | Evening | 2012 | March 27 | Evening |
| | August 17 | Morning | | August 15 | Morning |
| 2005 | November 3 | Evening | 2013 | November 1 | Evening |
| 2006 | March 25 | Morning | 2014 | March 22 | Morning |
| 2007 | June 8 | Evening | 2015 | June 6 | Evening |
| | October 28 | Morning | | October 26 | Morning |
| 2008 | None | | 2016 | None | |
| 2009 | January 14 | Evening | 2017 | January 12 | Evening |
| | June 5 | Morning | | June 3 | Morning |

June 14, 2001
1:00 – 1:15 AM
Seeing 5/10
Central Meridian 288°

## Observing Mars

Our captivation with Mars began in the late 1800s when Percival Lowell declared that Mars had canals built by its inhabitants. Mars has no canals, but the fascination with this red planet continues because there is evidence indicating that this planet may have or still harbors microbial life. Additionally, Mars has frozen water at its poles and beneath much of its surface, which is the most important substance needed to establish any future colonies.

In the first half of this 21st century, the United States and other countries will deluge Mars with numerous exploratory spacecraft and surface rovers — maybe even a manned mission. Our understanding of this planet will dramatically increase over the coming years. I hope it continues to bring surprises and joy to our understanding of life in the Universe.

### Locating Mars

The tables on page 101 indicate Mars' position by constellation until 2017. If the constellation is visible in the night sky, so will the planet. Mars is easy to find in the sky near opposition because it is bright and red in color, shining steadily around magnitude –2. When not at opposition, its magnitude and conspicuousness fade to +2.

### Most favorable times to observe Mars

Mars is small, so it is best observed around opposition when it is closest to the Earth and appears its largest. Oppositions with Mars occur about every 26 months; however, some oppositions bring us closer together than others. Depending on where the two planets meet in their elliptical orbits, the distance between Earth and Mars at opposition can vary from 35,000,000 to 63,000,000 miles. This difference effectively doubles the size of Mars in a telescope. The table at the top of page 97 indicates the opposition dates, that is, the best dates for viewing Mars.

Drawing is a convenient way to record your observations of Mars' surface features. This drawing was made using a high-quality 4-inch refractor with magnifications around 300x. It shows a mirror image of Mars: left and right are reversed because a right angle diagonal was used for comfortable viewing (page 49). "Central Meridian" refers to the central longitude as calculated using a table in a *Sky & Telescope* magazine article. The seeing is a gauge of atmospheric viewing quality. Compare this drawing to the *Hubble Space Telescope* pictures on the next page.

# Observing Mars

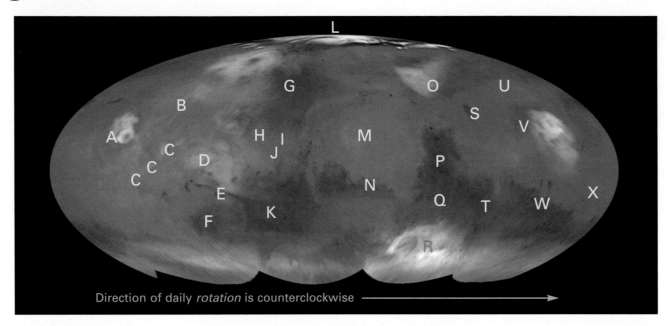

Direction of daily *rotation* is counterclockwise ⟶

## Major Surface Features of Mars

**A.** Clouds atop Mars' highest point and largest volcano, *Olympus Mons*
**B.** *Arcadia* Plain
**C.** Chain of three large volcanos
**D.** *Tharsis* Plain
**E.** *Valles Marineris* chasm
**F.** *Solis Lacus*
**G.** *Mare Acidalium*
**H.** Landing site of *Viking 1,* 1976
**I.** Landing site of *Pathfinder,* 1997
**J.** *Chryse*
**K.** *Mare Erythraeum*
**L.** North pole of Mars
**M.** Plain of *Arabia*

**N.** *Sinus Sabaeus*
**O.** *Utopia*
**P.** *Syrtis Major* (some report this as being bluish in color)
**Q.** *Iapygia*
**R.** *Hellas,* a giant impact crater that look whitish.
(This is Mars' lowest point. Don't mistake it for Mars' south pole.)
**S.** *Alcyonius Nodus*
**T.** Mare *Tyrrhenum*
**U.** Landing site of *Viking 2,* 1976
**V.** *Stymphalius Lacus*
**W.** *Mare Cimmerium*
**X.** *Memmonia* Plain

**Notes:** The south pole is shrouded in the lower clouds.
Names of features vary slightly among reference sources.

## Longitude centered on 285°
*Rotation* ⟶

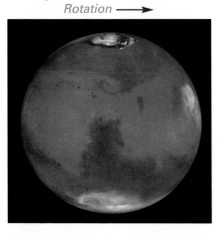

## Longitude centered on 195°
*Rotation* ⟶

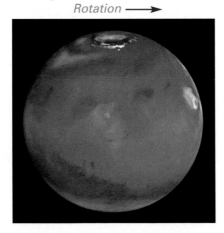

## Longitude centered on 110°
*Rotation* ⟶

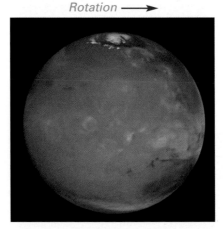

## Longitude centered on 25°
*Rotation* ⟶

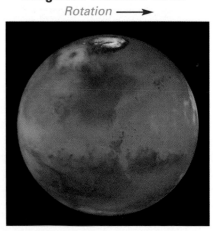

This set of pictures was taken by the *Hubble Space Telescope* that orbits Earth. They cover most of Mars' surface with the exception of its south pole. The north pole is at the top of these pictures. This set of pictures accurately depicts the surface coloration of the red planet and can serve as a reference for your observations; however, through a telescope, Mars appears much paler and shows less contrast than in these pictures.

The large white roundish area at the bottom of the left picture (longitude 285°) is *Hellas* (R above) and is not the south pole of Mars. Either or both poles are visible during oppositions, but the north pole is the larger and easier to see. All longitudes on Mars are west longitudes, so their range is from 0° to 359°. The center longitude for each of these picture is also called the Central Meridian.

## Opposition Dates and Angular Size of Mars

| Year & Date | | Arc Second Angular Size |
|---|---|---|
| **2003** | **August 28** | **25"** |
| 2005 | November 7 | 19" |
| **2007** | **December 24** | **16"** |
| 2010 | January 29 | 14" |
| **2012** | **March 3** | **14"** |
| 2014 | April 8 | 15" |
| **2016** | **May 22** | **18"** |
| 2018 | July 26 | 24" |

**TABLE NOTES:** These are the dates when Mars is closest to Earth and will appear at its largest. The optimal viewing period is from three weeks before to three weeks after these dates. Mars will also be at it brightest during these times. Arc size is indicated in arc seconds ("). See page 93 for a comparison of planet sizes as they appear in the sky. Magnifications of 150x to 300x or higher are recommended in order to view the most details on Mars.

## Observing Mars

Although surface coloration and the north polar cap can be seen in small to moderately sized telescopes (4-inch to 6-inch), they are subtle. For this reason, Mars is often disappointing to first-time viewers. Here are some suggestions to help maximize your observation of Mars' surface features around the time of opposition.

**1** Try to observe Mars often, one month before to one month after opposition. Repetitive viewing will increase your familiarity with this planet and increase your chance of observing on a good night. Additionally, you will be able to see its different sides and all of its surface markings if you observe over a period of time. Mars' rotation on its axis is only 37 minutes different from Earth's, so if you observe the planet at the same time each night, you will pretty much return to viewing the same side.

**2** Use a minimum magnification of 100x; however, 200x to 300x or higher is preferable. Achieving higher magnifications depends on your telescope and atmospheric conditions.

**3** Observe Mars when it is highest in the sky in order to minimize atmospheric disturbance. This will occur around midnight during opposition. It is more difficult to see the surface markings when Mars is low in the sky. The worst part about observing at midnight is staying up or waking up. But it is worth it, since Mars is only at opposition every few years.

**4** When you are looking at Mars through a telescope, you will notice that there are split-second moments when the view of the surface appears clear. It is during these moments of clarity that you will get your best glimpses. It is a rare night when you can look directly at Mars and plainly see its subtle surface markings. The poles usually stand out. You will either see one or both, depending on the opposition.

**5** Several months before opposition, the popular monthly astronomy magazines will carry in-depth articles about observing the red planet. I highly recommend purchasing these issues; these timely pieces are invaluable because they often include current maps of the surface markings and tables for calculating the side of Mars visible when you observe.

**6** On page 55, there is a picture of several colored filters that thread into the bottom of eyepieces. Filters such as these are sometimes used to enhance viewing of the planets, especially Mars and Jupiter. I have personally found that these filters provide only subtle enhancement of surface features. However, for Mars, red and orange filters show the surface markings best, while blue ones highlight the atmosphere and clouds. There are lighter and darker colored filters. Purchase the lighter colored filters because the darker filters make it difficult to see any surface markings.

**7** Don't expect to easily see Mars' two moons, Phobos and Deimos, since their magnitudes are respectively 12 and 13. Phobos orbits closest and will be at most one planet diameter away while Deimos can be as far as three planet diameters away. You can find their exact positions (at the time you are observing) by using computer planetarium software like *Starry Night Pro*.

**8** If you follow the suggestions above and still cannot see surface markings, here are some possible reasons.

**a)** Your telescope optics may not be adequate or may not be properly aligned. Ask someone at a telescope store or an astronomy club member to check out your telescope. **b)** The turbulence in Earth's atmosphere may be affecting telescope image quality, so keep trying. **c)** Remember, if you take your telescope from the warm interior of your home to the cold outside, it will take *at least* fifteen minutes for the telescope optics to cool and settle down — up to an hour for an 8-inch SCT. The image of Mars during this time will be blurry. **e)** Finally, wind storms on Mars could be kicking up dust and obliterating the surface markings. Review the popular monthly astronomy magazines for the latest internet sites to check on current weather conditions on Mars.

# Observing Jupiter

## Observing Jupiter

The largest planet in the solar system is easy to locate and yields details more readily than any other planet. Next to Saturn's rings, this is the planet most often observed.

Jupiter was one of the first objects viewed by Galileo with his small, homemade telescope in 1610. His observations of the four brightest moons revolving about this giant gave credence to the Sun being the center of the Universe, instead of Earth. In his honor, these four moons are called the Galilean moons.

Fast forward to July 1994 — comet Shoemaker-Levy 9 slams into Jupiter. This collision provided direct evidence that Jupiter has possibly served as a "cometary magnet," thus providing time for life to develop on Earth.

Jupiter has provided us with more insights about the nature of our solar system than any other planet. He truly is a king in both history and size.

### Locating Jupiter

This amber jewel is easy to find in the sky because it is bright and prominent, shining boldly above magnitude –2 most of the time. Sirius, the brightest star in the whole sky, shines only at –1.4. See the Superior Planets Constellation Table for its location in the night sky (page 101). Also see the Opposition Table on the next page.

### The Galilean moons

The four Galilean moons are visible with well-focused binoculars. In fact, they would be visible to the naked eye if it were not for the bright glare of Jupiter. All four are similar in size to our Moon but revolve around their planet much faster than ours. See closeup pictures on page 16 and table to the right.

Almost everyone enjoys coming back to the Galilean moons because they provide an ongoing display of beautiful, ever-changing patterns. I often look at Jupiter just to see the moons. I enjoy their beauty, but for me, they are a constant reminder of the dynamic nature of our Universe.

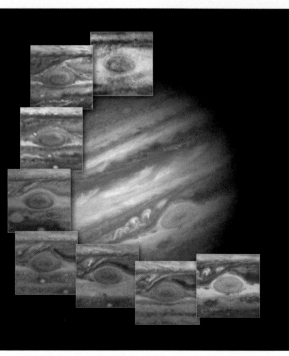

Eight snapshots of the Great Red Spot from the *Hubble Space Telescope* show variations in size, shape and color. This 14,000-mile-wide hurricane-type storm rotates counter-clockwise once in about seven days with wind speeds topping 270 miles per hour. Some detail within the spot can be seen in telescopes with diameters as small as 8 inches.

Movement of the two inner moons can be noticed in as little as 5 to 15 minutes. Sometimes only 2 or 3 moons are visible, because the others are temporarily behind the planet. At other times, there are transits, which is when a moon passes in front of Jupiter, casting a round shadow on its clouds. The shadow is easily seen, but the actual moon is usually more difficult to spot because it blends in with Jupiter's clouds.

Although Jupiter has dozens of moons, only the four Galilean moons are easily observed. Amalthea, Jupiter's fifth brightest moon, shines at magnitude 14.1, which is as faint as Pluto and is the visual limit of a 12-inch telescope.

When Jupiter is visible in the sky, the popular monthly astronomy magazines publish a graph indicating the daily positions of the four moons. You can also find their position by using computer planetarium software like *Starry Night Pro*. I generally don't care about calculated positions because I enjoy being surprised.

### Cloud belts & rotation

Jupiter has numerous cloud belts, but the North and South Equatorial Belts (**N** and **S** respectively in the illustration) are the two most distinguished on the planet. They are plainly visible in small telescopes and appear as two "thick" parallel bands on opposite

sides of a center line. A narrow band (**A**) called the North Temperate Belt, just above the North Equatorial Belt can also be seen. Other cloud details can be observed in its many belts with higher magnification, larger aperture telescopes and good seeing conditions.

All of the cloud belts are parallel to each other and perpendicular to the axis of rotation. Like with Mars, drawing is a convenient way to record your observations.

Jupiter rotates on its axis in a little less than 10 hours, so you can easily notice movement of the Great Red Spot in 30 minutes.

## Galilean Moons

| Moon[1] | Average Distance from Planet[2] | Revolution Period | Diameter | Visual Magnitude[3] |
|---|---|---|---|---|
| IO (I) | 262,000 miles | 1.77 days | 2,255 miles | 5.0 |
| **EUROPA (II)** | **416,900 miles** | **3.55 days** | **1,950 miles** | **5.3** |
| GANYMEDE (III)[4] | 664,900 miles | 7.16 days | 3,270 miles | 4.6 |
| **CALLISTO (IV)** | **1,171,000 miles** | **16.69 days** | **2,980 miles** | **5.6** |

[1]The Roman numeral designation of these moons is also provided. [2]Distance measured from center of planet. [3]Visual magnitude at opposition. [4]Ganymede is the largest moon in our solar system, larger than Mercury and Pluto.

## Great Red Spot

The Great Red Spot (**G** on the illustration) is a giant circulating vortex located on the southern edge of the South Equatorial Belt. As shown in the picture, its color and shape vary over time. I remember how much darker and more prominent it appeared in the 1970s, but has paled considerably since. The spot has been visible for as long as we have been observing the planet. It may be possible for it to dissipate; however, it would probably reform. This oval is approximately 14,000 or so miles wide (depends how you want to measure it).

### Opposition Dates for Jupiter

| Year & Date | | Year & Date | |
|---|---|---|---|
| 2002 | *No opposition* | **2010** | **September 21** |
| **2003** | **February 2** | 2011 | October 28 |
| 2004 | March 3 | **2012** | **December 2** |
| **2005** | **April 3** | 2013 | *No opposition* |
| 2006 | May 4 | **2014** | **January 5** |
| **2007** | **June 5** | 2015 | February 6 |
| 2008 | July 9 | **2016** | **March 8** |
| **2009** | **August 14** | 2017 | April 7 |

**TABLE NOTES:** These are the dates when Jupiter is closest to Earth and will appear at its largest (see more about its apparent size on page 93). Around the opposition date, Jupiter is rising in the eastern sky as the Sun is setting in the west. At these times, it is at it brightest and will be highest in the southern night sky around midnight, sometimes overhead. Jupiter is visible in the night sky for about 3 months before and after the opposition date.

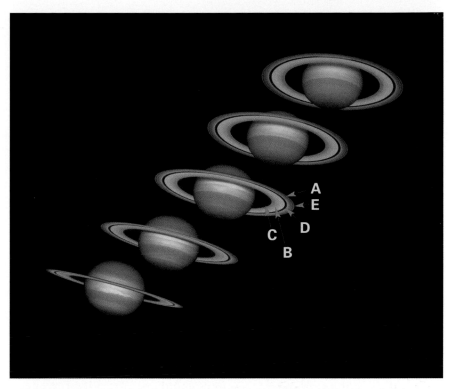

The inclination of Saturn's rings varies because they, along with the planet's axis, are tilted about 25° to its orbit around the Sun. From Earth's vantage point, this allows us to see the rings in different positions as Saturn completes an orbit every 29 years. These pictures were captured by the *Hubble Space Telescope* from 1996 to 2000.

The magnificent rings of Saturn are actually a series of ringlets. The outer **A** ring is separated from the bright **B** ring by a 2,900-mile gap called the Cassini division (**D**). The inner dark **C** ring, also known as the Crepe ring, is difficult to see in small telescopes. There is a faint gap in the outer **A** ring called the Enke division (**E**) that requires good seeing conditions and a moderate-diameter telescope of around 10 inches. The diameter of the **A** ring is about 170,000 miles. As you can see in the pictures, the cloud belts of Saturn appear much plainer that those on Jupiter.

## Observing Saturn

The magnificent rings of Saturn make this planet visually unique. Galileo was one of the first scientists to observe and draw it. He depicted it as three orbs, two smaller orbs on opposite sides of a larger one. At first thought, this might seem like a ludicrous rendition of the ringed planet, until you realize that he was using a very small telescope (about 1 inch in diameter) and very low magnification. Additionally, since he was one of the first to turn a telescope towards the heavens, he had no context for the shape, size, color or features of *any* celestial object. His drawing was amazingly accurate given the circumstances.

The rings always beg questions. In 1980 and 1981, the *Voyager* missions provided close-up views of them and helped answer the most long standing ones. They are relatively thin, with a thickness varying from perhaps 30 to 350 feet, and are a collection of countless ringlets, like the grooves on a record (for those who remember them). These ringlets are made up of billions of chunks of water ice, averaging about an inch across. The ice cubes in your freezer represent their makeup and size fairly well. Each ice chunk orbits Saturn just like our Moon orbits Earth. The diameter of this system of rings is about 250,000 miles, which includes fainter rings beyond the brightest pictured on this page.

Why does Saturn have a ring system? The total amount of material in the rings is small and would be equivalent to a comet about 60 miles (97 km) in diameter. One theory is that Saturn's rings may be fragments of a comet that got too close to the planet. If this is the case, Saturn's rings may not be that old (a million years or so) and may not be permanent. The rings are positioned in an area around the planet where tidal-type gravitational forces are greatest, enough to shear a comet into pieces and prevent the pieces from clumping together. All of the gas giants in our solar system have ring systems, but none compare to Saturn's. The rings of Uranus and Neptune appear to be composed of rocks

# Observing Saturn

instead of ice. Ring systems may be a common feature of larger gaseous planets.

The spacecraft *Cassini* is on its way to the ringed planet and is scheduled to be placed into orbit around 2004. Our knowledge of the planet, its rings and moons will soar once we start receiving data from this explorer.

## Locating Saturn

This yellowish-amber colored planet is fairly easy to find in the sky with the naked eye because it shines steadily with an average magnitude of 0. See the Superior Planets Constellation Table on page 101 to locate Saturn. The Opposition Dates Table in the next column indicates the time of the year when Saturn will appear its largest and brightest in the sky.

## Saturn's moons

Titan, Saturn's largest moon, is also the second largest moon in our solar system after Jupiter's Ganymede. Titan is easy to see because it is the brightest "star" near the ringed planet, but it can be positioned farther away than you might think, up to four ring diameters. Much closer to Saturn are four additional moons which can be glimpsed with small telescopes. These moons are much fainter than the Galilean moons of Jupiter and are very close to the ring system, resembling little specks of light. When Saturn is visible in the sky, the popular monthly astronomy magazines publish a graph indicating the daily positions of these five moons or you can use computer planetarium software like *Starry Night Pro* to find their positions.

### Saturn's Brightest Moons

| Moon | Average Distance from Planet[1] | Revolution Period | Diameter | Visual Magnitude[2] |
|---|---|---|---|---|
| ENCELADUS | 147,900 miles | 1.4 days | 311 miles | 11.8 |
| TETHYS | 183,300 miles | 1.9 days | 659 miles | 10.3 |
| DIONE | 234,900 miles | 2.7 days | 699 miles | 10.4 |
| RHEA | 326,800 miles | 4.5 days | 951 miles | 9.7 |
| TITAN[3] | 758,100 miles | 15.9 days | 3,200 miles | 8.4 |

[1]Distance measured from center of planet. [2]Visual magnitude at Saturn's opposition. The visual limit of a 4-inch telescope is magnitude 12. [3]Titan is the second largest moon in our solar system and is larger than Mercury and Pluto.

## The rings

Saturn's rings are easily seen in a small telescope with magnification as little as 40x. Higher magnifications will reveal more detail. When Galileo first observed Saturn in 1610, the rings were plainly visible, but in 1612, the rings were edge on and could not be seen. This no doubt created a stir and was, to say the least, puzzling. Although Saturn is synonymous with "rings," they do turn edge on every 14 years and effectively disappear for about a year. (This is not the time to show your friends Saturn because they will not believe that what they are looking at is the ringed planet. Instead, they are more likely to think that you don't know what you are talking about!)

Saturn's rings are visible most of the time. However, as Saturn circles the Sun, the rings vary in the degree that they are "open," or inclined toward Earth. During half of Saturn's 29 year revolution around the Sun, we see the top side of the rings, and the bottom side for the other half. The appearance of Saturn's rings changes because the axis of the planet is tilted by about 25° to the plane of its orbit. This allows us to see the rings from various positions or angles as Saturn orbits the Sun.

There are three major divisions in the visible rings labeled, from outermost to innermost, A, B and C. Between rings A and B, there is 2,900 mile gap called the Cassini Division. This gap is visible in small telescopes and most apparent when the rings are opened. The middle B ring is the widest and brightest of the three rings and overwhelms the innermost faint C ring (known as the "crepe" ring), making it difficult to see in smaller telescopes.

## Cloud belts

Saturn's cloud belts are not as distinct as Jupiter's. Close-up pictures of Saturn by *Voyager 1* and *2* also revealed that the clouds are not as complex. However, you should be able to see several light colored belts when observing with a small telescope.

### ORIENTATION of Rings

| Dates | Orientation |
|---|---|
| 2000 – 2005 | Rings Open Southward |
| January 2009[1] | Rings Edge-On |
| 2014 – 2020 | Rings Open Northward |

[1]Rings not visible for up to 6 months before and after this date.

### Opposition Dates for Saturn

| Year & Date | | Year & Date | |
|---|---|---|---|
| 2002 | December 17 | 2010 | March 21 |
| 2003 | December 31 | 2011 | April 3 |
| 2004 | No opposition | 2012 | April 15 |
| 2005 | January 13 | 2013 | April 28 |
| 2006 | January 27 | 2014 | May 10 |
| 2007 | February 10 | 2015 | May 22 |
| 2008 | February 24 | 2016 | October 15 |
| 2009 | March 8 | 2017 | October 19 |

**TABLE NOTES:** These are the dates when Saturn is closest to Earth and will appear at its largest (see more about its apparent size on page 93). Around the opposition date, Saturn is rising in the eastern sky as the Sun is setting in the west. It is also at it brightest during this time and will be highest in the southern night sky around midnight, sometimes overhead. Saturn is visible in the night sky for about 3 months before and after the opposition date.

# Superior Planets Constellation Table

These tables are to aid you in locating Mars, Jupiter and Saturn in the sky. They indicate, by month, which constellations these planets are in. Use them in conjunction with the corresponding Opposition Dates Tables for each of these planets (pages 97, 99 & 100). For the most part, if a constellation listed below is visible at night, so is the corresponding planet. The tables below can also provide you with a sense of the easterly movements of these planets through the constellations of the zodiac as well as their retrograde motion (page 92). The constellations of the zodiac complete a circle all the way around the celestial sphere. The Sun and all the planets move around this circle because all their orbits are nearly in the same plane.

## 2002

| | Jan | Feb | Mar | Apr | May | Jun | Jul | Aug | Sep | Oct | Nov | Dec |
|---|---|---|---|---|---|---|---|---|---|---|---|---|
| Mars | Psc | Psc | Ari | Tau | Tau | Gem | Cnc | Leo | Leo | Vir | Vir | Vir |
| Jupiter | Gem | Gem | Gem | Gem | Gem | Gem | Gem | Cnc | Cnc | Cnc | Cnc | Leo |
| Saturn | Tau | Tau | Tau | Tau | Tau | Tau | Tau | Tau | Tau | Tau | Tau | Tau |

## 2003

| | Jan | Feb | Mar | Apr | May | Jun | Jul | Aug | Sep | Oct | Nov | Dec |
|---|---|---|---|---|---|---|---|---|---|---|---|---|
| Mars | Lib | Oph | Sag | Sag | Cap | Aqr | Aqr | Aqr | Aqr | Aqr | Aqr | Psc |
| Jupiter | Cnc | Cnc | Cnc | Cnc | Cnc | Cnc | Leo | Leo | Leo | Leo | Leo | Leo |
| Saturn | Tau | Tau | Tau | Tau | Tau | Gem | Gem | Gem | Gem | Gem | Gem | Gem |

## 2004

| | Jan | Feb | Mar | Apr | May | Jun | Jul | Aug | Sep | Oct | Nov | Dec |
|---|---|---|---|---|---|---|---|---|---|---|---|---|
| Mars | Psc | Ari | Tau | Tau | Gem | Gem | Cnc | Leo | Leo | Vir | Vir | Lib |
| Jupiter | Leo | Leo | Leo | Leo | Leo | Leo | Leo | Leo | Vir | Vir | Vir | Vir |
| Saturn | Gem | Gem | Gem | Gem | Gem | Gem | Gem | Gem | Gem | Gem | Gem | Gem |

## 2005

| | Jan | Feb | Mar | Apr | May | Jun | Jul | Aug | Sep | Oct | Nov | Dec |
|---|---|---|---|---|---|---|---|---|---|---|---|---|
| Mars | Oph | Sgr | Sgr | Cap | Aqr | Psc | Psc | Ari | Ari | Ari | Ari | Ari |
| Jupiter | Vir | Vir | Vir | Vir | Vir | Vir | Vir | Vir | Vir | Vir | Vir | Lib |
| Saturn | Gem | Gem | Gem | Gem | Gem | Gem | Cnc | Cnc | Cnc | Cnc | Cnc | Cnc |

## 2006

| | Jan | Feb | Mar | Apr | May | Jun | Jul | Aug | Sep | Oct | Nov | Dec |
|---|---|---|---|---|---|---|---|---|---|---|---|---|
| Mars | Ari | Tau | Tau | Tau | Gem | Cnc | Leo | Leo | Vir | Vir | Lib | Lib/Sco |
| Jupiter | Lib | Lib | Lib | Lib | Lib | Lib | Lib | Lib | Lib | Lib | Sco | Sco |
| Saturn | Cnc | Cnc | Cnc | Cnc | Cnc | Cnc | Cnc | Cnc | Leo | Leo | Leo | Leo |

## 2007

| | Jan | Feb | Mar | Apr | May | Jun | Jul | Aug | Sep | Oct | Nov | Dec |
|---|---|---|---|---|---|---|---|---|---|---|---|---|
| Mars | Oph/Sgr | Sgr | Cap | Aqr | Psc | Psc | Ari | Tau | Tau | Gem | Gem | Gem |
| Jupiter | Oph | Oph | Oph | Oph | Oph | Oph | Oph | Oph | Oph | Oph | Oph | Sgr |
| Saturn | Leo | Leo | Leo | Leo | Leo | Leo | Leo | Leo | Leo | Leo | Leo | Leo |

## 2008

| | Jan | Feb | Mar | Apr | May | Jun | Jul | Aug | Sep | Oct | Nov | Dec |
|---|---|---|---|---|---|---|---|---|---|---|---|---|
| Mars | Tau | Tau | Gem | Gem | Cnc | Cnc | Leo | Leo | Vir | Vir | Lib | Oph |
| Jupiter | Sgr | Sgr | Sgr | Sgr | Sgr | Sgr | Sgr | Sgr | Sgr | Sgr | Sgr | Sgr |
| Saturn | Leo | Leo | Leo | Leo | Leo | Leo | Leo | Leo | Leo | Leo | Leo | Leo |

## 2009

| | Jan | Feb | Mar | Apr | May | Jun | Jul | Aug | Sep | Oct | Nov | Dec |
|---|---|---|---|---|---|---|---|---|---|---|---|---|
| Mars | Sgr | Cap | Aqr | Psc | Psc | Ari | Tau | Tau | Gem | Cnc | Cnc | Leo |
| Jupiter | Cap | Cap | Cap | Cap | Cap | Cap | Cap | Cap | Cap | Cap | Cap | Cap |
| Saturn | Leo | Leo | Leo | Leo | Leo | Leo | Leo | Leo | Vir | Vir | Vir | Vir |

## 2010

| | Jan | Feb | Mar | Apr | May | Jun | Jul | Aug | Sep | Oct | Nov | Dec |
|---|---|---|---|---|---|---|---|---|---|---|---|---|
| Mars | Cnc | Cnc | Cnc | Cnc | Leo | Leo | Leo | Vir | Vir | Lib | Oph | Sgr |
| Jupiter | Aqr | Aqr | Aqr | Aqr | Psc | Psc | Psc | Psc | Psc | Psc | Aqr | Aqr |
| Saturn | Vir | Vir | Vir | Vir | Vir | Vir | Vir | Vir | Vir | Vir | Vir | Vir |

## 2011

| | Jan | Feb | Mar | Apr | May | Jun | Jul | Aug | Sep | Oct | Nov | Dec |
|---|---|---|---|---|---|---|---|---|---|---|---|---|
| Mars | Cap | Cap | Aqr | Psc | Ari | Tau | Tau | Gem | Gem | Cnc | Leo | Leo |
| Jupiter | Psc | Psc | Psc | Psc | Psc | Psc | Ari | Ari | Ari | Ari | Ari | Psc |
| Saturn | Vir | Vir | Vir | Vir | Vir | Vir | Vir | Vir | Vir | Vir | Vir | Vir |

## 2012

| | Jan | Feb | Mar | Apr | May | Jun | Jul | Aug | Sep | Oct | Nov | Dec |
|---|---|---|---|---|---|---|---|---|---|---|---|---|
| Mars | Leo | Leo | Leo | Leo | Leo | Leo | Vir | Vir | Lib | Sco/Oph | Sgr | Sgr |
| Jupiter | Ari | Ari | Ari | Ari | Ari | Tau | Tau | Tau | Tau | Tau | Tau | Tau |
| Saturn | Vir | Vir | Vir | Vir | Vir | Vir | Vir | Vir | Vir | Vir | Vir | Lib |

## 2013

| | Jan | Feb | Mar | Apr | May | Jun | Jul | Aug | Sep | Oct | Nov | Dec |
|---|---|---|---|---|---|---|---|---|---|---|---|---|
| Mars | Cap | Aqr | Psc | Psc | Ari | Tau | Gem | Gem | Cnc | Leo | Leo | Vir |
| Jupiter | Tau | Tau | Tau | Tau | Tau | Tau | Gem | Gem | Gem | Gem | Gem | Gem |
| Saturn | Lib | Lib | Lib | Lib | Vir | Vir | Vir | Vir | Lib | Lib | Lib | Lib |

## 2014

| | Jan | Feb | Mar | Apr | May | Jun | Jul | Aug | Sep | Oct | Nov | Dec |
|---|---|---|---|---|---|---|---|---|---|---|---|---|
| Mars | Vir | Vir | Vir | Vir | Vir | Vir | Vir | Vir | Lib | Oph | Sgr | Cap |
| Jupiter | Gem | Gem | Gem | Gem | Gem | Gem | Cnc | Cnc | Cnc | Cnc | Leo | Leo |
| Saturn | Lib | Lib | Lib | Lib | Lib | Lib | Lib | Lib | Lib | Lib | Lib | Lib |

## 2015

| | Jan | Feb | Mar | Apr | May | Jun | Jul | Aug | Sep | Oct | Nov | Dec |
|---|---|---|---|---|---|---|---|---|---|---|---|---|
| Mars | Aqr | Psc | Psc | Ari | Tau | Tau | Gem | Cnc | Leo | Leo | Vir | Vir |
| Jupiter | Leo | Cnc | Cnc | Cnc | Cnc | Leo | Leo | Leo | Leo | Leo | Leo | Leo |
| Saturn | Sco | Sco | Sco | Sco | Lib | Lib | Lib | Lib | Lib | Sco | Sco | Oph |

## 2016

| | Jan | Feb | Mar | Apr | May | Jun | Jul | Aug | Sep | Oct | Nov | Dec |
|---|---|---|---|---|---|---|---|---|---|---|---|---|
| Mars | Vir | Lib | Sco | Oph | Sco | Lib | Lib | Sco | Oph | Sgr | Cap | Cap |
| Jupiter | Leo | Leo | Leo | Leo | Leo | Leo | Leo | Vir | Vir | Vir | Vir | Vir |
| Saturn | Oph | Oph | Oph | Oph | Oph | Oph | Oph | Oph | Oph | Oph | Oph | Oph |

## 2017

| | Jan | Feb | Mar | Apr | May | Jun | Jul | Aug | Sep | Oct | Nov | Dec |
|---|---|---|---|---|---|---|---|---|---|---|---|---|
| Mars | Aqr | Psc | Ari | Tau | Tau | Gem | Cnc | Cnc | Leo | Vir | Vir | Vir |
| Jupiter | Vir | Vir | Vir | Vir | Vir | Vir | Vir | Vir | Vir | Vir | Vir | Lib |
| Saturn | Oph | Oph | Sgr | Sgr | Sgr | Oph | Oph | Oph | Oph | Oph | Oph | Sgr |

**Ari** = Aries
**Aqr** = Aquarius
**Cap** = Capricornus
**Cnc** = Cancer
**Gem** = Gemini
**Leo** = Leo
**Lib** = Libra
**Oph** = Ophiuchus
**Psc** = Pisces
**Sco** = Scorpius
**Sgr** = Sagittarius
**Tau** = Taurus
**Vir** = Virgo

Starting at Pisces, the order of the constellations of the zodiac eastward is Pisces, Aries, Taurus, Gemini, Cancer, Leo, Virgo, Libra, Scorpius, Ophiuchus, Sagittarius, Capricornus and Aquarius. Ophiuchus is not a traditational zodiacal constellation but its boundary overlaps the ecliptic which is the path (great circle) that defines the zodiac.

# Observing Uranus, Neptune and Pluto

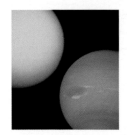

## Observing Uranus & Neptune

If any two planets could be called twins, they would be Uranus and Neptune. These two gas giants not only orbit next to each other but are also similar in size and color. Although Uranus is visible to the naked eye, it was not discovered until 1781, with Neptune following in 1846. Unfortunately, these planets are too far away for you to observe any surface clouds; however, just finding and observing them brings a satisfaction that most people will never experience.

### Locating Uranus and Neptune

Uranus and Neptune are much harder to find than the five closer planets because they are much fainter and thus less conspicuous. Planetarium programs like *Starry Night Pro* can help you locate their exact position from night to night. Additionally, on a yearly basis, the popular monthly astronomy magazines have charts for locating these twin planets. However, the easiest way to find them is to use a computerized GO TO telescope, because they have the position of the planets programmed into their hand controllers.

Although Uranus can be seen with the unaided eye, it is indistinguishable from other 5th and 6th magnitude stars, which is the limit that our eyes can see. During the years 2002 to 2017, Uranus will move east from the eastern part of the constellation Capricornus to the middle of Pisces, staying close to the ecliptic. It will be at opposition during August from 2002 to 2005, September from 2006 to 2012 and October from 2013 to 2017.

Unless you have a GO TO telescope, Neptune requires some persistence to find, since it is not visible to the naked eye; however, this 8th magnitude planet is visible with binoculars or a small telescope. During the years 2002 to 2017, Neptune will move east from the western part of the constellation Capricornus to just about the middle of Aquarius, staying very close to the ecliptic. It will be at opposition during August from 2002 to 2015, and early September for 2016 and 2017.

### Observing Uranus and Neptune

Uranus' greenish color and relative brightness distinguish it from surrounding stars but this planet appears starlike since magnifications of over 100x are required even to discern it as a small disk. Uranus' rings and clouds cannot be seen in amateur telescopes.

Neptune's pretty bluish color distinguishes it from surrounding stars; however, this planet appears more starlike than Uranus since magnifications of over 200x are required to discern a hint of a disk. Neptune's rings and surface clouds cannot be seen in amateur telescopes.

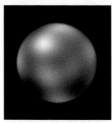

## Observing Pluto

Pluto was found by Clyde Tombaugh in 1930 after an exhaustive photographic search. Since then and despite 70 years of advancing science, little is known about this planet because of its distance and small size (its diameter is only 1,429, miles compared to our Moon's 2,160). Additionally, Pluto is the only planet that an exploratory spacecraft has not visited, and until one does, its secrets will remain out of reach.

### Locating and observing Pluto

Pluto is difficult to locate and see because it is so faint. Its magnitude hovers around 14, which is the visual magnitude limit of a 12-inch diameter telescope. And because it is so faint, visually it is difficult to distinguish from surrounding stars of similar magnitude (there are many more faint stars than bright ones).

So, how is Pluto observed visually? GO TO telescopes won't help you here. To see Pluto through an eyepiece, you will need a telescope at least 14 inches in diameter, dark skies, detailed star charts and three to four consecutive nights of comparative viewing. There are no off-the-shelf star charts that display magnitudes down to 14, so other sources are needed. The yearly *Astronomical Calendar* by Guy Ottewell is one of my favorites (the popular monthly astronomy magazines also publish a locating chart once a year). He includes Pluto's path superimposed on a detailed star chart. This chart enables you to plan your observation of Pluto when it is positioned near brighter and/or more easily identifiable reference stars. Pluto's faintness makes it impossible to know for certain whether you have seen it after just one night of observation, because it will appear just like the other fainter stars. Amateurs thus verify their observation of Pluto by observing for three or four consecutive nights in order to see it move (all the planets move against the background of stationary stars). Two consecutive days of observation may not be enough to see movement, but three days is often adequate. Obviously, drawing the area observed will help in determining the movement of the "star" planet. For the most part, Pluto will appear as one of the faintest stars seen, no matter the size of the telescope. Needless to say, Pluto is an object for the better equipped and more advanced amateur. Pluto's moon Charon cannot be seen with amateur telescopes.

During the years 2002 to 2017, Pluto will slowly move east from the constellation Ophiuchus to Sagittarius. In 2002, it will be above the star *Sabik* in Ophiuchus and by the end of 2017 it will be northeast of Sagittarius' bowl. Opposition occurs in June for these 16 years. Pluto has the greatest orbital inclination of any planet and thus can appear at a considerable distance from the ecliptic compared to the other planets (see page 11).

# Observing Deep Sky Objects
## AS WELL AS VARIABLE AND DOUBLE STARS

Deep sky objects include nebulae, star clusters and galaxies, that is, distant objects beyond our solar system. Binary and variable stars are not considered deep sky objects, but I have included them in this section to "round out" the kinds of objects that are observed by amateur and professional astronomers. The star charts in this book indicate the position of numerous deep sky objects.

### Deep sky objects overview

All of these objects are pictured and discussed in Part I of this book, but I will briefly review them here.

**Galaxies.** Galaxies represent groupings of billions of stars. All galaxies lie outside our Milky Way Galaxy at distances in the millions to billions of light years. The most distinct looking galaxies are categorized as "**spiral**," which have several curved arms radiating from a bulged center or nucleus. However, by far the most common galaxy is the **elliptical** which resembles a ball or elongated ball. There are also irregularly shaped galaxies with "mixed-up" insides. Galaxies are faint and appear brightest in larger amateur telescopes. The most well-known, and one of the few that can be seen with the naked eye, is the Andromeda Galaxy, M31 on Chart I (object #89).

**Nebulae.** The word nebulae is a general term that refers to gaseous hydrogen clouds. These clouds reside inside galaxies. For the most part, amateurs and professional astronomers can observe only the closest nebulae, those in our Milky Way Galaxy.

There are several types of nebulae: galactic clouds, planetary nebulae and supernova remnants. **Galactic clouds** represent birthing places of stars. They can appear dark, like silhouettes or bluish/reddish in color because they either reflect starlight or create their own light. These nebulae are located mostly in the arms of our Milky Way Galaxy. The best example is the Great Orion Nebula, M42, shown on Chart C (object #22). **Planetary nebulae** (the name has nothing to do with the planets, it's just an old name that stuck) represent the remains of outer atmospheres from "large" stars in their death throes. These nebulae are spherical, ringed or have diametrically opposed lobes. The best example is the Ring Nebula, M57 on Charts F & G (object #69). **Supernova remnants** are nebulae created from

The center of the well-known Andromeda Galaxy is visible to the naked eyes (catalog designations of M31 and NGC 224). In all, this galaxy spans a length in the sky of six Moons widths. See Chart I, object #89.

the explosions of very large stars at the ends of their lives. M1 on Chart B (object #20) is a good example. Supernova remnants are rare compared to other nebulae. On the average, nebulae are faint and appear best in larger amateur telescopes. However, there are a handful that are magnificent even in small telescopes.

**Star clusters.** The term "star cluster" is a general term referring to an open cluster, galactic cluster or globular cluster. An **open cluster** represents a group of stars born together out of the same nebula, anywhere from a dozen to a thousand. Open and galactic clusters are similar, but a **galactic cluster** is a young cluster residing within an arm of our galaxy or other spiral galaxies. **Globular clusters** are distinctly different from open or galactic clusters, being a collection of several thousand to a million stars compacted into the shape of a ball. Our galaxy has about 200 globular clusters surrounding it in a spherical halo. Clusters are easier to observe than nebulae and galaxies, so many are visible in small telescopes. However, globular clusters really come alive in larger telescopes, more than you would think from viewing them in smaller telescopes.

### Variable stars & AAVSO

Any star that changes in actual brightness over a period of hours to days or years is considered a variable star. Stars change in brightness for a few different reasons. For the record, twinkling stars are not variable stars. *Twinkling is caused by atmospheric turbulence and is most noticeable when stars are near the horizon.* Traditionally, variable stars are not considered deep sky objects, but I have included them here because they are just as challenging to find and observe as deep sky objects.

Variable stars are divided into two categories. Algol in Perseus (Chart B, object #12) is an example of an extrinsic variable star known as an eclipsing binary. Algol is orbited by a significantly fainter star that passes between Algol and Earth, blocking and lowering Algol's light and magnitude for a period of several hours.

Most variable stars change in brightness due to intrinsic physical changes that occur within the star's structure. The Cepheid variables are the best known type. These stars expand and contract, changing their overall size by as much as 30%,

# Observing Deep Sky Objects

and therefore their brightness varies by as much as one magnitude.

The American Association of Variable Star Observers (AAVSO) is an organization whose members (mostly amateurs) observe variable stars, record their magnitudes and submit data to a central office on a regular basis. The collected data is reviewed by the professional community for trends and anomalies. Amateurs wishing to participate in this should check out the AAVSO website (www.aavso.org). Two of the most famous comet discoverers of the 20th century, Leslie Peltier and David Levy, were active participants in AAVSO.

### Double, binary and multiple stars

Double stars can be either optical or binary. Optical double stars appear to be close to each other because they are in the same line of sight. For example, the Moon and Venus sometimes appear close to each other in the sky but we know that they are really far apart.

About half of all stars are binary or multiple stars. A binary is a pair of stars orbiting each other, while multiple stars represent a system of three or more stars revolving around each other. A good example is Mizar (Chart A, object #5). Casually, we refer to Mizar as a binary star; however, it is a multiple star system. In a small telescope at 50x, Mizar can be separated into two stars, known as Mizar A (the actual Mizar) and Mizar B. However, each of these stars has another star revolving around it. This multiple star system has a total of four stars. The two stars that make up Mizar (Mizar A) revolve around each other in 20.5 days, while Mizar A and B take about 10,000 years to revolve around each other.

Numerous double stars are indicated on the charts. Most can be observed with small, well-collimated telescopes with magnifications from 50x to 200x.

## OBSERVING DEEP SKY OBJECTS

Deep sky objects are markedly different (fainter) than the planets, Moon or Sun, so they are observed differently. Below are some suggestions for observing these objects.

**1** Since deep sky objects are faint, it is best to observe them when the Moon is

The Great Hercules Cluster, designated M13 or NGC 6205 is a favorite globular cluster in the northern hemisphere. See Chart F, object #63.

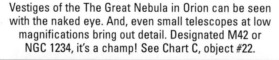

Vestiges of the The Great Nebula in Orion can be seen with the naked eye. And, even small telescopes at low magnifications bring out detail. Designated M42 or NGC 1234, it's a champ! See Chart C, object #22.

not out because its light whitewashes the night sky along with most fainter objects. The fainter deep sky objects cannot be seen when the Moon is out. As you can imagine, the Moon is a bane for those studying deep sky objects.

**2** Situate or position your telescope away from bright or glaring lights. If this is impossible, at least keep your back to these lights.

**3** Deep sky objects can only be observed when the sky is at its darkest, generally around or after astronomical twilight in the evening.

**4** Once outside at your observing site, let your eyes "dark-adapt" for a good 15 minutes before observing fainter deep sky objects (see page 41). Eat up this time by looking at some of your favorite brighter objects.

**5** To preserve your dark-adapted eyes, use only a red-light flashlight to look at your reference material or for writing notes. Using a white-light flashlight can destroy or interfere with your night vision.

**6** If you have never found a deep sky object, begin with easier objects from the charts — those that are bright and conspicuous, like the Pleiades, Mizar, Albireo, the Great Orion Nebula, the Andromeda Galaxy and so forth. Some of the objects on the star charts are fairly easy to find and see, while others require more diligence and/or dark skies.

**7** If you continue having difficulty finding deep sky objects, enlist the help of others. If this is not practical, search for these objects in many short sessions over several days, weeks or months, instead of long, drawn-out sessions. You may find that failing to see these objects is not your fault, but simply due to your sky, especially if you must contend with light pollution.

**8** If light pollution is a problem, try observing these types of objects when they are higher in the sky, near the zenith. More often than not, you may simply have to observe away from your area. I live on the immediate outskirts of Tucson, so half of my sky is immersed in the city's glow, but the other half is okay; however, I still have to travel about 30 miles (with all my equipment) to get to reasonably dark skies for serious deep sky exploration.

**Using averted vision to see deep sky objects.** Averted vision means viewing a faint object using peripheral vision instead of looking directly at it. Why do this? Objects that are faint, at the threshold of what our eyes can see, disappear if you stare or look at them directly. This is because our eyes have a reduced number of light receptacles in the center of the retina which makes this area literally "blind" (called the blind spot) to objects with very low brightness. In observational astronomy, a "trick" to seeing fainter objects (including fainter stars) is to use peripheral vision. This often helps to see objects that may not be there on first inspection.

## M objects, NGC & IC objects and Moore

Over the past two centuries, astronomers have compiled numerous catalogs of celestial objects, some very specialized and others more general. The specialized catalogs are most often used by professional astronomers whereas the general catalogs are used by amateurs and professionals alike. Below are descriptions of the most popular catalogs.

**M objects of Charles Messier.** The most popular catalog of celestial objects was compiled by Frenchman Charles Messier (1730–1817) in the late 1700s. This catalog is still widely used today and its 110 deep sky objects represent the biggest and brightest visible from the northern hemisphere. In astronomy circles, whenever you hear someone say the letter "M," followed by a number from 1 to 110, it refers to an object in this catalog. Included are the Great Orion Nebula (M42), Pleiades (M45), Great Hercules Cluster (M13), Ring Nebula (M57) and many more. It just so happens that at least one of every type of deep sky object is represented in this catalog. Various books and resources on the Messier objects are available at most telescope stores.

Charles Messier was a comet hunter who started cataloging fuzzy appearing objects in order to avoid mistaking them for comets, but soon expended the catalog to deep sky objects in general.

All of the Messier objects can be seen with a small telescope, and a few can even be seen with the naked eyes. Many can be glimpsed with binoculars. Once a year, around the New Moon in March, it is possible to see all but one of these objects in a single night. This is commonly called the Messier Marathon.

The Crab Nebula is the first object and only supernova remnant listed in the Messier catalog (designated M1 or NGC 1952). Supernova remnants represent the rarest type of nebulae. Chart B, object #20.

Most of us have heard about the Seven Sisters or Pleiades because of the charming stories associated with these stars. This cluster is one of the few visible to the naked eye. Although this cluster looks like a little dipper, it is not the "Little Dipper"! Chart B, object #14.

**New General Catalogue (NGC) and IC addendum.** It became apparent in the 1800s that a thorough catalog of deep sky objects would be invaluable to astronomers worldwide in their study of the celestial sphere. In 1888, J. L. E. Dreyer published a comprehensive compilation entitled, *New General Catalogue of Nebulae and Clusters of Stars* (NGC), listing 7,840 deep sky objects in the northern and southern hemispheres. By 1908, an additional 5,386 objects were added by Dreyer to what is called the *Index Catalogue* (IC). These catalogs represent the last major compilations of galaxies, nebulae and clusters. With the advent of astrophotography, the number of objects, mostly galaxies, that could be recorded on film became too numerous to sensibly catalog. Professional astronomers looking deep into the cosmos for the faintest objects use photographic atlases instead of traditional star charts.

*NGC 2000.0*, edited by Roger Sinnott and published by Sky Publishing Corporation (www.skyandtelescope.com) is the only modern book listing all 13,226 NGC and IC objects along with their current celestial positions and original descriptions. Many star charts and atlases include the NGC and IC objects. The hand controllers on GO TO telescopes (page 52) normally include all the NGC and IC objects as well as brief descriptions.

A larger telescope, 12 inches in diameter or greater, is required to observe all the NGC and IC objects. This is because most of the objects are faint galaxies. I generally observe with a 4-inch refractor and have found that I can see many, but not all, of the open, galactic and globular clusters listed in the NGC/IC catalogs, but most of the listed galaxies are beyond its grasp.

**C objects of Moore's Caldwell catalog.** Patrick Caldwell-Moore is the consummate amateur who popularized astronomy on British TV and can be thought of as the Carl Sagan of the Brits. In the early 1990s, he compiled his own catalog of 109 celestial objects located throughout the northern and southern hemispheres (a number of them can only be viewed from the southern hemisphere). His cue for 109 objects was the Messier count, but his list consists of the more interesting and sometimes challenging NGC/IC objects. Many telescope stores sell a laminated card listing his chosen objects.

# Observing Deep Sky Objects

**Overlapping designations.** Celestial catalogs are independent of each other, so an object can often be listed in several catalogs, thus acquiring different designations. Almost all of the Messier objects have NGC numbers (but the numbers are not the same). Most amateurs refer to an object by its name or M number, if it has one. Otherwise, NGC or IC numbers are used. There are unofficial lists of objects that have "proper" names, but even this can get confusing because some objects have several names or are duplicated. The Omega Nebula and Swan Nebula are both M17 (Chart G) and there is a separate northern and southern hemisphere "Jewel Box" (NGC 6231 & NGC 4755 on Charts G & J).

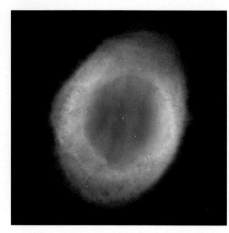

The Ring Nebula (M57) is a well-known example of a planetary nebula, representing the shedded atmosphere of a dying star. Chart F & G, object #69.

## Tips for Finding Deep Sky Objects

If you have a GO TO telescope, finding deep sky objects is just a matter of pressing a few buttons. However, if your telescope does not have such wizardry, you must find objects the "old fashioned" way — manually moving and pointing your telescope using star charts as your guide.

I love my GO TO telescope mounts but I also enjoy finding objects manually. Personally, I think you should try your hand at finding objects manually from time to time. This will provide practice in learning the constellations and using star charts. Additionally, it will give you a better sense of the lay and movements of the celestial sphere.

**How hard is it to manually find celestial objects?** If you can navigate your car using a street map, you should be able to translate those same skills into finding celestial objects. However, if you have trouble with vehicular navigation, it only means that you might have to practice more.

Dark-adapted eyes, dark skies (a sky away from city lights) and moonless nights are either essential or helpful when observing deep sky objects because these objects are faint! If all three conditions are satisfied, most Messier objects are easily found because they stand out amongst surrounding stars, even in small telescopes. However, the opposite can be true if just one of these conditions is not met.

**What will these objects look like through a telescope?** Except for a few deep sky objects, all are much, much fainter than photos. Additionally, the vivid colors and miniscule detail captured by photos cannot be seen visually. Stars and planets show colors but nebulae and galaxies look whitish. Don't let this dissuade you from marching forward to find and observe these objects. Views through the telescope are real and captivating. There is something about seeing them "live," a vividness that cannot be conveyed through photographs. Star clusters are most often prettier than in pictures. Globular clusters come *alive* with larger telescopes and details of objects *can* be glimpsed by spending time studying them. There is a whole universe out there, so go out and have fun seeing it firsthand.

### General Viewing Considerations

**1** Review the section on General Observing Considerations on pages 40 & 41, as well as Using Your Telescope starting on page 49. Make sure you are familiar and comfortable with the operation of your telescope before observing.

**2** To locate an object, always use eyepieces that provide low magnification, around 50x. Low-powered eyepieces yield the greatest field of view, that is, you see more of the sky at one time, which makes it easier to come across an object. Any eyepiece that delivers 50x magnification has a field of view of 1° or more, which is equivalent to two Moon widths.

**3** Ensure that your finder (traditional or reflex-sight) is well aligned to the view through the eyepiece. Good pointing accuracy of the finder increases the likeli-

hood of finding objects quickly. Occasionally, the object you are trying to locate will be in the eyepiece after you have pointed the telescope with the finder. More often, the object is not in view and you have to move the telescope around to find it. *See examples below for strategies.*

**4** Although the star charts is this book are good for finding many objects, you may eventually want to purchase more detailed charts that go to fainter magnitudes, like *Sky Atlas 2000.0* by Wil Tirion and Roger Sinnott (Sky Publishing Corporation).

**5** If the thought of finding deep sky objects seems daunting, work on finding the biggest and brightest first and ease into the "harder" later. In this book, objects described as binocular objects (on the charts) are good starting points for first telescope objects.

**6** Initially, practice finding objects for short periods of time instead of long, drawn-out sessions. If you are having difficulty finding objects, plan on many short sessions over a period of time and stick with the easiest objects noted on the charts.

**7** If you are having a very difficult time finding objects, seek the help of a friend, the advice of a telescope store or a local astronomy club.

## Examples of Strategies for Finding Deep Sky Objects

**A** The Great Orion Nebula (M42) is easy to find and see, but the nearby nebula M78 is harder. Let's start with M42. This nebula represents an easy type of object to locate because it is visible to the naked eye (not in light-polluted skies). The challenge with locating M42 is navigating the constellations of the night sky. To observe this wonder, find the constellation Orion (one of the brightest patterns in the sky), then its belt of three prominent stars, and finally "drop down" from the belt stars to the sword stars. The middle of three faint stars that comprise the sword is the Great Orion Nebula. To observe it, aim your telescope, using your finder. The nebula should appear at or in a low magnification eyepiece field of view of around 50x. If it is not visible in the eyepiece, move your telescope a little from side to side and up and down to bring it into view. Increase your magnification to get a better view of the Trapezium that lies within, (Chart C). M78 is a bit more challenging because unlike M42, it is not visible to the naked eye. This nebula is found using basic figures of geometry — in this case, a right angle. Point the finder at a spot in the sky that is at a right angle (90° angle) from the left belt star, at a distance equal to the width of the three

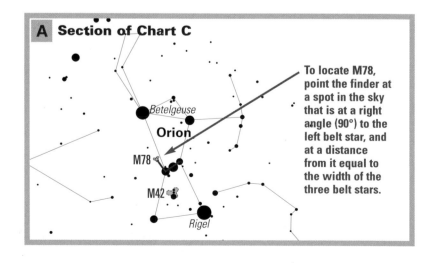

**A Section of Chart C**

Betelgeuse
Orion
M78
M42
Rigel

To locate M78, point the finder at a spot in the sky that is at a right angle (90°) to the left belt star, and at a distance from it equal to the width of the three belt stars.

# Observing Deep Sky Objects

belt stars. This is one of the few that I often "peg," getting it positioned in the eyepiece with the first aiming of the scope. But the difficulty with this nebula is not so much finding it as seeing it. It is *much* fainter than M42 and is more easily seen in dark skies than in light-polluted ones.

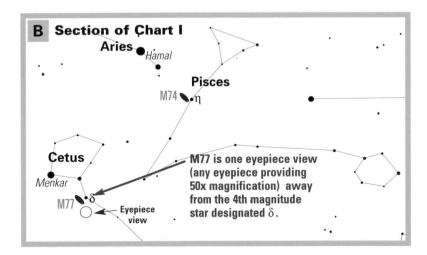

**B** As long as you can see some of the "fainter" stars that make up the constellation Cetus, finding the location of galaxy M77 is relatively easy, but seeing this galaxy is another matter. It is located within 1 arc degree of the 4th magnitude star designated by the Greek letter δ, which is the first star below the "head" of the sea monster. A Plössl eyepiece providing a magnification of about 50x has a field of view spanning an arc degree, so by placing the star δ *Ceti* at one edge of the eyepiece field of view, it is possible to find the galaxy on the opposite side. The difficulty with seeing this galaxy is that it is very faint and may go unnoticed if the skies are not dark. Spiral galaxies that are orientated more "edge-on" to our line of sight appear visually brighter than those more "face-on." M77 is a spiral galaxy that is more "face-on," so this adds to its overall faintness (referred to as having a low surface brightness). The nucleus of this galaxy appears starlike and there is a faint star near its edge, both causing some confusion in its identity for first-time observers using smaller telescopes.

M74 in Pisces is similar to M77 but fainter. It is another face-on galaxy that is 1.3 degrees from a 4th magnitude star in Pisces designated by the Greek letter η. You may have to use adverted vision to see this galaxy.

**C** The pair of galaxies known as M81 and M82 are all-time favorites because both are bright and close enough to each other to be viewed in the same low-power eyepiece field of view. These galaxies can also be seen in some

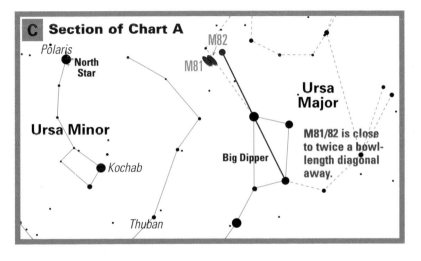

light-polluted skies. However, locating them can be challenging because they are not near any conspicuously bright stars. I find them by aiming the finder at a spot in the sky that is twice the length of extension of a diagonal of the Big Dipper's bowl. Starting at this point, I then slowly move the telescope up and down and side to side until I come across either galaxy. M82 stands out the most and looks like a cigar because it is an edge-on, irregular, spiral-type galaxy. What happens if I can't locate them? I reposition the telescope to the original spot and search again. Usually this proves fruitful. Why reposition it to the original spot? Because you will find that moving the telescope "around" to find an object will most likely position the scope at a considerable distance from the area of the object. I have bad nights when I can't seem to find anything, so I give up and come back later or try another night.

**D** **Potpourri:** On this chart, I have indicated, using colored lines, the geometry for providing "spots" to aim the finder at. M70 is halfway between two stars. M22 is one of the vertices that roughly completes a parallelogram. M8 is about twice the distance of a handle and bowl star away. M7 is close to twice the distance of the two indicated stars while M6 forms a shallow triangle between the stars shown. M55 seems like it is floating in the middle of nowhere until you realize that it is in line with two of the bowl stars. M17 is a little harder to locate but if you can see fainter stars, you can draw a line between two of them and drop down one-third of the way from the star in Scutum to get close to it. M17 is bright and easily spotted when you come across it. I know that many people don't like geometry, but finding deep sky objects is often a case of just using *simple* geometry with the stars.

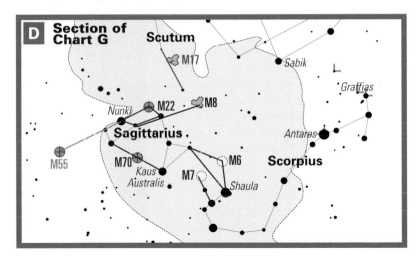

**When all else fails.** The galaxies within the Virgo Cluster of Galaxies indicated in star Chart E are difficult to see because they are small and faint. Moreover, they are difficult to find and positively identify because 14 of them are located in a relatively small area of the sky without any conspicuous naked-eye or other distingushing stars. So, unless you have a "detailed" star chart, it is impossible to positively identify each of these galaxies. To find and identify them, you need a star chart that shows stars to fainter magnitudes, like the one on page 71. Navigation of the telescope is accomplished by moving it, from one set of stars to another, using a low-powered eyepiece and the star chart for guidance. In other words, you match up the stars in your eyepiece with those on your chart, then move the telescope a bit, and again, match up the new stars in your eyepiece with those on the chart. To start, use the star Vindemiatrix as an anchor because it can be positively identified. This is a tedious process, but it works. Note: If you are using a refractor or SCT with a right-angle diagonal for comfortable viewing (page 49), your images through the eyepiece will be mirror images, with left and right reversed. This can complicate matching the stars. A way around this is to scan the chart into your computer and flip the image with a graphics program.

# Comets & Meteors

**Comets** are spectacular to behold. They can span the sky with a splendor unequaled by any other astronomical object. They bring astronomy to entire continents, and their grand displays unite us in awe of the Universe. In early civilizations, comets were harbingers of the future because something as impressive as the unexpected appearance of a comet in the sky had to be significant. Depending on the culture, a comet represented either a good or bad omen. Today, we can enjoy comets as neither good nor bad, but as the spectacular objects that they are. It is good fortune when we get the opportunity to view one of these marvelous treasures of our solar system.

## The most famous comet

Halley's comet (pronounced HAL-lee) was named in honor of the English astronomer Edmond Halley (1656–1742) who concluded that the great comet of 1682 was the same one that had appeared in 1531 and 1607. Its regularity along with its brightness have made it the most familiar comet in the solar system. Comet Halley returns about every 76 years. Its last appearance was in 1985, so it won't be back until 2061. Its orbit brings it in closer than Venus and out between Neptune and Pluto.

## The size and composition of comets

The nuclei of comets, that is, their solid bodies, vary in size with diameters ranging from just a few to perhaps 150 miles. Pictures of Comet Halley's nucleus show that it resembles a potato in shape, with dimensions of approximately 6 by 10 miles.

The often used phrase "dirty snowball" aptly describes the composition of comets, for they are a mixture of various ices and sand-type dust.

As comets approach the Sun and heat up, the ices that make up their nuclei sublime, that is, they change directly from solids to gases, to become the comae and tails. This starts to occur when comets reach the distance that Jupiter is from the Sun.

Comae can have diameters ranging from 125,000 to 1.2 million miles and they always obscure the small nuclei. Comet tails can stretch for millions of miles; the longest was Hale-Bopp's reaching 140 million miles. The solar wind and pressure from sunlight always push tails away from the Sun. Sometimes comets develop two tails: a yellowish-white dust tail and a blue

Comet Hale-Bopp appeared in the night skies from 1996 to 1997. It had two tails, one of white dust, the other a blue ion.

ion tail (blue from fluorescing ions). Either one or both tails may be present.

Comets can exhibit jets, which are spurious eruptions that shoot out from the nuclei. These develop when pockets of ice volatiles are exposed and warmed by the Sun. A jet can turn on and off, depending on the rotation of the nucleus and exposure to the Sun.

A comet is considered to be an asteroid until it develops a coma or tail. Many comets are not visible to the naked eye and require the use of a telescope.

## When will the next comet appear?

Normally, astronomers cannot predict when bright, naked-eye comets will appear. Most comets come from the outer regions of our solar system and do not become noticeable until they get "close" to the Sun. These comets await individuals like Gene and Carolyn Shoemaker or David Levy who gaze up and discover them so they can be announced to the world. Unexpected gifts are often remembered the most, and so it is with comets. These unexpected and marvelous guests leave us with the fondest memories.

## Observing comets

The naked eye, binoculars and telescopes at low magnifications can be used to observe large visible comets. In my opinion, binoculars mounted on a tripod are the ideal observing instrument. Binoculars will enable you to see most or all of a comet in the same field of view while the tripod will help steady the binoculars and allow easy extended viewing.

## Meteors

On a typical clear night, while looking at the sky for 10 to 15 minutes, you stand a good chance of seeing a meteor, commonly called a shooting star. In fact, about seven meteors per hour can be seen normally. But at specific times of the year, there are meteor showers which may allow you to see 10 to 200 meteors per hour. And, on rare occasions, if you are very fortunate, you may encounter a storm that displays tens of thousands of meteors per hour.

## Meteoroid, meteor and meteorite

These terms are often confused. A **meteoroid** is a small rock in space. When a meteoroid enters the Earth's atmosphere, we view it as a white luminous streak called a **meteor**. If the meteoroid survives its journey through the atmosphere and happens to reach the Earth's surface as a "rock," it is then called a **meteorite**.

## Meteor characteristics

Most meteors are caused by meteoroids the size of a grain of sand. Atmospheric speeds reach up to 45 miles per second or 162,000 miles per hour, and trail heights range from 30 to 60 miles above the Earth's surface. A very bright meteor, about the brightness of Venus, is called a fireball. An exceedingly bright meteor, much brighter than a fireball, is called a bolide. Bolides light up the whole sky like a giant camera flash, producing strong shadows. They may be accompanied by sound and often leave a lingering trail. The brightest may be seen during the day since meteors pierce the atmosphere unceasingly day and night.

## Meteor showers: legacy of comets

Meteor showers are produced from sand-size silicate particles left behind by comets. About a dozen showers occur every year when the Earth passes through semi-permanent swarms of cometary debris that also orbit the Sun.

Meteors associated with showers appear to radiate from a point in the celestial sphere, so showers are named after the constellation from which the meteors seemingly originate. The reason why they appear to radiate from a specific constellation is because the sand particles orbit in the same direction as the constellation.

New showers will be established when future cometary debris crosses Earth's orbit. Existing showers will eventually fade away as debris dissipates. The Perseids have been around for a thousand years, while there is no indication of the Quadrantids further back than 200 years. Shower intensity varies and cannot be predicted accurately from year to year. Some forecasts are available in the popular monthly astronomy magazines.

## Meteor storms

One of the last great meteor storms was associated with the Leonids in 1966. For a period of about an hour, more than a hundred thousand meteors pierced the sky. To say the least, watching meteors rain down, filling the entire sky, would be awesome! Unfortunately, most of us will never see a meteor storm. Unlike total solar eclipses, storms are rare and cannot be predicted accurately.

The debris from Comet Tempel-Tuttle, which circles the Sun every 33.2 years, creates the Leonids. On average, the debris from this comet produces a meteor count of only 10 per hour, but it has concentrated pockets responsible for most of the storms seen in the past few hundred years. This comet is not normally visible to the naked eye, but nevertheless, it frequently visits the inner solar system, and regularly leaves behind a trail of debris. These debris fields overlap, creating pockets with higher than normal particle counts that are responsible for producing the storms.

The Leonids and Draconids are currently the only known showers capable of becoming storms. However, the debris from future comets, that is, new comets that come in from afar, have the potential to produce similar displays if the Earth passes through their wake.

## Observing meteors & showers

Meteors are observed best with the naked eye. It is not practical to view them with binoculars or a telescope because they last just a fraction of a second and extend over arcs greater than what can be viewed through these instruments. Additionally, their appearance and paths in the sky cannot be predicted.

The first time you see a meteor, you will probably say, "What was that?" And, unless you are looking in the direction of its path, you may only catch it out of the corner of your eye, but, even then, it will be exciting!

Meteors not associated with showers are called sporadic meteors. Both sporadic meteors and shower meteors can appear anywhere in the sky. Although the meteors from showers originate from a small area in the sky, this will not be immediately apparent. And when watching showers, it is not necessary to face the associated constellation, because the meteors will appear all around you. The best way to watch a shower is to get comfortable with proper clothing and furniture. I like sitting in an outdoor chair and changing my direction from time to time. I have seen others fully extended on lawn chairs or sleeping bag mattresses. Lying on your back, facing up, provides the greatest view of the sky, but this position may be awkward for some.

The most favorable time to observe meteors or showers is from around midnight to early morning, before the Sun rises, when the Earth is rushing head-on into the meteoroids. And the viewing is best when the Moon is not out, because the moonlight easily white-washes the sky, making it difficult to see any meteor.

### Yearly Meteor Showers

| Shower[1] (Constellation) | Peak | Date[2] (Active Period) | Hourly Rate[3] |
|---|---|---|---|
| QUADRANTIDS (Bootes)[4] | Jan 3 | (Jan 1 – Jan 5) | 60 – 200 |
| LYRIDS (Lyra) | Apr 22 | (Apr 16 – Apr 25) | 15 – 20+ |
| Eta ($\eta$) AQUARIDS (Aquarius) | May 5 | (Apr 19 – May 28) | 60 |
| Southern Delta ($\delta$) AQUARIDS | July 29 | (July 12 – Aug 19) | 20 |
| PERSEIDS (Perseus) | Aug 12 | (July 17 – Aug 24) | 120 – 160 |
| DRACONIDS (Draco) | Oct 8 | (Oct 6 – Oct 10) | 5[5] |
| ORIONIDS (Orion) | Oct 21 | (Oct 2 – Nov 7) | 20 |
| Southern TAURIDS (Taurus) | Nov 5 | (Oct 1 – Nov 25) | 5 |
| Northern TAURIDS | Nov 13 | (Oct 1 – Nov 25) | 5 |
| LEONIDS (Leo) | Nov 17 | (Nov 14 – Nov 21) | 10[5] |
| GEMINIDS (Gemini) | Dec 14 | (Dec 7 – Dec 17) | 120 |
| URSIDS (Ursa Minor) | Dec 22 | (Dec 17 – Dec 26) | 10+ |

[1]Showers have traditionally been named after the constellation they appear to radiate from. [2]Peak date is approximate and may vary by a day from year to year. [3]Hourly rate is frequency or number of meteors per hour around the Peak date. [4]The Quadrantids was named after an obsolete constellation recognized in the 1800s. Today, this shower is sometimes referred to as the Bootids, after the constellation Bootes. [5]These showers have the potential to produce meteor storms, with spectacular displays of thousands of meteors per hour.

# Aurorae and Other Splendors

**Aurorae** are beautiful swaths of colored light that blanket an area of the night sky. Subtle or bold, they may shimmer, fold and sizzle. The years 1999 to 2002 provided extraordinary displays because this period marked a height of solar activity which occurs about every 11 years. Solar outbursts during these times trigger these beautiful events. Aurorae occur when massive quantities of charged particles (electrons and protons — the parts of hydrogen atoms) are hurled from the Sun and interact with our atmosphere. These particles are corralled and funneled by Earth's magnetic field to collide with the molecules in the upper atmosphere. This excites oxygen and nitrogen to glow in green and red colors. The northern hemisphere aurorae are commonly referred to as the Aurora Borealis, and those in the southern hemisphere as Aurora Australis.

**Observing.**
Aurorae appear at their brightest and most dazzling in the regions closest to the poles on Earth, where the magnetic fields are the strongest. However, during periods of peak solar activity, they have been observed lower than 30° north or south latitude. However, these displays lack the brilliance and vividness of their polar counterparts. Overall, aurorae span large areas of the sky. Their colors can be green, red or dull white. Some of their shapes include ribbon arcs, spiked arcs, folded curtains, rays, flames, patches of soft glow, etc. They can shimmer, move and pulsate.

I have only seen one aurora display in my life. Unfortunately, it appeared as just faint white patches that slowly changed in brightness but displayed none of the beauty shown in many photographs. You can sign up for emails that predict aurorae based on the Sun's activity at www.spaceweather.com.

## The green flash
One of the earliest references to the green flash was in the 1882 novel *Le Rayon Vert*, by Jules Vernes. For the longest time, the green flash was considered a rare event, and seeing one was like winning today's lottery. What is the green flash? It is a flash of green that appears as the last vestige of the Sun drops below the horizon. The green flash represents nothing more than seeing the second to last color in the spread of the spectrum, which spans from red, orange and yellow to green and blue. As the Sun sets, the atmosphere near the horizon acts like a prism for the last light, with green and blue being the last colors to be pulled under. We normally don't see a blue flash because this color is easily scattered by the atmosphere, but green sometimes gets through. There have been reports of a blue flash, but this represents the rarest of this type of event, visible only with the clearest atmospheric conditions.

**Observing.**
Many people report seeing the green flash when out at sea, but it is visible over land. You have the best chance of seeing it when the horizon appears clear and the

color of the Sun stays "true" to the end. Your chances of seeing it are greatly reduced when the atmosphere creates a reddish Sun, which will scatter any green before it reaches your eyes. In my own observations, the green is very fleeting and could easily be missed. In fact, I would say that most people would not notice the hint of green if they did not know about its occurrence. I have only seen the flash over land it hasn't appeared like a flash, but more like a "quick roll into and out of green for a split second" before the Sun fades into the horizon. I would be interested in your experiences. You observe this event with your naked eyes, so you must wait until the Sun is almost down before looking.

### Zodiacal light

Little beknownst to most, there is a giant cloud of dust that shrouds the inner planets of our solar system. This dust reflects sunlight, and under the right conditions can be seen as a faint glow in the western sky after sunset, or in the eastern sky before sunrise. And because this cloud is flattened along the plane of the solar system (remember, the planets orbit the Sun in pretty much the same "flattened" plane), its faint glow follows the ecliptic, that is, the constellations of the zodiac.

**Left page.** Aurorae are more common at higher latitudes around the Earth's poles, but occasionally a display occurs at lower latitudes, as captured by this picture taken from Kitt Peak in Tucson, Arizona, latitude 32°N.

**Observing.** The zodiacal light is best observed when the ecliptic is perpendicular to the horizon. This happens in February and March evenings in the western sky and in September and October mornings in the eastern sky. The zodiacal light is easily washed out, so look for it under dark skies, away from city lights. Watch for it when it firsts gets dark or before it gets light. It can be shaped somewhat like a large, fat flame coming up from the horizon with its tip stretched toward the zenith. Its brightness is similar to the fainter parts of the Milky Way Band, but it can also be as bright as the southern summer band.

### Moon and Sun halos

I frequently get questions about Moon halos when they appear in the sky. Halos can appear around the the Sun and Moon and are similar to rainbows but are produced by higher altitude clouds containing hexagonal (pencil-shaped) ice crystals instead of raindrops. The halos around the Moon particularly stand out in the night sky and look mysterious because of the Moon's play with the thin and wispy clouds housing the crystals.

**Below.** A Sun halo is caused by hexagonal-shaped water crystals in higher-altitude clouds. These same crystals can produce halos around the Moon. Rainbows are created from round raindrops instead of crystals.

# Astrophotography
## TAKING PHOTOS OF THE NIGHT SKY

The Universe is beautiful, and it is only natural to want to photograph it. Now, I don't want to bridle your enthusiasm, but it is probably better to take astrophotography in small steps and with some thought because overall, it is a bit harder than "point and shoot." So, If you purchased this book as your introduction to astronomy, but are really using it as a fast track to astrophotograpy, I just want to say one thing: "Slow down, partner!"

Astronomy needed photography. The idea got rolling in 1882 after David Gill photographed Comet Halley and noticed that there were many more stars surrounding the comet than could be seen with the eyes. In the years following, astronomers quickly discovered that film (originally glass plates) could record stars much fainter than the eyes could see, and record details in nebulae and galaxies that could not be viewed directly. Imaging the sky also provided permanent records that astronomers could study further. In essence, astrophotography opened a door to a very faint Universe that was beyond the reach of our eyes only.

Astrophotography is a skill. It can be learned like anything else, and with practice, you get better. Today, it is possible for amateurs to get pictures that rival some of those taken at professional observatories. But specialized accessories and equipment are needed to achieve this result. One of the challenges of astrophotography is keeping pace with technology because film, digital cameras and image processing software are constantly improving. Although astrophotography is easier today than ever before, it still requires a commitment of time, energy and money.

### Some terminology
Below are frequently used terms related to astrophotography. There are also many others, but these pop up often.

**Single Lens Reflex camera (SLR).** Camera of choice when using film for astrophotography. Lenses are detachable. Adapters allow SLRs to attach to eyepiece focusers. Manual SLRs are best, since these do not require a battery to operate the shutter.

**Digital camera.** Any of the new consumer digital cameras on the market (these are similar to, but not the same as CCD cameras defined below). Digital cameras can be used for some astrophotography but are not designed to take time exposures, which are required for many objects.

**Guidescope.** A smaller telescope attached to the main telescope (this is not a finderscope) used to keep the telescope "on course." All motorized telescopes do not "follow" stars with perfect accuracy. A reticle-type eyepiece is used in conjunction with the guidescope to keep a guide star (a randomly but conveniently selected star) in the cross hairs. The guide star is maintained in the cross hairs by making small nudges to the mount using a hand controller that has directional buttons.

**Slow-motion control.** The ability to minutely control the speed and direction of the motors that drive the telescope. Necessary for making minor pointing corrections for extended exposures. This is an advanced practice.

**CCD camera (Charged-Coupled Device).** A digital camera designed specifically for astrophotography. These recording devices do not look like regular digital cameras and require a computer to operate (laptops are often used). Cost varies from the high hundreds to thousands of dollars. Overall, CCDs provide the best images of celestial objects.

### Prelude to astrophotography examples
All but the simplest astrophotography is beyond this book, so I will briefly outline below what it takes to photograph various objects. If you have a high interest in learning astrophotography, I recommend visiting a telescope store and browsing through their astrophotography books (call them first for an inventory). If this is inconvenient, check out the books sold by Sky Publishing at www.skyandtelescope.com. Astrophotography isn't just the act of taking a picture, it's the cumulative total of purchasing specialized equipment, becoming skilled in its use and finally becoming adept at processing the image with computer software.

**1 Above middle.** The easiest type of astrophotography is to take "star trail" photographs. The longer the exposure, the longer the trails. This picture was taken using the camera setup shown at left. All I did was aim and keep the shutter open for 15 minutes.

**Left.** The setup for taking star trail photos — an SLR camera on a tripod with a shutter release cable. An SLR camera is a must for astrophotography because it allows taking time exposures. Additionally, it can be fitted with adapters to attach to telescopes. Time exposures are accomplished by setting the shutter speed to "B" and locking the shutter open with the shutter release cable, **A**.

## 1 Easiest Astrophotography ★ No Telescope

**Photos of:** Trails of stars as they march across the sky.

**Examples:** See picture numbered **1** on previous page.

**Equipment:** SLR camera, shutter release cable and tripod. Film speed from 100 to 800. See bottom picture on previous page for setup.

**Discussion:** If you have an SLR camera, you can take these kinds of photos. Simply set your camera on a tripod, point it toward the night sky and take a time exposure (shutter speed dial set on "B"), anywhere from a few minutes to an hour or longer. Experiment with film and exposures. The shutter release cable is needed to lock the shutter open for the duration of the exposure. *Don't undervalue this type of astrophotography.* I have seen some of the prettiest "sky" pictures taken using this method. For creative ideas, check out the popular monthly astronomy magazines because they showcase amateur photos.

## 2 Simple Astrophotography with a Telescope

**Photos of:** Moon and Sun. **WARNING: You must attach a solar filter to your telescope to take pictures of the Sun (see page 87).**

**Examples:** See pictures numbered **2** in this section.

**Equipment:** SLR camera with T-ring and T-adapter (see picture on page 115), shutter release cable and telescope. Film speed from 100 to 400.

**Discussion:** You can take pictures of the Moon and Sun with any telescope on a stable mount. The telescope does not have to be motorized. Remove any eyepiece from the eyepiece holder and slide in your SLR with its attached T-ring and T-adapter. Aim the scope at the Moon and focus through the camera's viewfinder. Use your camera's metering system to determine a starting point for an exposure, but don't trust this for an ideal exposure. Take several pictures using different shutter speeds than those determined by your camera's metering system. It is important to use the shutter release cable when "snapping" these photos. Pushing the actual shutter on the camera with your finger will move or produce vibration in the telescope and make your photos blurry. Also, keep a log of film speed and exposure time to eliminate future trial and error. This type of astrophotography is called *prime focus* photography. How can you make the Moon or Sun bigger? One solution is to use a 2x or 4x barlow lens placed in front of the camera.

**Right.** An SCT ready for astrophotography. The SCT is one of the most popular and versatile telescopes, but how do you use it effectively for astrophotography? In order to take photos of star clusters, nebulae and galaxies, that is, objects which require extended exposures, you must purchase an optional accessory, **J**, called a wedge. The wedge allows tilting of the base of the SCT so that its main axis can be pointed to a celestial pole, **K**. Adjustments are made at both **L**s to accurately aligned the telescope to this point in the sky. In essence, the wedge creates an equatorial-configured mount (see page 50) which is an absolute necessity for long time exposures. If a wedge were not used for long time exposures, the stars in your photos would become elongated (very much so around the edge of the image area and less at the center). A wedge is not required for taking photos of the Moon, Sun and planets because the exposure time for these objects is just a fraction of a second.

This SCT, as shown, is not totally ready to take photos through the telescope. A camera and guiding unit must be attached at **M**. A guiding unit it attached first at **M**, and the camera is then attached to it. The guiding unit is called an "off-axis" guider and allows keeping the telescope on target during the length of the exposure. It performs the same function as the guidescope on the telescope shown above but is a little trickier to use.

A SLR camera, **N**, is shown "piggybacked" onto the SCT. The lenses on cameras have wide fields of view compared to telescopes and allow photographing whole constellations or larger areas of the sky. These types of photographs generally require longer exposures, so some guiding may be needed.

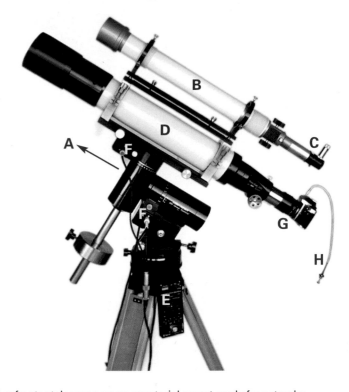

**Above.** A refractor telescope on an equatorial mount ready for astrophotography. The polar axis, **A**, must be accurately aligned (pointed) to the North Celestial Pole if you are in the northern hemisphere. The guidescope, **B**, with a reticle eyepiece, **C,** is used to keep the telescope **D** on course. Minute adjustments are made by looking through the guidescope's reticle eyepiece and then pressing directional buttons on the hand controller **E**. This activates either motor **F** to very slowly redirect the telescope. All telescope mounts exhibit some "drift" because their motors are not perfectly timed to the Earth's rotation and because polar alignments are usually not "dead-on." The SLR camera with T-ring and T-adapter (see picture on page 115) is slid into the eyepiece focuser, **G**. A shutter release cable, **H** is used to lock the shutter open during exposures.

# Astrophotography

 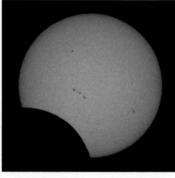

**2** **3** **Above.** Pictures of the Moon and Sun can be taken with any telescope that has a steady mount. All you need is an SLR camera fitted with a T-ring and T-adapter so that it fits into the focuser. A shutter release cable is used to snap the picture in order to keep the telescope as steady as possible. Always take several photos at different exposures.

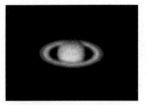 

**3** **Above.** These pictures of the planets Saturn and Jupiter were taken by handholding a digital camera in front of an eyepiece. It is easiest to do this with motorized telescopes. I took many pictures and processed the best using Adobe Photoshop. The yellow-greenish cast of these pictures is a factor caused by the camera's digital chip.

## 3 Intermediate Astrophotography with a Motorized Telescope

**Photos of:** Constellations, Moon, Sun, planets.

**Examples:** See pictures numbered **3** in this section.

**Equipment:** SLR camera with lens, T-ring and T-adapter (see picture on next page), shutter release cable, digital camera and motorized telescope on an equatorial mount or wedge if it is an SCT. Film speed from 100 to 800.

**Discussion:** A motorized telescope makes it immensely easier to take photos of the Moon, Sun and planets because you do not have to constantly nudge the telescope to keep these objects in view. If you are using an SCT to photograph these three objects, it is not necessary to use a wedge because the exposures are short. If you have a digital camera, try holding it over an eyepiece to take pictures of these bright objects. Use an eyepiece that has a rubber eyeguard to prevent the lenses from touching. Better yet, companies like Tele Vue sell adapters to mount digital cameras in front of an eyepiece, but these adapters rely on the camera lens having filter threads, a feature not found on all digital cameras. This type of photography is called *afocal* photography. Similar to afocal is *eyepiece projection*, which allows taking photos of the planets using an SLR: The SLR without its lens is positioned above an eyepiece, housed in an eyepiece projection unit (the camera is held in the unit by a T-ring). Pictures of the planets cannot be taken using *prime focus* photography (discussed in 2 above) because they will appear very small on the film. Finally, pictures of whole constellations are not taken through the telescope but with cameras "piggybacked" on to it (see SCT on page 113). The telescope and its mount is the "host" used to follow the stars. Obviously, different lenses can be attached to the camera for wide angle or "closeup" shots.

## 4 Advanced Astrophotography with Film or CCD Imaging

**Photos of:** Star clusters, nebulae, galaxies (and the planets/Moon/Sun).

**Examples:** See pictures numbered **4** in this section and pictures on pages 29, 30 and 31.

**Equipment:** Everything mentioned above plus CCD camera, laptop computer, autoguider (electronic version of a guidescope), software programs, film scanner and various other accessories.

**Discussion:** This is the most difficult type of astrophotography. It requires the largest investment of time and money. For the most part, CCD cameras have replaced film for recording images of all celestial objects. Their advantage is that they can record images in a fraction of the time of film and obtain greater detail. A bonus of CCD cameras is that they work fairly well in light polluted areas. Although CCD cameras function similarly to

**3** **Left.** This beautiful picture of the Sagittarius/Scorpius area (Chart G) of the sky was taken by Scott Tucker using a large professional format film camera piggybacked onto a telescope similar to the one shown at the top of the previous page. The exposure was 20 minutes with a 165mm focal length lens which is equivalent to about an 85mm for a 35mm film format camera.

digital cameras, the chips in digital cameras will not work for taking pictures of nebulae and galaxies. Imaging faint objects requires long exposures, and thus a mount that is well polar-aligned. On the average, amateur astrophotographers prefer true equatorial mounts over an SCT with a wedge. Additionally, any mount must be well guided, that is, it must have a means to follow stars precisely. Medium priced CCD cameras ($3,000 plus) often incorporate an "auto-guider chip" whose function is to track just one star, keeping the telescope on target. These autoguiders are interfaced with the slow-motion controls of the mounts and can literally keep a star fixed on one pixel of a CCD chip. For amateurs, CCD imaging technology has advanced to the point that photographs taken with small telescopes of 12 inches in diameter or less can rival those taken from some professional observatories. They certainly will surpass the photographs taken from the largest telescopes of just 40 years ago.

The Flaming Star Nebula, IC 405 in Auriga as captured by Scott Tucker. He used a 6-inch refractor with an exposure of 75 minutes on professional Kodak film (ISO film speed of 100). Pictures like this represent a considerable investment in time and equipment. Additionally, many things can go wrong during an exposure to ruin the photo, including equipment failure and environmental factors like wind or clouds.

**Left**. Closeup of an SLR equipped with a T-ring, **A**, and 2-inch diameter T-adapter, **B**. These are necessary to slide the camera into a 2-inch eyepiece focuser in order to take photos through a telescope. The T-adapters are universal but the T-rings are specific to the lens mount of the camera's manufacturer.

Galaxy M82 in Ursa Major (Chart A, objects #2&3). This picture was taken by Dean Koenig, using a 12.5 inch Cassegrain-type reflecting telescope called a Ritchey-Chretien coupled to an advanced CCD camera. He took three photos with 12-minute exposures through a red, green and blue filter which were combined in a software program like Adobe Photoshop to produce the colors.

The Cone Nebula, NGC 2264 in the constellation Monoceros. Dean Koenig used a 7-inch refractor and an advanced CCD camera to capture this beautiful image. He made four exposures. The first was 135 minutes using a special hydrogen-alpha filter to capture the fine detail. Then he took 5-minute exposures with red, green and blue filters to achieve color. All four images were combined in a software program like Adobe Photoshop to produce this final picture.

# Time

Most of this book is informational with little commentary. However, in this section I will allow myself to begin with commentary. The United States has isolated itself from the rest of the world by continuing to embrace the English system of measurement instead of the metric system. We are the only major country left using this "old" method of measurement. We need to define a five-year transition period and change over. Personally, I'd rather continue with pounds and miles for the rest of my life, but it is more important to be in step with everyone else when it comes to measurement. The metric system is here to stay.

Why is it here to stay? Because the metric system is based on units that are multiples of ten. A meter is 1,000 millimeters, a kilometer is 1,000 meters. A liter, about equal in volume to a quart, has 1,000 millimeters. What makes the metric system sensible is that the math for any system based on multiples of ten is *much* easier to perform than systems based on units of 12, like our English system of measurement. So why was there ever a system of 12? There are advantages, a simplicity to conducting "everyday" commerce or other measurements using divisions of 12 rather than divisions of 10. Simply, it is much easier to divide units of 12 into equal parts than units of 10.

What does all this have to do with time? The clock is based on units of 12. I think one of humankind's most ingenious ideas was the division of the day into 24 hours, the hours into 60 minutes and the minutes into 60 seconds (seconds are further divided into tenths). All of these numbers represent units of 12 (60 = 12 x 5). With these divisions, the day is easily divided into halves, thirds and quarters, and the hours and minutes can further be divided into fifths and tenths. All of this adds up to incredible flexibility in dividing our time into convenient intervals that are whole numbers, instead of some dangling decimal or fraction if based on units of 10. Although I applaud the metric system for its simplicity and straightforwardness, I find, like many of those in the past, that a system based on 12 can be most convenient for commerce, time and "angles." One-quarter of a dozen is the whole number 3, while it is 2.5 for 10. The compass point

Where time begins. The prime meridian or 0° longitude passes through the Old Royal Observatory at Greenwich, England, just outside London.

system is based on 360° (12 x 30) instead of 100° because this allows the most equal part divisions. One hundred is evenly divisible by 1, 2, 5, 10, 25, 50 and 100. But 360 is evenly divisible by 1, 2, 3, 4, 5, 6, 8, 9, 10, 12, 15, 18, 20, 24, 30, 36, 40, 45, 60, 72, 90, 120 and 180, which makes it much more flexible for dividing into equal parts.

## Time, divisions & practices

Since the Earth continuously turns on its axis, where and when do time and the days start and stop? Most of this was hashed out over the last 100 years at international forums on the subject. The last took place in 1928. Here are the resolutions of these timely events:

**Apparent Solar Time.** This is the time that is indicated on a sundial. It would be impractical to use Apparent Solar Time because cities or towns just a short distance apart would have slightly different times.

**Standard Time Zones.** The Earth is divided into 24 time zones, each 15° wide in longitude (remember, lines of longitude pass through the poles, latitude lines are parallel to the equator). Everyone in a time zone sets their clocks to the same time. The time difference between adjacent time zones is one hour. In the middle of the oceans, the time zone boundaries are straight vertical lines; however, over populated land, they are often irregular because they have been redefined to take into account political, economic and social considerations. The continental United States is spanned by four standard time zones.

**Standard Time or Local Standard Time.** The time on our clocks which is based on the 24 standard time zones, as defined above.

**Daylight Saving Time (DST).** The practice of advancing the clocks from Standard Time by one hour from the first Sunday in April to the last Saturday in October (in the US). DST is sometimes referred to as Summer Time. Most, but not all of the world changes its clocks to Daylight Saving Time. This practice of changing the clocks has been a societal decision. The following locations in North America do not observe DST: Hawaii; most of Arizona; most of Indiana; most of Saskatchewan, Canada; Puerto Rico; Virgin Islands and most of Mexico.

## Coordinated Universal Time Broadcast Frequencies

| Signal Origination | Station and Location | Shortwave Broadcast Frequencies[1] |
|---|---|---|
| US | WWV at Fort Collins, Colorado | 2.5, 5, 10 & 20 MHz |
| Canada | CHU at Ottawa, Ontario | 3.330, 7.335 & 14.670 MHz |

[1]If your radio is digital, you may have to enter these frequencies as multiples of 1,000, so that 2.5 becomes 2500, 10 becomes 10000 and 3.330 becomes 3330.

**Universal Time (UT).** Astronomical events are expressed in Universal Time, which is the Standard Time at the Old Royal Observatory in Greenwich, England. The location of the Old Royal Observatory was chosen to be longitude 0° in 1884. The beginning of every new day starts here. Universal Time is not adjusted for Daylight Saving Time. Expressed using the 24-hour clock, Universal Time must be converted to obtain Local Standard Time.

**Coordinated Universal Time (UTC).** In North America, the WWV radio station in Fort Collins, Colorado and the CHU radio station in Ottawa, Ontario, Canada broadcast Universal Time 24 hours a day on shortwave radio frequencies. The broadcasting of this time is known as Coordinated Universal Time. The abbreviation UTC was adopted from the French word order. These radio broadcasts use tones to mark the seconds and have an automated voice announcement at the beginning of each minute. Amateur and professional astronomers use UTC to accurately record astronomical events. Additionally, many home clocks incorporate radio receivers that quietly and automatically adjust the clock's time using the UTC signals.

**Greenwich Mean Time (GMT).** Universal Time was originally referred to as Greenwich Mean Time. The term Universal Time was adopted in 1928 by the International Astronomical Union. UT is still occasionally referred to as GMT.

**International Date Line.** The International Date Line is the 180° longitude line that bisects the Pacific Ocean and is exactly opposite the longitude 0° line that passes through Greenwich, England. This longitude has been designated as the line where the calendar date changes. Since it falls mostly over the ocean, the different dates that occur on opposite sides affect no major populated areas.

### Twilight, dawn & dusk

Twilight is the time before sunrise and after sunset. It represents the transition period between day and night. Before sunrise, the twilight period is commonly referred to as dawn, and after sunset, dusk. Twilight is caused by the scattering of sunlight from the atmosphere. There are three recognized twilight periods as described below.

**Civil twilight.** The period beginning at sunset and ending when the Sun is 6 arc angle degrees (12 Sun diameters) below the horizon. In the morning, before sunrise, Civil twilight begins when the Sun is 6 degrees below the horizon, and ends at sunrise. Civil twilight is the last or first time of the day when normal daylight activities can be conducted.

**Nautical twilight.** Begins in the morning or ends in the evening when the the Sun is 12 degrees below the horizon. At this time, the horizon at sea is not visible but the planets and brighter stars are.

**Astronomical twilight.** The Sun must be 18 degrees below the horizon for Astronomical twilight to end in the evening and begin in the morning. When the Sun is 18 or more degrees below the horizon, everyone would agree that it is night, and it is dark enough for all astronomical objects to be seen.

### Working with Universal Time (UT)

If you read any astronomical literature, including the popular monthly astronomy magazines, you will quickly discover that Universal Time is often used to express the occurrence of astronomical events. This is done to avoid confusion with time zones. But given the UT time, what *is* the equivalent local standard time for your location? Depending on the actual Universal Time and your location, you could witness an astronomical event as much as a day before the Universal Time noted for the event.

There are several factors that must be taken into consideration when changing Universal Time to local standard time. First is the Time Zone difference between your location and Greenwich. Second is consideration of Daylight Saving Time. Third is that the local standard time date may be one day prior to the UT date; and lastly, 24-hour UT time must be converted to 12-hour time.

## Twilight Rules of Thumb

| | |
|---|---|
| **CIVIL Twilight** | **Ends 30 minutes after Sunset**<br>*Starts 30 minutes before Sunrise* |
| **NAUTICAL Twilight** | **Ends 60 minutes after Sunset**<br>*Starts 60 minutes before Sunrise* |
| **ASTRONOMICAL Twilight** | **Ends 90 minutes after Sunset**<br>*Starts 90 minutes before Sunrise* |

## 24-Hour to 12-Hour Conversion Chart

| 24 Hour | 12 Hour |
|---|---|
| 0[1] | MIDNIGHT 12 A.M.[2] |
| 1 | 1 A.M. |
| 2 | 2 A.M. |
| 3 | 3 A.M. |
| 4 | 4 A.M. |
| 5 | 5 A.M. |
| 6 | 6 A.M. |
| 7 | 7 A.M. |
| 8 | 8 A.M. |
| 9 | 9 A.M. |
| 10 | 10 A.M. |
| 11 | 11 A.M. |
| 12 | NOON 12 P.M.[2] |
| 13 | 1 P.M. |
| 14 | 2 P.M. |
| 15 | 3 P.M. |
| 16 | 4 P.M. |
| 17 | 5 P.M. |
| 18 | 6 P.M. |
| 19 | 7 P.M. |
| 20 | 8 P.M. |
| 21 | 9 P.M. |
| 22 | 10 P.M. |
| 23 | 11 P.M. |

[1]Although 0 hour & midnight represent the same time, the date of midnight is one day prior to 0 hour.
[2]You may encounter differing uses of A.M. and P.M. associated with Noon and Midnight in different sources.

# Time

## Universal Time Zone Differences

The numbers below the Time Zones indicate the difference in **hours** between Local Standard Time and Universal Time. *The number in parentheses is the difference during Daylight Saving Time.*

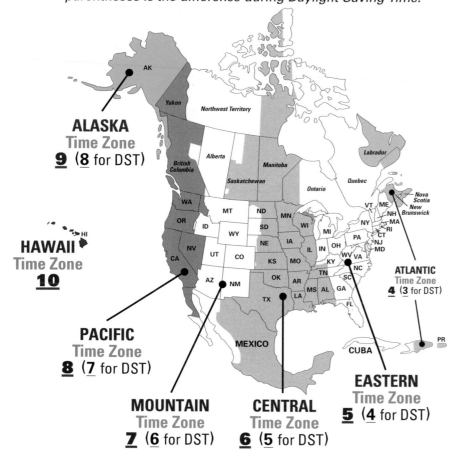

**ALASKA**
Time Zone
**9** (**8** for DST)

**HAWAII**
Time Zone
**10**

**PACIFIC**
Time Zone
**8** (**7** for DST)

**MOUNTAIN**
Time Zone
**7** (**6** for DST)

**CENTRAL**
Time Zone
**6** (**5** for DST)

**EASTERN**
Time Zone
**5** (**4** for DST)

**ATLANTIC**
Time Zone
**4** (**3** for DST)

**TO CHANGE**...Universal Time (UT) to your Local Standard Time, *subtract* the *BLUE number* for your Time Zone from the UT. *Use the DST number* (Daylight Saving Time number) from the first Sunday in April to the last Saturday in October.

*The following locations do not observe Daylight Saving Time: Hawaii, most of Arizona, most of Indiana, most of Saskatchewan, Puerto Rico, Virgin Islands, most of Mexico, so you always use the BLUE number.*

## Changing UT to Local Standard Time

The procedure, as well as examples, for changing UT to Local Standard Time are outlined below, and in the illustration above.

### STEPS FOR CHANGING UT TO LOCAL STANDARD TIME

**a** *From the last Sunday in October to the first Saturday in April,* find your location on the map above and note the BLUE Time Zone number.

**or**

**b** *From the first Sunday in April to the last Saturday in October,* note the BLACK DST number in parentheses

if your location observes Daylight Saving Time (DST).

**c** Subtract the Time Zone number (or DST number) from the Universal Time. Subtract whole hours only.

**d** If the Time Zone number is larger that the UT hour, then first add 24 to the UT hour and then subtract the Time Zone number from this larger number. When 24 is added to the UT time, the date of the local standard time will be one day prior to the UT date.

**e** Use the conversion table on page 117 to change 24-hour time to 12-hour time.

### Basic Example

*Change the UT of August 4, 19:56 to local standard time if you are in New York.* **Answer:** *August 4, 3:56 P.M.*

**1** Look up the Time Zone number for New York using the map to the left (in this case, use the DST number) → 4

**2** Subtract 4 from 19:56 → 19:56 – 4 = 15:56

**3** Change 15:56 to 12-hour time by referring to the table on page 117 → 15:56 = 3:56 P.M.

**4** The date does not have to be changed because the Time Zone number is less than the UT hour of 19.

### Date Change Example

*Change the UT of Tuesday, April 1, 2:38 to local standard time if you are in San Diego, CA.* **Answer:** *March 31, 6:38 P.M.*

**1** Look up the Time Zone number using the map to the left for San Diego → 8

**2** You cannot subtract 8 from the 2 in 2:38 because 8 is larger than 2, so add 24 to 2:38 → 26:38

**3** Now subtract 8 from 26:38 → 26:38 – 8 = 18:38

**4** Change 18:38 to 12-hour time by referring to the table on page 117 → 18:38 = 6:38 P.M.

**5** The date changes to March 31 because subtracting 8 from 2:38 UT backs into the previous day. Whenever you add 24 to the UT, the local date will always be one day prior to the UT date.

# Appendix:  Resources

## Telescope Reviews

**Todd Gross' Weather and Astronomy Site**
www.weatherman.com

**Cloudy Night Telescope Reviews**
www.cloudynights.com

**The Telescope Review Web Site** by Ed Ting
www.scopereviews.com

**Affordable Astronomy Equipment Reviews**
members.tripod.com/irwincur/index.html

## Major Telescope Manufacturers

**Celestron**
www.celestron.com

**Meade Instruments Corporation**
www.meade.com

**Tele Vue**
Quality refractors and eyepieces
www.televue.com

## Major Planetariums

**Adler Planetarium,** Chicago, IL
www.adlerplanetarium.org

**Albert Einstein Planetarium,**
Smithsonian, Washington, DC
www.nasm.edu/nasm/planetarium/einstein.html

**Hansen Planetarium,** Salt Lake City
www.hansenplanetarium.net

**Hayden Planetarium,** New York, NY
www.amnh.org/rose

**Griffith Observatory Planetarium,**
Los Angeles, CA (reopens 2005)
www.griffithobs.org/Planetarium.html

## Outdoor Telescope Events

Check the popular monthly astronomy magazines for listings of amateur astronomy events. One of the largest that I recommend for beginners and families is the

**RTMC Astronomy Expo** held near Big Bear City, California at the end of May
www.rtmc-inc.org

## Popular Monthly Astronomy Magazines

**Sky & Telescope**
www.skyandtelescope.com

**Astronomy**
www.astronomy.com

**SkyNews** (Canadian)
www.skynewsmagazine.com

## Star Charts

**Guide to the Stars** by David Levy
Published by Ken Press
www.whatsouttonight.com

**Sky Atlas 2000.0**
by Wil Tirion and Roger Sinnott
Published by Sky Publishing
www.skyandtelescope.com

## General Astronomy Internet Sites

www.astronomy.com

www.skyandtelescope.com

www.space.com

www.nasa.gov

science.nasa.gov

## National Organizations

**Astronomical Society of the Pacific**
General membership. Newsletters. Educator support. Books and science materials.
www.astrosociety.org

**The Planetary Society**
Supports planetary exploration. Newsletter.
planetary.org

**The Astronomical League**
A federation of astronomical societies and clubs.
Awards. Newsletter. Catalog.
www.astronomicalleague.com

## Eclipse Tours

Check ads in the popular monthly astronomy magazines for eclipse tours.

## Major Observatories

These observatories have visitor's centers that are open during the day. A few have evening observing programs, but these generally require reservations. Call ahead for hours/tours, etc.

**Kitt Peak** near Tucson, AZ
www.noao.edu/kpno

**McDonald** near Fort Davis, TX
vc.as.utexas.edu

**Mount Palamor** near Pasadena, CA
www.astro.caltech.edu/palomar

**Grifford** in Los Angeles, CA  (reopens 2005)
www.griffithobs.org

**Mauna Kea** on Hawaii
www.ifa.hawaii.edu/mko

**Lowell** in Flagstaff, AZ
www.lowell.edu

## Space Weather Reports

Science news and information about the Sun-Earth environment.
www.spaceweather.com

## Buying, Selling and Trading Telescope Equipment

A premier site for telescope equipment. Skip ebay.
www.astromart.com

## Astronomy Bed & Breakfast

**The Sky Watcher's Inn**
Benson, Arizona
Featuring a 20-inch telescope, many others and wonderful breakfasts.

www.communiverse.com/skywatcher
tel/fax (520) 615-3886

## Astronomy Radio Show

**Let's Talk Stars**
Hosted by famous comet discoverer David Levy.
www.letstalkstars.com

# Appendix:  Resources

## A Favorite Astronomy "Adventure" Book

**Starlight Nights:  The Adventures of a Star-Gazer** by Leslie C. Peltier
Read about the passions of a famous comet discover. Published by Sky Publishing.
www.skyandtelescope.com

## Astronomical Almanacs

Both *Sky & Telescope* and *Astronomy* magazines publish yearly almanacs that are available from newsstands at the end of each year. Two other, wonderful but more advanced almanacs are:

**Observer's Handbook**
Royal Astronomical Society of Canada

**Astronomical Calendar** by Guy Ottewell
Published by Universal Workshop

## AAVSO

The American Association of Variable Star Observers is open to amateur participation in measuring the brightness of variable stars.
www.aavso.org

## Telescopes & Accessories

Check your yellow pages for local dealers. In smaller communities, camera stores often carry telescopes. Or, purchase one of the popular monthly astronomy magazines for dealer ads.

## Satellite Tracking Website

Check this website to find out when the International Space Station and other satellites can be seen overhead.
www.heavens-above.com

## Educational Resources

For books, slides, posters or science items, get catalogs from the following:

**Astronomical Society of the Pacific**
www.astrosociety.org

**Sky & Telescope**
www.skyandtelescope.com

## Astronomy Textbook

One of the most comprehensive textbooks on astronomy that is well-written, expensive, but worth it.

**Foundations of Astronomy**
6th Edition or later
by Michael Seeds
Published by Brooks/Cole

## Planetarium Software

Mac or Windows. Complete planetarium program to display sky anywhere on Earth. Find out where the planets are, and lots more.

**Starry Night Pro** by Space Com

## International Dark-Sky Association

An organization that promote keeping our skies dark so everyone can enjoy the night sky.
www.darksky.org

# Credits

The background photograph on the front cover is the Trifid Nebula in Sagittarius, designated M20 and described on page 23.
It is not indicated on the charts but is located just north of the Lagoon Nebula, object #73 on Chart G.

Front cover. Background: NASA AND JEFF HESTER, Telescope: Ken Graun. Page 3. Earth: NASA, Saturn: JPL. Page 4. Ken Graun and Kris Koenig. Page 5. Eclipse: AURA/NOAO/NSF, Ken Graun. Page 6: Left to right by columns: NASA AND JEFF HESTER; NASA, ESA, MOHAMMAD HEYDARI-MALAYERI (OBSERVATOIRE DE PARIS, FRANCE); NASA AND THE HUBBLE HERITAGE TEAM (STSCI/AURU), NASA AND THE HUBBLE HERITAGE TEAM (STSCI/AURU). Page 7: AURA/NASA/ESA. Page 8. Eclipse: AURA/NOAO/NSF, Nebula: JEFF HESTER AND PAUL SCOWEN (ARIZONA STATE UNIVERSITY) AND NASA. Page 9. Sun: AURA/NOAO/NSF, Prominence: AURA/NOAO/NSF, Mercury: NASA, Inset of Mercury: NASA, Inset of Venus: JPL. Page 10. Sun: NASA/ESA. Page 11. Mercury: NASA, Venus: NASA/ARC, Earth: NASA, Mars: AURA/NASA/ESA, Jupiter-Saturn-Uranus-Neptune: JPL, Pluto: NASA/ESA, Asteroid: ARECIBO OBSERVATORY, Comet: BILL AND SALLY FLETCHER. Page 12. Venus top: JPL, Spacecraft: NASA/JPL, Venus bottom: JPL, Astronauts: NASA, Inset of Earth: NASA. Page 13. Middle four pictures: NASA, Inset of Moon: UCO/Lick Observatory, Inset of Mars: AURA/NASA/ESA. Page 14. Volcano & polar cap: JPL, Globe: NASA AND THE HUBBLE HERITAGE TEAM (STSCI/AURA), Bottom panorama: JPL. Page 15. Ida: JPL, Inset of asteroid: ARECIBO OBSERVATORY. Page 16. Middle: JPL, Moon: UCO/LICK OBSERVATORY, Four Galilean moons: DLR, Inset of Jupiter: JPL. Page 17. JPL. Page 18. JPL, Inset of Pluto: NASA/ESA. Page 19. Comet: BILL AND SALLY FLETCHER, Jupiter: NASA (STSCI), Inset of comet: NASA (STSCI). Page 20. BILL SCHOENING, VANESSA HARVEY/REU PROGRAM/NOAO/AURA/NSF. Page 21. NASA/ESA/HST. Page 22. 1: AURA/NASA/ESA, 2: HUBBLE HERITAGE TEAM (AURU/STSCI/NASA), 3a: NOAO/AURA/NSF, 3b: GMOS TEAM, 3c: NASA, ESA, R. DE GRIJS (INSTITUTE OF ASTRONOMY, CAMBRIDGE, UK), 4a: NOAO/AURA/NSF, 4b: NASA AND JEFF HESTER, 5a: N.A. SHARP, MARK HANNA, REU PROGRAM/NOAO/AURA/NSF, 5b: N.A. SHARP, REU PROGRAM/NOAO/AURA/NSF, 6a: .P. HARRINGTON AND K.J. BORKOWSKI (UNIVERSITY OF MARYLAND), 6b: JAY GALLAGHER (U. WISCONSIN)/WIYN/NOAO/NSF. Page 24. Top: NASA, ESA AND D. MAOZ (TEL-AVIV UNIVERSITY AND COLUMBIA UNIVERSITY0, Bottom: NASA AND THE HUBBLE HERITAGE TEAM (STSCI/AURA). Page 25. NIGEL SHARP, NOAO/AURA/NSF. Page 26. Panorama: NASA/COBE/DIRBE, Inset: NASA. Page 27. Clockwise from top left: EUROPEAN SOUTHERN OBSERVATORY, Ken Graun, Larry Moore. Page 28. A: BILL SCHOENING/AURA/NOAO/NSF, B,C,D: JEFF HESTER AND PAUL SCOWEN (ARIZONA STATE UNIVERSITY) AND NASA. Page 29. Dean Koenig. Page 30. Dean Koenig. Page 31. Scott Tucker. Page 32. Top: NASA, ESA, AND MARTINO ROMANIELLO (EUROPEAN SOUTHERN OBSERVATORY, GERMANY), Bottom: ANGLO-AUSTRALIAN OBSERVATORY/ROYAL OBSERVATORY EDINBURGH. Page 33. A. DUPREE (CFA), NASA, ESA. Page 34. A: NASA AND THE HUBBLE HERITAGE TEAM (STSCI/AURA), B: AURA/STSCI/NASA, C: WIYN/NOAO/NSF, NASA AND THE HUBBLE HERITAGE TEAM (STSCI/AURA), D: NASA AND THE HUBBLE HERITAGE TEAM (STSCI/AURA). Page 37. Top: NASA AND JEFFREY KENNEY AND ELIZABETH YALE (YALE UNIVERSITY), Bottom: NASA AND THE HUBBLE HERITAGE TEAM (STSCI/AURA). Page 38: NASA. Pages 39 to 58. All pictures by Ken Graun except 15-inch Dobsonian on page 47 by Discovery Telescopes. Page 66: BILL SCHOENING/NOAO/AURA/NSF. Page 69: TODD BOROSON/NOAO/AURA/NSF. Page 77. BILL SCHOENING/NOAO/AURA/NSF. Pages 82/83. Ken Graun. Pages 84/85. Moon halves: UCO/LICK OBSERVATORY, Full Moons: UCO/LICK OBSERVATORY. Page 87. Telescopes: Ken Graun, Full Sun/Sunspot: AURA/NOAO/NSF, Promimence: Vincent Chan. Page 88. Top: AURA/NOAO/NSF, Middle two: Ken Graun, Bottom: Larry Moore. Page 89: Ken Graun. Page 90. Total eclipse: BILL LIVINGSTON/NOAO/AURA/NSF. Page 91. Solar eclipse: BILL LIVINGSTON/NOAO/AURA/NSF, Lunar eclipse: NASA. Page 94. Inset of Mercury: NASA, Bottom: Ken Graun. Page 95. Inset of Venus: NASA/ARC, Inset of Mars: MALIN SPACE SCIENCE SYSTEMS, Drawing: Ken Graun. Page 96. STEVE LEE (UNIVERSITY OF COLORADO), JIM BELL (CORNELL UNIVERSITY), MIKE WOLFF (SPACE SCIENCE INSTITUTE) AND NASA. Page 98. Middle: NASA (STSCI), Inset of Jupiter: JPL. Page 99. Top: JPL, Inset of Saturn: NASA (STSCI). Page 102. Inset of Uranus/Neptune: JPL, Inset of Pluto: NASA/ESA. Page 103. BILL SCHOENING, VANESSA HARVEY/REU PROGRAM/NOAO/AURA/NSF. Page 104. Top: N.A. SHARP, REU PROGRAM/NOAO/AURA/NSF, Bottom: BILL SCHOENING/NOAO/AURA/NSF. Page 105. Top: JAY GALLAGHER (U. WISCONSIN)/WIYN/NOAO/NSF, Bottom: ANGLO-AUSTRALIAN OBSERVATORY/ROYAL OBSERVATORY EDINBURGH. Page 106. NASA AND THE HUBBLE HERITAGE TEAM (STSCI/AURA). Page 108. BILL AND SALLY FLETCHER. Page 110. ADAM BLOCK/NOAO/AURA/NSF. Pages 111 to 113. Ken Graun. Page 114. Top four: Ken Graun. Bottom: Scott Tucker. Page 115. Top: Scott Tucker. Bottom two: Dean Koenig. Page 116. Ken Graun. Back cover. Background: NASA AND JEFF HESTER, Telescope & planisphere: Ken Graun, Rocker: NASA, Saturn: JPL. All illustrations in this book are by Ken Graun.

# Glossary

**Absolute Magnitude.** The magnitude of a star if it were placed at a distance of 10 parsecs from Earth. The Sun's absolute magnitude is +4.8, and most stars range from −5 to +15. Absolute magnitude is used for comparing the actual brightness of stars.

**Absolute Zero.** The coldest possible temperature, at which all molecular motion stops. Absolute zero is 0K, −273° C or −459° F.

**Albedo.** The amount of sunlight reflected from a planet, moon or asteroid. Albedo is normally expressed as a decimal between 0 and 1 (or the equivalent percentage). A mirror would have an albedo of 1 (reflects 100% of sunlight); Venus has a high albedo of 0.65 (65%); the Earth, 0.37 (37%) and the Moon, 0.11 (11%).

**Altazimuth Telescope Mount.** A mount that moves in altitude and azimuth, allowing a telescope to move "up" and "down" vertically (altitude) and rotate horizontally to any compass point (azimuth). Everyone is familiar with this mount because it is the type used with binoculars at tourist attractions. This mount has become increasing popular because of its simplicity and low cost. Most professional telescopes today use computer controlled altazimuth mounts.

**Altitude.** For an altazimuth telescope mount, altitude refers to the movement of the telescope "up" and "down" vertically from the horizon to directly overhead. Altitude also refers to a measurement system, where the height of an object above the horizon is expressed in arc degrees. This measurement system ranges from 0° at the horizon to 90° at the zenith (of the observer).

**Angstrom (Å).** A unit of measurement that once was widely used to express the wavelength of light. The angstrom is being replaced by the nanometer (abbreviated nm). An angstrom is 10–10 meters; a nanometer is 10–9 meters, so 10 Å = 1 nm.

**Annular Eclipse.** An eclipse of the Sun by the Moon in which the whole Moon moves in front of the Sun but does not completely cover the Sun. Because the Moon's orbit is an ellipse, its distance to the Earth varies. Annular eclipses occur when the Moon is a little farther away than normal, making its arc diameter a little smaller than the Sun's. During a total eclipse of the Sun, the Moon's arc diameter is slightly larger than the Sun's.

**Aphelion.** The point in a planet's, asteroid's or comet's orbit where it is farthest from the Sun. Since all celestial objects have elliptical orbits, they have a closest and farthest point from the object they orbit.

**Apochromatic.** Optical term that refers to the highest quality telescope optics which are free of spherical, chromatic and other optical aberrations. The term is usually associated with refractor telescopes.

**Apogee.** The point in the orbit of the Moon or an artificial satellite where it is farthest from the Earth. Since all celestial objects have elliptical orbits, they have a closest and farthest point from the object they orbit.

**Arc Degree (°).** Unit of angular measurement used in astronomy. One arc degree is the same as one compass point degree. There are 360 arc degrees in a circle; each arc degree is divided into 60 arc minutes; and each arc minute is divided into 60 arc seconds. Arc seconds are further divided into tenths. The word "arc" is usually omitted when using this measurement system, but this omission can cause confusion when minutes (time) are used in the same dialog with arc minutes. The Sun and Moon are both about 1/2 of an arc degree (30 arc minutes) in angular diameter. Notation example: 6° 26' 3.2"

**Arc Minute (').** 1/60 of an arc degree. The Moon is about 30 arc minutes in diameter.

**Arc Second (").** 1/3600 of an arc degree or 1/60 of an arc minute.

**Ascending Node.** The point at which the orbit of a solar system mem-ber, like one of the planets, crosses the celestial equator or ecliptic from south to north (in declination). See also Descending Node.

**Asterism.** A recognizable or distinguished group of stars. Often a subgroup of a constellation. The Big Dipper is an asterism of the constellation Ursa Major.

**Asteroid.** A large, irregularly shaped "rock" that circles the Sun. Most asteroids orbit in a belt between Mars and Jupiter. The largest asteroid, Ceres, is 568 miles (914 km) in diameter and takes approximately 4.6 years to circle the Sun. Asteroids are also referred to as minor planets.

**Asteroid Belt.** Most asteroids orbit the Sun in a belt between Mars and Jupiter. These asteroids represent remnants left over from the formation of the solar system.

**Astrology.** Astrology is not astronomy! Astronomy is a science; astrology is not. Astrology is a system of predictions based on planetary and lunar positions. Although astronomy and astrology share some terminology and concepts, astrology's foundation is not based on the scientific gathering and analysis of information; hence it is an arbitrary system. Until modern times, astronomy and astrology were linked together. In the early 1600s, Johannes Kepler, who discovered the laws that govern the orbits of the planets, used astrology to help earn a living. Kings, queens and nobles hired astrologers to predict their futures (obviously, making positive or favorable predictions helped an astrologer to stay in business). Astrological predictions offer a feeling of control and power in a chaotic world.

**Astronomical Unit (AU).** Unit of distance in astronomy. One astronomical unit is 92,955,800 miles (1.48 billion km), the average distance from the Earth to the Sun.

**Aurora (plural: Aurorae).** A beautiful display of illumination in the night sky caused by charged particles from the Sun spilling into the atmosphere. These displays are concentrated around the polar regions of the Earth. In the northern hemisphere, the aurorae are called Aurora Borealis (Northern Lights) and in the southern hemisphere, Aurora Australis. Their red and green colors can shimmer, move and pulsate in large diffuse patches, ribbons or folded curtains. Their shape and intensity can change in minutes.

**Autumnal Equinox.** Occurs on or near September 23. At this time, the Sun is crossing the celestial equator from north to south. This occasion is one of two during the year (the other is at the vernal equinox) when day and night are equal in length.

**Averted Vision.** An observing technique which helps one see faint objects. Instead of looking directly at a faint object, you look slightly away from it, using peripheral vision for viewing. In the dark, our peripheral vision is more sensitive to faint light than direct vision.

**Azimuth.** For an altazimuth telescope mount, azimuth refers to the rotation of the telescope in a circle, around the horizon to any compass point. Azimuth is also part of a measurement system. Azimuth starts with 0° at true North and arcs eastwardly, through 360° of the compass.

**Barlow Lens.** A barlow lens increases the magnification of eyepieces, usually by a preset factor of 2 or 3. Barlows are popular because one barlow effectively doubles the range of magnification possible from a set of eyepieces. Barlow lenses fit into a telescope's eyepiece holder. Eye-pieces are then inserted into the barrel of the barlow.

**Barred Spiral Galaxy.** Similar to a spiral galaxy except that the center bulge has a straight arm, or "bar" passing through it. The curved arms then radiate off the ends of the bar. Our Milky Way galaxy is a moderately barred spiral galaxy.

**Bayer Letters.** The formal name of the lowercase Greek letters assigned to the brightest stars in each of the constellations.

**Big Bang.** The predominant theory detailing the creation of the Universe. This theory states that all the matter in the Universe was once compressed together and then rapidly expanded or exploded to form the galaxies that exist today.

**Binary Star.** A pair of stars where one revolves around the other (actually, each star revolves around a mutual center of gravity). Binary stars have revolutions that can last just days or thousands of years.

**Black Hole.** An astronomical body with a density so great that the resulting gravity will not even let light escape from its surface. Black holes cannot be directly observed, but there are telltale signs that indicate their presence. A black hole can

# Glossary

be created from a star with as little as three times the mass of our Sun. As massive stars age and burn out, their remaining matter collapses upon themselves, creating black holes, the densest objects in the Universe. Some galaxies have giant black holes at their centers. A rudimentary idea of a black hole was formed in the late 1700s.

**Brown Dwarf.** A "star" that never ignited because it did not have sufficient mass to produce nuclear fusion. It is essentially a ball of hydrogen gas. Brown dwarfs are difficult to locate because they do not give off visible light.

**Catadioptric Telescope.** Any telescope that uses a combination of lenses and mirrors to focus light.

**CCD (Charged-Coupled Device).** A term often used for the digital imaging technology used in astronomy. This is the same technology as digital cameras.

**Celestial Equator.** A great circle that is the projection of the Earth's equator onto the sky. The celestial equator has declination 0° (corresponding to a latitude of 0°).

**Celestial Horizon.** The meeting of the sky and the horizon. At sea, the celestial horizon is unobstructed and perfectly round.

**Celestial Meridian.** A celestial meridian is a great circle that divides the sky into eastern and western halves. This circle passes through the observer's zenith and the North and South Celestial Poles. On Earth, a meridian is a longitude line.

**Celestial Sphere.** At one time, it was thought the Sun, Moon, planets, comets and stars resided on the inside of a giant sphere called the Celestial Sphere. Today, it is a convenient term to indicate the visible Universe.

**Chromatic Aberration.** Optical term referring to the inability of a refracting lens to focus all colors of light at the same point. This aberration is particularly noticeable in lower-quality binoculars, refractor telescopes and eyepieces as orange and blue halos around viewed objects.

**Coma (Comet).** The large, cloudy veil that forms around the nucleus of a comet when it gets close to the Sun. The coma is the brightest part of a comet.

**Coma (Telescope).** An optical aberration that occurs in short focal length reflectors, causing stars toward the edge of an eyepiece's field of view to appear elongated instead of as points of light.

**Comet.** Sometimes referred to as "dirty snowballs," because they are composed mostly of dust and ices. As comets approach the Sun, the ices vaporize, creating the bright, reflective, gaseous coma and tail. Most comets have highly elliptical orbits and take hundreds to thousands of years to revolve around the Sun.

**Conjunction.** The alignment of two or more solar system members as viewed from Earth. Conjunction usually applies to the Sun, Moon and planets. When two or more planets, the Moon and a planet (or planets) or the Sun and a planet (or planets) appear very close to one another in the sky, they are said to be in conjunction. The inferior planets, Mercury and Venus, are at Inferior Conjunction when they are directly between the Earth and the Sun. They are at Superior Conjunction when they are on the opposite side of the Sun from the Earth. In both cases, these planets will rise and set with the Sun. A superior planet, Mars through Pluto, is in conjunction when it is on the opposite side of the Sun from the Earth (Sun and planet rise and set at the same time).

**Constellation.** A group of visible stars that has been assigned a name. The stars in a constellation usually form a pattern that aides in their recognition. The visible stars were first categorized into constellations thousands of years ago and are associated with lore. Today the constellations are not just named groups of stars, but also include the area of sky around the stars. Each constellation has a boundary just like each state in the United States. Probably the most easily recognizable constellation is Orion because of its bright stars and striking pattern. There are a total of 88 constellations.

**Corona.** The "atmosphere" of the Sun above the photosphere (visible surface). It extends outward from the Sun for several million miles and is visible during a total solar eclipse as the irregular white halo surrounding the Moon.

**Cosmology.** The study of the Universe as a whole, on its grand scale.

**Cosmogony.** The study of the origin and evolution of the Universe.

**Crater.** A concave depression on a planet, moon or asteroid created from the impact of a comet, asteroid or meteoroid.

**Crater Rays.** Bright streaks that radiate from some craters on the Moon. They are the result of the ejection of reflective material from craters during their formation (from cometary or meteoroid impacts).

**Crescent.** A phase of the Moon between New Moon and either First or Last Quarter.

**Dawn.** The time in the morning around sunrise.

**Daylight Saving Time.** The advancing of clocks from Standard Time by one hour. Most of the world changes to Daylight Saving Time. In the US, the clocks are advanced from the first Sunday in April through the last Saturday in October. The practice of advancing the clocks occurs for social, rather than scientific reasons.

**Declination (also Dec or d).** Latitude-type coordinate used to indicate the position of an object in the sky. Declination is equivalent to and is expressed in the same manner as latitude. 0° declination is at the celestial equator (0° latitude is at the equator). The north celestial pole has declination +90°, the south celestial pole, −90°. Declination is used in conjunction with Right Ascension to determine coordinates of celestial objects.

**Deep Sky Objects.** Refers to galaxies, nebulae, globular clusters and open clusters. Although the term connotes objects that are distant and faint, some deep sky objects are bright and span a large area of the sky. The Andromeda galaxy, for example, spans more than six Moon diameters and can be seen with the naked eye. The stars, planets and other members of our solar system are not considered deep sky objects.

**Descending Node.** The point at which the orbit of a solar system member, like one of the planets or a comet, crosses the celestial equator or ecliptic from north to south (in declination). See also Ascending Node.

**Dobsonian Telescope.** Named after John Dobson, who in the 1970s popularized astronomy through larger, simpler and cheaper Newtonian telescopes. The key to this concept was the use of simple but effective altazimuth mounts.

**Double Star.** Double stars can be optical or binary. Optical doubles are two stars that appear visually very close to each other because they just happen to be in the same line of sight. On the other hand, binary doubles, also called binary stars, are a pair of stars that revolve around each other.

**Dusk.** The time around sunset.

**Dwarf Star.** Our Sun is a typical dwarf star. The term "dwarf" refers to luminosity rather than to size. More than 90% of stars are classified as "dwarfs," but they represent the average stars.

**Earthshine.** Sunlight reflected off the Earth which slightly illuminates the dark side of the Moon facing Earth (that is, the side that is not being directly lit by sunlight). Earthshine is especially noticeable when the Moon is a crescent. During this time, the highlands and maria can be glimpsed on the dark side through a telescope.

**Eccentricity.** A number between 0 and 1 used to indicate the elongation of an ellipse. An eccentricity of 0 indicates a circle; and ellipses with eccentricities close to 1 would look similar in shape to a submarine.

**Ecliptic.** The apparent path that the Sun describes in the sky over the course of a year. The ecliptic is a great circle (cuts the sky into two halves) and crosses 12 constellations — the constellations of the zodiac. The Sun appears to revolve around the Earth once a day, but this movement does not "create" the ecliptic. The ecliptic is described from the Earth revolving around the Sun. Since the background stars remain stationary, it appears from the Earth as if the Sun slowly moves in a circle against the background stars over the course of a year.

**Ellipse.** An oval or elongated circle. All celestial orbits (of planets, moons, comets, binary stars) are ellipses and not circles. An elliptical orbit may be very close to a circle, as is the case of Venus' orbit, or highly elongated as with comets.

**Elongation.** The arc angle distance between the Sun and a solar system member (planet, Moon, comet or asteroid) as viewed from Earth.

**Emission Nebula.** A nebula that produces its own light from the stimulation of its gas by ultraviolet radiation from a nearby star or stars.

**Equatorial Mount.** A type of mount that facilitates observing and photographing celestial objects because an observer has to make only one movement to keep an object centered in the eyepiece. Equatorial mounts have two perpendicular axes. The polar axis points to the north celestial pole; the other axis is positioned 90° to the polar axis. Until the mid-1970s, the majority of telescopes at professional observatories were equatorial mounts. Today, most professional telescopes have computer-controlled altazimuth mounts because they cost less than equatorial mounts. Equatorial mounts are also called German equatorial mounts because the idea originated in Germany.

**Equinox.** See Vernal Equinox or Autumnal Equinox.

**f/number.** See Focal Ratio.

**Field of View.** The expanse of sky that can be seen through binoculars or a telescope. Expressed in degrees (arc degrees), field of view can be true or apparent. True field of view is the actual amount of sky that can be seen through a telescope or binoculars. For example, if you look through a telescope and you see the whole Full Moon, nothing more and nothing less, then the true field of view for that eyepiece is 1/2° or 30 arc minutes (30'). Apparent field of view is a design attribute of an eyepiece. The greater an eyepiece's apparent field of view (usually ranges from 50° to 83°), the larger is the true field of view. A difference in apparent field of view is like the difference between looking out a large and small window.

**First Quarter.** Phase of the Moon, halfway between New and Full, when the Moon is "half" lighted on the right or eastern side.

**Fission.** The splitting apart of atoms which was the process employed in early nuclear weapons. This is not the mechanism that fuels stars.

**Flamsteed Numbers.** Numbers assigned to the stars, by constellation, to aid in identification. Flamsteed numbers are an expansion of the system that identifies the brightest stars with Greek letters.

**Focal Length.** The distance from the primary mirror or objective lens to the point where light comes to a focus. Usually expressed in millimeters.

**Focal Ratio (f/ratio).** The ratio of the focal length of a telescope to the diameter of the primary mirror or objective lens. A focal ratio is calculated by dividing the diameter of the primary or objective into the focal length of the telescope (the units of measurement must be the same for the focal length and primary/objective diameter).

**Full Moon.** Phase of the Moon when the lighted side presents a full, circular disk in the sky. The Full Moon rises as the Sun sets.

**Fusion.** The process that fuels the stars and our Sun. Fusion occurs when four hydrogen atoms fuse to form one helium atom. The resulting helium atom is 1% less in mass than the four hydrogen atoms. The energy from the Sun comes from this 1% difference in mass. Fusion is triggered by the tremendous pressure from the sheer mass of stars.

**Galactic Cluster.** Relatively young open clusters found in the spiral arms of our galaxy. The spiral arms have the highest concentrations of hydrogen gas, where stars are born.

**Galaxy.** A basic grouping in the Universe. Galaxies represent a collection of billions to hundreds of billions of stars that are gravitationally bound. They are generally circular, like a disk or spherical in shape. All galaxies are outside of our Milky Way galaxy.

**Giant Star.** This term refers more to a star's relative luminosity than its actual size. A giant star is in a later stage in the evolution of average dwarf stars, like the Sun, where the star is brighter than normal.

**Gibbous.** The phase of the Moon between First and Last Quarter, (through Full Moon). During this time, the Moon is considered to be respectively a waxing and waning gibbous Moon.

**Globular Cluster.** This deep sky object is a tight group of up to a million stars resembling a ball (like a cotton ball). Globular clusters are not galaxies, but are parts of galaxies. The globular cluster M13 in Hercules is just visible to the naked eye at a dark location.

**GMT.** See Universal Time.

**Great Circle.** Any circle in the sky that divides the sky in half (creating two equal hemispheres). Examples are the celestial equator and the ecliptic.

**Green Flash.** A flash of green light that sometimes appears at the moment the Sun dips below the horizon. Green flashes are more often seen at sea.

**Greenwich Mean Time.** See Universal Time.

**Harvest Moon.** The Full Moon closest to the autumnal equinox, which occurs around September 23.

**Hertzsprung-Russell Diagram.** A famous diagram in astronomy that shows the relationship between the luminosity and surface temperature of stars.

**Hubble Space Telescope (HST).** Launched into orbit 375 miles (600 km) above Earth in 1990, this 94-inch (2.4 meters) diameter telescope has revolutionized astronomy by providing the most detailed images of the Universe.

**Huygens Eyepiece.** The first true eyepiece, invented by Christian Huygens in the 1700s, uses two lens elements.

**IC (Index Catalogue of Nebulae and Star Clusters).** A listing of more than 5,000 deep sky objects compiled by J. L. E. Dreyer in 1908 and still in use. The majority of IC objects are faint galaxies. Also see NGC.

**Inferior Conjunction.** See Conjunction.

**Inferior Planets.** Mercury and Venus — the two planets that orbit closer to the Sun than Earth.

**Inner Planets.** The four planets — Mercury, Venus, Earth and Mars — that orbit inside the asteroid belt.

**Ion.** An atom or molecule that has gained a positive or negative charge by acquiring or losing outer electrons.

**Jupiter.** The 5th planet from the Sun. Jupiter is famous for its Great Red Spot, cloud bands and four bright moons. Comet Shoemaker-Levy 9 collided with Jupiter in July 1994. Astronomers believe that Jupiter may act like a gravitational magnet and has probably incurred the largest proportion of comet and meteoroid impacts in our solar system, thus giving Earth a chance to harbor life.

**Kellner Eyepiece.** A "medium line" eyepiece with three or more lens elements. Kellner eyepieces are superior to Ramsden eyepieces but do not perform as well as Orthoscopic or Plössl eyepieces.

**Kelvin (K).** A temperature system based on absolute zero (the lowest temperature possible) and the Celsius scale. 0K is absolute zero; 273K is 0° C and 373K is 100° C. Note that the little circle used to denote degrees is not used with the K.

**Last Quarter.** Phase of the Moon, between Full and New, when the Moon is half lighted on the left or western side. Also referred to as Third Quarter.

**Libration.** A slight up-and-down and side-to-side movement of the Moon that enables observers on Earth to see more than just half of its surface — in fact, close to 59%. The Moon's elliptical orbit combined with its small axial tilt allow for glimpses around its edges.

**Light-Year (l.y.).** Unit of distance in astronomy. One light year is the distance light travels in one year. Since light travels at the rate of 186,282 miles per second, it will travel 5,880,000,000,000 miles (almost 6 trillion miles) in one year. It takes light 1.3 seconds to travel the distance from the Earth to the Moon and 8.3 minutes to travel from the Sun to the Earth. Our solar system is about 11 light hours in diameter and our galaxy is about 100,000 light years in diameter.

**Local Group.** A group of about 30 galaxies that includes our galaxy and the Andromeda galaxy. Galaxies are clumped together in groups throughout the Universe.

**Lunar Eclipse.** The blockage of the sunlight illuminating the Moon by Earth's shadow. Lunar eclipses can occur only at Full Moon and do not occur every month because the Moon's orbit is inclined to Earth's orbit. This usually places the Moon above or below Earth's shadow.

**Maksutov Reflector.** A catadioptric telescope that has a deeply concave front correcting lens. Maksutov reflectors can provide better image quality over a larger field of view than Newtonian and Schmidt-Cassegrain reflectors.

# Glossary

**Mare (plural: Maria).** Original name given by Galileo to the smooth, dark plains on the Moon because they resemble bodies of water. Mare is the Latin word for sea. The maria were created by lava flow.

**Mars.** The 4th planet from the Sun. Mars appears reddish but is actually pale brown. Mars became well known for its "canals," the result of erroneous observations made in the early 1900s. The canals do not exist. Mars is the most hospitable planet in our solar system (after Earth) and its north polar cap contains huge amounts of frozen water. Mars may have harbored primitive life in the past, and will hopefully be visited by humans before 2050.

**Mercury.** The closest planet to the Sun. Mercury resembles the Moon because it is pitted with craters and has no atmosphere.

**Meridian.** See Celestial Meridian.

**Messier Objects.** A collection of 110 deep sky objects recorded and described around 1750 by Charles Messier of France. These objects include the brightest galaxies, nebulae, globular clusters and open clusters. Messier was a comet hunter, and cataloged these objects so other comet hunters would not mistake them for comets. Astronomers and scientists of the 1700s did not know what galaxies and nebulae were, but they knew these blurry objects did not move around the sky as did comets.

**Meteor.** The light trail in the sky created when a meteoroid enters Earth's atmosphere. Often called a shooting star.

**Meteorite.** A rock from space that has fallen to the ground.

**Meteoroid.** The term used to describe a space rock before it enters the Earth's atmosphere and becomes a white streak known as a meteor. Most meteoroids are about the size of a grain of sand and burn up completely in the Earth's atmosphere.

**Meteor Shower.** Meteors that appear to originate from a particular spot in the sky. Twelve major meteor showers occur every year. These showers are the result of the Earth passing through semi-permanent swarms of cometary debris that orbit the Sun.

**Micrometeorite.** A meteoroid as small as or smaller than a grain of sand.

**Milky Way.** A hazy, cloudy (milky) band that circles the night sky. This band is a permanent part of the sky and has an average width of five arc degrees (10 Moon diameters). The Milky Way is impossible to see in larger cities because of light and air pollution; however, it is very prominent in country skies. It appears milky because it is composed of countless stars — the bulk of the stars in our galaxy. With a telescope or binoculars, one can see that there are many more stars in the region of the Milky Way than in other areas of the sky. The Milky Way is also the name of our galaxy.

**Minor Planet.** The preferred term for an asteroid by astronomers.

**Multiple Star.** Three or more stars that are gravitationally bound and revolve around one another.

**Nadir.** The point directly below an observer. We each have our own nadir.

**Nebula (plural: Nebulae).** Gaseous cloud, comprised mostly of hydrogen, that resides in galaxies. Most nebulae are irregular in shape; however, some are spherical shells of hydrogen left by the collapse of a giant star. In spiral galaxies, the highest concentration of hydrogen gas is in the arms, where most new stars are born.

**Neptune.** The 8th planet is a gas giant and was discovered in 1871. It is slightly smaller than Uranus and has a very faint ring system.

**Neutron Star.** An extremely dense star created from the supernova explosion of a massive star. The compression from the explosion merges electrons and protons into neutrons. The mass of a neutron star ranges from 1.4 to 3 times that of our Sun, but it only has a diameter of about 12 miles (19 km). Since neutron stars give off very little light, they are often studied as pulsars with radio telescopes. Pulsar is a descriptive term for a neutron star that is highly magnetized and spins rapidly, anywhere from 4 to 200 times a second.

**NGC (New General Catalogue of Nebulae and Star Clusters).** A listing of nearly 8,000 deep sky objects compiled by J. L. E. Dreyer in 1888 and still used today. The majority of NGC objects are galaxies and open clusters. Overall, they are not as faint as Dreyer's list of 5,000 IC objects (Index Catalogue of Nebulae and Star Clusters). See IC.

**New Moon.** The Moon is considered New when it is between the Earth and Sun. It cannot be seen at this time because it is near the Sun.

**Newtonian Telescope.** The simplest and most widely used reflector telescope. First built by Isaac Newton in 1668, this telescope uses a parabolic mirror to focus light.

**Northern Lights.** See Aurora.

**Nova.** A nova explosion is cyclical, caused by the repeated infusion of hydrogen gas from a giant star to a white dwarf (binary pair).

**Occultation.** The eclipsing of one celestial body by another. The Moon frequently occults stars and the planets. Less frequent are occultations of a star by the planets or an asteroid.

**Open Cluster.** A group of up to several thousand stars that were born together and reside in close proximity to one another. Several open clusters are visible to the naked eye. The Pleiades in Taurus is the best known; however, most open clusters can be seen only with binoculars or a telescope.

**Opposition.** The alignment of one or more superior planets (Mars through Pluto) with the Earth and Sun. These planets are in opposition when they are directly "behind" the Earth, away from the Sun. The superior planets are closest to the Earth at opposition and they rise in the east as the Sun is setting in the west.

**Orthoscopic Eyepiece.** A four-element lens eyepiece that was very popular during the 60s and 70s. The Plössl lens design has superseded the orthoscopic eyepiece in popularity because it has a wider field of view.

**Outer Planets.** Jupiter, Saturn, Uranus, Neptune and Pluto: the planets that orbit outside the asteroid belt.

**Parabolic.** The adjective of the noun parabola, which is a mathematical shape that describes a curve found frequently in nature. This shape has the unique property of allowing incoming light to focus at the same point — something that a simple circle shape cannot do. The primary mirrors of Newtonian reflectors are parabolic.

**Parsec.** Unit of distance in astronomy. One parsec is about 3.2 light years. The parsec is derived by using the astronomical unit and trigonometry. It is the distance that one astronomical unit would have to be from the Earth in order for it to appear 1 arc second in length (1/3600 of 1 compass degree). The Moon is about 1,800 arc seconds.

**Penumbra (Eclipse).** The shadow adjacent to the dark umbra shadow. If you are in the penumbra shadow during a solar eclipse, you will see the Sun partially blocked by the Moon.

**Penumbra (Sunspot).** The lighter part of a sunspot that immediately surrounds the dark inner umbra.

**Perigee.** The closest point that the Moon or an artificial satellite comes to the Earth. Since all orbiting bodies have elliptical orbits, they have a closest and farthest point from the object they orbit.

**Perihelion.** The point in a planet's, asteroid's or comet's orbit where it is closest to the Sun. Since all solar system members have elliptical orbits, they have a closest and farthest point from the Sun.

**Photosphere.** The visible surface of the Sun. The photosphere is 125 miles deep (200 km), reaches a temperature of 10,000° F (5,500° C) and is comprised of granules, or cells, about 650 miles (1,050 km) in diameter. Sunspots are on the photosphere.

**Planetary Nebula.** A huge spherical shell, a ring or opposed lobes of hydrogen gas left by the collapse of a red giant or supergiant star. The gas is stimulated to emit its own light by ultraviolet radiation from the collapsed star. planetary nebulae can measure a light year or more in diameter (or greatest length) and can be seen with small telescopes.

**Planisphere.** A circular star chart that is used to find the constellations. The word planisphere refers to a sphere of stars plotted on a flat plane. Planispheres are handy charts for beginners and amateurs because unlike star charts in books, they can be adjusted to show the stars visible for a specific hour and day of the year.

**Plössl Eyepiece.** The most popular optical design for eyepieces. It utilizes four lens elements and provides a large apparent field of view (50° or greater).

**Pluto.** The 9th planet in our solar system. Discovered in 1930 by Clyde Tombaugh in Flagstaff, Arizona, after an extensive photographic search of the sky. Pluto's orbit is greatly inclined compared to the other planets. Its moon, Charon, is more than half Pluto's diameter.

**Population I and II Stars.** Population I stars, which include our Sun, are relatively young stars and contain a higher abundance of metals than the older Population II stars. Population I stars are often found in the arms of spiral galaxies. Globular clusters are composed mainly of the older Population II stars.

**Precession.** The Earth spins on its axis like a top. At the same time, the Earth's axis is slowly wobbling around a "giant" circle, similar to a top wobbling as it slows down. This wobble is known as precession and is caused by the gravitational pull from the Moon and Sun. The precession wobble describes a 47° arc diameter circle in the sky and it takes approximately 25,800 years for the Earth's axis to move and complete this circle. Today, the Earth's axis points toward Polaris, the North Star. In about 12,000 years, the axis will be pointing to the star Vega, in the constellation Lyra. Some ancient civilizations, including the Egyptians, knew about precession.

**Prominence.** Protrusion of ionized gas from the surface of the Sun. Large prominences can easily extend 10 to 30 Earth diameters from the photosphere and can loop back to the surface, creating beautiful arches.

**Proper Motion.** The apparent motion of the stars in the sky in relationship to the Sun. This motion is not the daily motion of the stars around the Earth, but represents the movement of stars with respect to one another. Generally, the stars that are closest to our Sun have the largest proper motions. Proper motion is measured in thousands of years.

**Pulsar.** See Neutron Star.

**Pyrex.** Annealed pyrex is the preferred glass for reflector telescope mirrors. Pyrex is significantly more stable with temperature variations than plate glass.

**Quadrature.** A separation in the sky of 90° between solar system members. A superior planet (Mars through Pluto) would be at quadrature with the Sun if the planet were at the zenith as the Sun was rising or setting.

**Quasar.** Extremely bright galaxy that outputs enormous amounts of energy over the entire electromagnetic spectrum. Quasars are the farthest and among the oldest objects in the Universe. The energy from quasar galaxies is produced from the interaction of enormous amounts of matter being pulled into giant black holes at the galaxies' centers.

**Radio Telescope.** An instrument used to study celestial objects by mapping their radio waves instead of light rays. Radio astronomy uses very large dish antennae.

**Ramsden Eyepiece.** An inexpensive eyepiece that uses two lens elements. Ramsden eyepieces often are included with inexpensive telescopes. They are not generally used today.

**Redshift.** A lengthening or stretching of the wavelength of light in the spectrum of a celestial body that is moving away from Earth. The redshift can be used to determine the speed of receding objects.

**Reflecting Telescope.** Any telescope that uses a concave mirror as the primary means for focusing light.

**Refractor Telescope.** Any telescope that uses a glass objective lens as the primary means for focusing light. Camera lenses and Galileo's telescope are refracting instruments. Refracting telescopes are more expensive per aperture inch than other telescopes. For the price of a quality 4-inch refractor, you could purchase a 16 to 18-inch Dobsonian reflector.

**Retrograde.** An apparent backward movement in the sky (as viewed from Earth) of the superior planets (Mars through Pluto). As the superior planets move in their orbits around the Sun, they appear to move slowly eastward against the background of stars. However, for several months each year, these planets reverse their course and move westward, then resume their eastward course. This apparent backward/ westward movement is called retrograde motion. This effect is created by a faster orbiting Earth "passing" the slower orbiting superior planets.

**Richest-Field Telescope (RFT).** A telescope with a low focal ratio, generally ranging from f/4 to f/6. You can see more sky in the eyepiece of a RFT than with higher focal ratio telescopes.

**Right Ascension (also RA or a).** West-to-east coordinate used in conjunction with Declination to determine the position of an object in the sky. Right Ascension is equivalent to longitude but is expressed differently. It is derived by dividing the celestial sphere into 24 hours. Each hour is further divided into 60 minutes and each minute into 60 seconds. Zero hours (0h) starts at the vernal equinox. Examples of R.A. are 12h 23.7m and 1h 14m 23s.

**Rille.** Fairly straight, long "lines" on the Moon's maria produced from faults on these plains.

**Saturn.** The 6th planet is magnificent in the sky with its beautiful ring system. Until the 1980s, it was thought these rings were unique to Saturn. The other gas giants (Jupiter, Uranus and Neptune) also have ring systems, but none are as spectacular as Saturn's.

**Schmidt-Cassegrain Telescope (SCT).** This catadioptric telescope has two mirrors and a front correcting lens. Its folded optical path makes it one of the most compact telescopes. The 8-inch SCT is a very popular amateur telescope.

**Seeing.** An observing term indicating the atmospheric viewing condition of the night sky. Often graded on a 1 to 10 scale with 1 the worst and 10 the best.

**Setting Circles.** Circular, graduated scales sometimes attached to the right ascension and declination axes of equatorial mounts that aid in locating celestial objects by using their RA and Dec coordinates.

**Sidereal.** The true orbital or rotational period of a planet, moon, asteroid or comet. This is the time it takes to complete one revolution or rotation. Earth's sidereal rotational period (23 hours, 56 minutes, 4 seconds) is obtained by measuring successive passages of a star in a fixed telescope. This is not used for clock time because if it were, in six month's time, noon would occur at midnight (4 minutes x 180 days = 12 hour change).

**Solar Eclipse.** Occurs when the Moon moves in front of the Sun, which can happen only at New Moon. There are three types of solar eclipses: total, partial and annular. A total eclipse occurs when the Sun is completely blocked by the Moon. An annular eclipse occurs when the Moon passes completely in front of the Sun, but does not totally cover the Sun. Partial eclipses occur when the Moon covers only a portion of the Sun.

**Solar Flare.** A spontaneous eruption on the surface of the Sun that releases enormous amounts of energy and energetic particles into the solar system. These eruptions cause the aurorae as well as radio and communication disruptions.

**Solar System.** A system composed of a star and revolving planets, asteroids and comets. We normally use the term to refer to our solar system; however, astronomers have found numerous nearby stars with their own orbiting planets.

**Solar Wind.** A wind in the solar system caused by the release of charged photons and electrons from the Sun. The solar wind is partially responsible for pushing a comet's tail away from the Sun.

**Solstice.** The time of year when the Sun is at its highest or lowest point in the sky. Also see Summer Solstice and Winter Solstice.

**Spectrum.** The light from the Sun, planets, stars, nebulae and galaxies can be directed through a prism (or diffraction grating) to obtain a spectrogram (photographic or digital image of a spectrum). Spectrograms look like long, horizontal bands marked with numerous dark parallel lines. The arrangement of these lines is used to identify the chemical makeup as well as the velocity of celestial objects.

**Spherical Aberration.** The inability of an optical system to focus all light rays at the same point. For example, the light rays from the outer edge of an objective mirror or lens may focus short or long compared to the light rays that pass near the center of the objective.

**Sporadic Meteor.** A meteor not associated with a shower. Between three and seven sporadic meteors can be observed every hour.

**Standard Time.** Local time, the time on our clocks. The continental United States has four standard time zones.

**Star Cluster.** An open cluster, galactic cluster or a globular cluster.

**Sublimate.** To change directly from a solid to a gas or from a gas to a solid without becoming liquid. The volatiles in a comet sublimate to create the coma and tail.

**Summer Solstice.** The day on which the Sun reaches its highest point in the sky (at noon), approximately June 21. The day with the most amount of sunlight (in the northern hemisphere).

# Glossary

**Sunspots.** Dark spots on the surface of the Sun. Sunspots rotate with the Sun. They continuously form, grow, decrease in size, and dissolve away. Often larger than the Earth, sunspots are cooler than the surrounding brighter photosphere (about 6,300° F or 3,500° C compared to 10,000° F or 5,500° C) and have intense magnetic fields.

**Supergiant Star.** A star with a diameter of around a 1,000 times that of our Sun. Because of their size, supergiants are very luminous; but they have low densities. Betelgeuse in Orion is a supergiant star.

**Superior Conjunction.** See Conjunction.

**Superior planets.** The planets that orbit beyond Earth — Mars, Jupiter, Saturn, Neptune, Uranus and Pluto.

**Supernova (plural: Supernovae).** An explosion of a massive star, at the end of its life, of such intensity that the light emitted can outshine the star's galaxy. A supernova is about 1,000 times brighter than a nova, and can remain brilliant for several weeks. Supernovae occur infrequently and are observed more often in galaxies other than our own. Supernovae have absolute magnitudes around −19.

**Synodic Period.** A relative period of revolution as viewed from Earth. For example, the time a superior planet takes to go from one opposition to the next, the time from one inferior conjunction with Venus to the next, or the time from one Full Moon to the next Full Moon. All of these examples represent revolution periods that are not a complete revolution around the Sun or Earth, but appear to be a complete revolution as viewed from Earth.

**Syzergy.** The alignment of three or more solar system members. New Moon and Full Moon are examples of three bodies lining up — the Sun, Earth and Moon.

**Terminator.** The "border" on the Moon between the lighted side and the dark side. The terminator is visible to observers on Earth when the Moon is in a phase other than Full or New. Craters near the terminator appear sharp and contrasty because of their shadows.

**Terrestrial Planets.** Mercury, Venus, Earth and Mars. These four planets share many characteristics.

**Third Quarter.** See Last Quarter.

**Transparency.** This term is often used in conjunction with "seeing," to gauge observing conditions. Transparency is the lowest magnitude star visible using the naked eyes.

**Twilight.** The transition time between day and night either before sunrise or after sunset. There are three officially defined twilights — civil, nautical and astronomical. Each is based on the Sun's arc angle distance below the horizon.

**Umbra (Eclipse).** An observer must be inside the Moon's umbra shadow to witness a total solar eclipse. The Moon must pass into Earth's umbra shadow for a total lunar eclipse to occur. The penumbra shadow immediately surrounds the umbra shadow.

**Umbra (Sunspot).** The inner and darkest part of a sunspot. The umbra is surrounded by the lighter penumbra.

**Universal Time (UT).** The occurrence of astronomical events is expressed in Universal Time in order to avoid confusion with time zones and Daylight-Savings Time. Universal Time was adopted by an international conference in 1884 and is the local time at the Old Royal Observatory in Greenwich, near London, England. Expressed using the 24-hour clock, Universal Time must be converted to Local Standard Time to adjust for time zone differences. The WWV radio station in Fort Collins, Colorado, as well as CHU in Ottawa, Ontario, Canada broadcast Universal Time 24 hours a day. These radio signal broadcasts are known as Coordinated Universal Time (UTC). Universal Time is sometimes referred to as Greenwich Mean Time (GMT).

**Uranus.** The 7th planet from the Sun was discovered by William Herschel in 1781. This gas giant is the third largest planet in our solar system and has a faint ring system.

**Variable Star.** A star whose brightness changes over a period of time. Stars change in brightness for various reasons. Some stars, like Algol in Perseus, change in brightness because they are eclipsed by dimmer companion stars. Other stars called Cepheid variables vary in brightness because they periodically expand and contact up to 30% in size.

**Venus.** The 2nd planet from the Sun is the brightest planet in the sky, reaching magnitude −4.6. Venus once was referred to as Earth's sister planet because its diameter is about the same as Earth's. However, this connotation is not used anymore because Venus' environment is totally hostile to life. Completely covered with clouds of sulfuric acid, Venus has an atmospheric pressure 90 times greater than Earth's and a surface temperatures reaching 900° F (480° C).

**Vernal Equinox.** One of two points in the sky where the ecliptic (the apparent path of the Sun over the course of a year) crosses the celestial equator. The other is the autumnal equinox. The vernal equinox is located in the constellation Pisces and represents the beginning of spring, when the Sun crosses the celestial equator from south to north. The vernal equinox is also the starting point for all celestial coordinates (R.A. 0h, Declination 0°). The Sun is at the vernal equinox on approximately March 21. Day and night are equal in length on this day.

**Vulcan.** A nonexistent planet that some thought might orbit between the Sun and Mercury.

**Waning.** Shrinking, decreasing. The Moon wanes as it decreases in size from Full to New. Opposite of waxing.

**Waxing.** Increasing, growing. The Moon is waxing as it increases in size from a Crescent to Full. Opposite of waning.

**White Dwarf.** The final stage in the life of some lower mass stars before they becomes cold, dark objects. White dwarfs have high densities; they are about the size of the Earth with the mass of our Sun. Sirius, the brightest star in the sky, has a white dwarf binary companion.

**Winter Solstice.** The day on which the Sun reaches its lowest point in the sky (at noon), which occurs approximately December 22. For the northern hemisphere, this is the day with the least amount of sunlight.

**Zenith.** The highest point in the sky, directly overhead. Everyone has his or her own zenith (unless you are carrying someone on your shoulders, then you share a zenith).

**Zodiac.** Twelve constellations make up the zodiac. These constellations lie along a great circle in the sky called the ecliptic, the apparent path the Sun travels in the sky over the course of a year. The ecliptic is created from the Earth's yearly revolution around the Sun.

# Index

# Index